jesus
and the
powers

jesus
and the
powers

CONFLICT, COVENANT,
AND THE HOPE OF THE POOR

RICHARD A. HORSLEY

Fortress Press
Minneapolis

JESUS AND THE POWERS
Conflict, Covenant, and the Hope of the Poor

Cover image: Jesus driving out the unclean spirit, ivory relief, 10th century by Hessisches Landesmuseum, Darmstadt, Germany/ The Bridgeman Art Library Nationality / copyright status: out of copyright
Cover design: Laurie Ingram
Book design: The HK Scriptorium, Inc.

Library of Congress Cataloging-in-Publication Data

Horsley, Richard A.
  Jesus and the powers : conflict, covenant, and the hope of the poor / by Richard A. Horsley.
       p. cm.
  Includes bibliographical references (p. 231).
  ISBN 978-0-8006-9708-2 (alk. paper)
  1. Jesus Christ—Teachings. 2. Sociology, Biblical. 3. Powers (Christian theology)—Biblical teaching. 4. Bible. N.T. Gospels—Social scientific criticism. I. Title.
  BS2417.S7H57 2010
  232.9'04—dc22

                                        2010017976

Contents

Abbreviations

b. Pesaḥ.	Babylonian Talmud, tractate *Pesaḥim*
Barn.	*Letter of Barnabas*
Cicero	
De or.	*De oratore*
Har. Resp.	*De haruspicum responso*
Rab. Perd.	*Pro Rabirio Perduellionis Reo*
Verr.	*In Verrem*
esp.	especially
ET	English translation
Gos. Pet.	*Gospel of Peter*
Gos. Thom.	*Gospel of Thomas*
Josephus	
Ant.	*Antiquities of the Jews*
Ag. Ap.	*Against Apion*
War	*Jewish War*
Julius Caesar	
Bell. Gall.	*Bellum Gallicum*
Juvenal	
Sat.	*Satirae*
m. Sheb.	Mishnah, tractate *Shebiʿit*
NRSV	New Revised Standard Version
orig.	original
par.	parallel
Philo	
Legat.	*Legatio ad Gaium*
Post.	*De posteritate Caini*

Pliny the Younger
    Ep.   *Epistulae*
Quintilian
    Decl.   *Declamationes*
repr.   reprint
Seneca
    Ben.   *De beneficiis*
    Ep.   *Epistulae morales*
Tacitus
    Agr.   *Agricola*
    Ann.   *Annales*
T. Mos.   *Testament of Moses*

Introduction

"You Shall Not Bow Down and Serve Them"

The Gospels are stories, exciting stories. We miss the excitement when we focus on particular verses in Bible studies or hear only separate "lessons" week by week in Sunday services. If we read the Gospels whole— or, better, hear them performed by a storyteller—they turn out to be dramatic stories about Jesus. The Gospel of Mark is particularly fast-moving.[1] The Gospels of Matthew, Luke, and John have pauses in the action for Jesus to deliver long speeches. But they also are stories of high drama.

CONFLICT, RENEWAL, AND POWERS

Among the many striking features of the Gospel stories, three in particular stand out:

1. The Gospel stories are full of *conflict*.[2] The dominant conflict is not between Jesus and his disciples but between Jesus and the high priestly and Roman rulers, and the conflict is not just religious but political. In Mark, the story has barely begun when the Pharisees and the Herodians, the representatives of those rulers, begin plotting to destroy Jesus. The primary conflict comes to a climax when Jesus marches up into Jerusalem at the head of a crowd that acclaims him as a liberator and then carries out a forcible protest demonstration in the temple. In Matthew, no sooner is Jesus born than King Herod sends out the death squads to massacre all the infants as a desperate device to kill the child who has just been born as the new, liberating messiah-designate. In Luke, after Jesus' dramatic speeches and actions against the Jerusalem rulers and their representatives, he is

1

accused before the Roman governor of perverting the people, forbidding them to pay tribute to Caesar, and generally of stirring up the people with his teaching. In the Gospel of John, Jesus marches into Jerusalem several times for confrontations with the high priestly rulers of Judea, who in turn seize Jesus and turn him over to the Roman governor for crucifixion, lest the Romans take military action against the whole people because of Jesus' disruptive activity. The Gospels are full of *political conflict*.

2. The Gospel stories portray Jesus as carrying out a *renewal of Israel*.[3] He carries out new actions of deliverance of the people reminiscent of the sea crossings and feedings in the wilderness led by Moses and the healings of Elijah. Jesus then appears with Moses and Elijah on a mountain and appoints twelve figures representative of (the twelve tribes of) Israel. He heals a twelve-year-old woman who is almost dead and a woman who has been hemorrhaging for twelve years, who evidently symbolize the Israelite people, nearly dead from having been bled dry by their rulers. Like the prophets of old, Jesus pronounces God's condemnation of the rulers for having exploited the people. Matthew, Luke, and John all, at several points in their stories, state explicitly that Jesus is fulfilling the longings and expectations of the people and particular prophecies spoken by prophets such as Isaiah. In the Gospel stories, Jesus stands squarely in the tradition of Israel and is carrying out a renewal of people. Jesus' renewal of Israel, moreover, is opposed to and by the rulers of Israel. In the climactic confrontation(s) in Jerusalem, Jesus declares God's condemnation of the rulers, and throughout the Gospels the rulers oppose Jesus and finally arrest, try, and execute him.

3. The Gospels are stories about a struggle between *opposing powers*, both at the political-economic level and at the spiritual level.[4] Herod sends out his military to suppress the threat represented by the newborn messiah. Caesar, having conquered subject peoples, has the political-military power to demand that they render tribute from their crops, which supply the energy needed to sustain people's lives. Jesus pronounces (God's) condemnation of the high priests for draining away to the Temple the people's resources, and he condemns their scribal and Pharisaic representatives for leading the people to violate the commandment of God to feed father and mother and for "devouring widow's livings." And the chief priests in Jerusalem and the Roman governor use their political power to arrest, try, and execute Jesus.

The power struggle rages also at the spiritual level. "Unclean spirits" or demons have seized control of certain people, in one case causing the demoniac to do extreme violence to himself as well as to members of his community. Jesus' exorcism of these spirits involves a struggle. The Gospels present Jesus' exorcisms and healings, as well as sea crossings and wilderness feedings, explicitly as *dynameis*, a Greek term that means "powers" but may be best translated as "acts of power." Indeed, Jesus' powers are threatening the dominant order.

The Pharisees accuse Jesus of casting out demons by the power of Beelzebul, the prince of demons. In response, Jesus insists that his exorcisms are, in effect, evidence that in the broader struggle between Satan and God for control of human life, the "strong man" has been bound. He declares that "the finger of God" has effected a new exodus-like deliverance. The two levels are thus closely interrelated. The people who witness Jesus' exorcism, moreover, declare that Jesus is acting with "authority/power," in contrast to the scribal representatives of the Jerusalem rulers. In the climactic confrontation in Jerusalem, the chief priests and elders in Jerusalem as well recognize that Jesus is acting with authority/power that they, the "authority figures," cannot match. In reassurance to his followers, whom he warns about the possibility that they may (also) be faced with "taking up the cross," he promises that the kingdom of God will (soon) be coming "with power."

ANACHRONISTIC ASSUMPTIONS

Insofar as political-religious conflict, renewal of Israel, and power(s) are so prominent, indeed central, in the Gospels, one would expect to find these same features in investigations of the historical Jesus, particularly insofar as the Gospels are the primary sources for such investigations. But rarely do any of these features crop up in interpretation of Jesus. There are a number of closely interrelated reasons for this, rooted in the worldview and assumptions of modern Western culture in general and in the field of New Testament studies in particular.

1. One of the principal reasons for this lack of attention to the conflict and the power struggle is that standard study of the historical Jesus does not consider the Gospels as stories, much less as historical sources, but as

containers for individual sayings of Jesus and little vignettes about Jesus, which are analyzed for the "data" from which conclusions can be drawn by the scholar.[5] Focused thus on text fragments that contain isolated bits of "data," scholars simply do not discern the broader patterns and relationships indicated in the Gospels and other sources for the historical context.

2. Another fundamental reason is that the field of New Testament studies, of which historical Jesus studies is a subfield, like Western culture generally, assumes that religion is separate from politics (and economics). Jesus is considered a religious figure. Hence, virtually by definition, he cannot have been political (or economic). This basic separation extends into the established academic division of labor in which reality is divided up for investigation, with political science charged with investigation of politics and religious studies or theology dedicated to investigation of figures such as Jesus or Muhammad or Gautama Buddha. In this modern Western division of reality into separate spheres, power is ordinarily understood as belonging to the political sphere, in both popular and academic discourse, and occasionally to economics. If religion has any power, it is confined to spirituality. Hence, again by definition, Jesus cannot have been involved in a power struggle.

3. With the combination of powerful individualism and the increasing marginalization of religion in the modern West, moreover, religion itself has been reduced to individual faith or belief. In contrast to traditional agrarian societies, in which religion was integral to fertility and economic production and the political-economic order, religion in contemporary Western societies is external or marginal to the relations and processes of economic production and political order.[6] As viewed by modern individualism and the reduction of religion to individual faith, particularly by modern liberals, Jesus was primarily an individual teacher of individuals about individual religious ethics or lifestyle.

4. Another reason for the inattention to the conflict and power struggle in historical Jesus studies is that, in the modern Western understanding, God, like Jesus, is associated primarily with religion, which is separate from politics and economics. This may be most clearly illustrated in the standard understanding that there is no conflict between "giving to Caesar the things that are Caesar's and to God the things that are God's" (Mark 12:13-17), that is, that Jesus instructs us to pay taxes to the political

authorities while giving our religious loyalty to God. In keeping with the same modern understanding of God, liberal interpreters have recently argued that "the kingdom of God," the very center of Jesus' teaching, was an individual, personal spiritual reality, an unmediated relationship with God.[7] The God of marginalized modern theology thus has a drastically reduced jurisdiction compared with the God of Israel, consistently portrayed in the Hebrew Bible (Old Testament) as comprehensively and directly concerned with political and economic affairs inseparable from religious loyalty. Similarly in biblical understanding, "the kingdom of God" refers to the comprehensive sovereignty of God.

Closely related to the reduction in the scope of reality over which "God" has jurisdiction is the continuing operation of an earlier theological emphasis that what was most important in both "Christianity" and its predecessor religion "Judaism" was "monotheism," the belief that there is only one God, not many. This, of course, was the ideal for Jewish and Christian faith, as stated in the Jewish Shema and in Christian creeds. In the Bible, from the Song of the Sea, the earliest Hebrew poetry ("Who is comparable to you, O YHWH, among the gods?" [Exod 15:11]) to the apostle Paul ("in fact there are many gods and many lords" [1 Cor 8:5]), it is understood that many gods/lords/powers are operative in the world. The theological emphasis on monotheism versus polytheism, however, tends to divert our attention from the reality of the multiple forces/gods that were impacting the lives of Jesus' contemporaries.

5. Moreover, interpretation of Jesus as part of New Testament studies, which is a subdivision of Christian theology, works with a standard theological scheme of the origins of Christianity as a new, supposedly more universal religion from the older, and supposedly more particularistic religion of Judaism. In this scheme, Jesus was the revealer, teacher, and healer of individual followers. Only after and as a result of the resurrection faith did a community or movement of his followers form. Jesus himself did not catalyze a movement. So theologically oriented interpreters focus mainly on the features of Jesus' "ministry" compatible with and developed by "early Christianity" as it spread primarily among "Gentiles" in the Hellenistic world. They see little or no reason to attend to the particular concerns and political conflicts in Galilee and Judea.

6. Finally, a principal reason for the lack of attention to "unclean spirits" and Jesus' "acts of power" in the Gospel stories is surely the modern

"scientific" frame of mind that developed in the wake of the Enlight-
enment reduction of reality to what was natural and comprehensible
by reason. Figures such as angels and demons were defined as unreal or
"supernatural." New Testament studies shared the Western scientific definition of reality; the field found the Gospel stories of healings and exorcisms to be "miracles" or "magic," due to "supernatural" causation. If Jesus'
exorcisms and healings were to be interpreted at all, they belonged to the
(individual) religious sphere, separate from the rest of life, and required
explanation in more "scientific" psychological or psychosomatic terms.
Standard critical study of Jesus took spirits and acts of power as elements
of an ancient worldview that had to be "demythologized" in order for
the teachings and acts of Jesus to become palatable for scientific-minded
modern individuals.

RETHINKING

In seeking to understand the historical Jesus in historical context, however, it makes sense to attempt to understand the worldview, assumptions, and culture of the ancient historical context, rather than to impose
modern Western assumptions and worldview onto the Gospel sources.
Of course, it is impossible not to be determined in all sorts of ways by our
own culture, viewpoint, and assumptions. But we can at least attempt to
appreciate other cultures and to be self-critical of our own culture and
viewpoint—particularly of the assumptions and approach in which professional scholarly interpreters have been trained.[8]

1. It should not be all that difficult to learn to read the Gospels, our
principal sources, as whole stories. Gospel interpreters have been doing
this for the last thirty years, with many treating the Gospels as modern
novellas or short stories, but at least some have attempted to appreciate
them as ancient stories in an ancient context.[9] Far more than mere containers of "data," the Gospels present broader portrayals of Jesus in which
the particular episodes are components. The Gospel stories (and the
parallel speeches in Matthew and Luke, presumably derived from their
common "source," Q) are our principal guide to the significance of those
particular components in the historical context of Jesus' mission and
movement. What have been taken as individual sayings are not separate

in the Gospels, and probably were never isolated from some communication context. They are, rather, components of speeches or of dialogue episodes on particular issues.

2. More difficult is how we can change our conceptualization to deal with the political-religious conflict, the (renewal of) Israelite tradition, and the powers and power struggle that are principal features of the Gospel stories of Jesus and of Jesus in historical context for which they are the principal sources. Since we are all virtually "socialized" into what are problematic modern Western assumptions and concepts that keep us from seeing significant features in the sources, it will take deliberate and concerted effort to think differently.

Not just in the Gospel sources but in ancient life in general, religion was inseparable from politics and economics. To allow the dimensions of reality to come back together, it may be necessary to use awkward hyphenated terms such as "political-economic-religious." Such a term is necessary to comprehend the institution of the temple-state in Jerusalem. The Temple was the center of the Judean economy, where people sent a portion of their crops as tithes and offerings, as well as the sanctuary where sacrifices were offered to God/the Most High. The high priest was, in effect, the local "head of state," appointed by the Roman governor in the first century C.E., and the priestly aristocracy was charged by the Romans with collection of the tribute paid to Rome. Caesar was not only the emperor but the "son of god," who was honored in temples and shrines throughout the Greek cities as the Lord and Savior who had brought salvation and peace and security to the world. The synagogues in which Jesus proclaimed the "kingdom of God" and exorcised demons were not (yet) religious buildings but the local village assemblies that were the form of local governance as well as gatherings for prayers.[10] The prayer that Jesus taught his followers focused on the people's need for bread and on their debts, that is, on economic issues.

3. The dominant conflict portrayed in the Gospels was political-economic-religious, as illustrated by the juxtaposition of the people's economic need addressed in the Lord's Prayer, on the one hand, and the combination of Caesar's demand for tribute and the high priestly demand for tithes and offering, on the other. The dominant division and conflict in ancient Roman Palestine were not between Judaism and Hellenism or between Jews and Gentiles, but between the people living in village

communities and the Roman rulers and the high priests and Herodian kings they appointed over the people.[11] Not only the Gospels but other sources as well, such as the histories of the wealthy Judean priest Josephus, portray the conflict between people and rulers. He includes accounts of widespread revolts and many resistance movements among the Judean and Galilean people against the Herodian and high priestly rulers as well as against Roman rule around the time of Jesus (see further chapter 3 below).

4. Contrary to modern Western individualistic assumptions, the ancient Galileans and other people among whom Jesus worked were embedded in the fundamental social forms of family and village community.[12] As exemplified in some of the movements included in Josephus's histories, leaders adapted "roles" or "scripts" from Israelite tradition in their relations with their followers in particular social circumstances. Inasmuch as the episodes and speeches in the Gospel traditions of Jesus were shaped by popular social memory for some decades before inclusion in the Gospels, we cannot know precisely "what Jesus really said" or "what Jesus was really like"—other modern concepts. What mattered historically was how what Jesus said and did affected people in the historical context and resulted in movements and in the Gospel traditions that those movements developed. What is significant historically, what we are after in our historical investigation, and what is important to understand is Jesus-in-movement-in-context.[13]

5. If Jesus was leading a renewal of Israel, as indicated in the dominant agenda and many of the component episodes of the Gospels, then he must have been not only embedded in Israelite tradition but interacting with his followers and opponents on the basis of Israelite tradition. We thus need to understand how Israelite tradition was alive and operative in the historical context and how Jesus may have built on aspects of Israelite tradition in the conflictual context of Roman Galilee and Judea.[14] We cannot understand the political-religious conflict that the Gospels represent Jesus as having with the rulers without appreciating how prominent conflict with rulers was in the Israelite tradition. Gaining such appreciation will require intensive critical acquaintance with Israelite tradition, not just as it appears in books later included in the Hebrew Bible, but in other Judean texts such as the *Psalms of Solomon* and key Dead Sea Scrolls. Moreover, with the recently dawning awareness that literacy was

limited mainly to scribal circles,[15] the present approach will also require greater sensitivity to how cultural tradition (social memory) operated differently among ordinary people from the way it was cultivated by the literate elite.[16]

6. Most difficult for us children of the Enlightenment may be to recognize the reality and operations of powers, particularly those that do not operate according to the canons of reason that still function as the criteria of the real. Yet, while demons or Satan or "the finger of God" may still seem quite alien to our rational-technological modern Western culture, the operations of powers in today's world have become more familiar in public discourse than they were when the assumptions and concepts of New Testament studies became standardized.

A century ago power was understood primarily in political-military terms. Europeans and European Americans had come to dominate other peoples because of their military might. In the early twentieth century, international relations were dominated by the "great powers," such as Great Britain, Germany, France, Russia, and the United States. Power was now clearly political-economic-military, generated and displayed partly in the respective empires. After World War II, the two great "superpowers," both possessing enough nuclear power to annihilate the earth, faced off in the Cold War. With the collapse of the Soviet Union, the United States came to dominate the "new world order" as the sole superpower. During the last decade, political theorists have discussed the relative effectiveness of wielding the "hard power" of military attacks or the "soft power" of diplomacy (often backed by the threat of military action).[17]

But power has been experienced and, often in retrospect, discussed in its other aspects as well. Psychological theorists such as Sigmund Freud drew attention to the reality of irrational drives that resisted rational personal and social control. In national and international affairs, the Nazi Party mobilized the powers of racism and fascism into the extremely destructive nationalistic political-military power in Germany, leading to the invasion of the rest of Europe and the mass slaughter of Jews in the Holocaust. Economists now discuss the power of the unregulated "free-market" economy, supposedly rational in its operations, in terms of the "irrational exuberance" that created the "housing bubble." It was the collective "greed" of the CEOs of megacorporations and the managers of "zombie banks" that led to the collapse of the globalized market economy in 2008. We are thus now coming to recognize that in today's world there are various kinds of power, or a number of powers, usually interrelated.

With such public awareness, albeit often in retrospect, of the operations of superhuman powers in the contemporary world, it may not be such an intellectual stretch to recognize the reality and operations of some corresponding powers in ancient Galilee and Judea under Roman rule. Awareness of the recent aggressive use of "hard power" by the United States in the invasion of Iraq enables us more readily to recognize the "shock and awe" of the standard Roman military destruction, slaughter, enslavement, and public crucifixion in conquests of peoples such as the Galileans and Judeans (in the accounts of Josephus and Tacitus). Recent discussion of the irrational exuberance and corporate greed that have operated so disastrously in the capitalist market should enable us to recognize the irrational exuberance and greed of the Roman elite who built up huge fortunes during the early Roman Empire by exploiting provinces such as Judea.

In recent decades, presidents, senators, and leading social scientists at major universities have been driven by fear of "the Evil Empire." So it should not be difficult to appreciate how ancient Judean intellectuals such as the Pharisees feared that a popular prophet who was gaining a following through his exorcisms was working in the power of the demonized ancient Canaanite god Beelzebul. The military-industrial complex, nuclear tests, and the regular military exercises of "war games" during the Cold War were the political-economic and military counterpart to the ideological dualism between "the forces of freedom" and the "forces of Communism." That our own society was caught up in such an ideological dualism may help us to understand those other ancient Judeans intellectuals who left the Dead Sea Scrolls, who were rehearsing for a holy war against the Romans in the confidence that the prince of light and God would be fighting on their side against Belial, the prince of darkness, who would be fighting on the Romans' side.

POWER, THE POWERS, AND POWER RELATIONS

If it is possible for us to appreciate the reality of the powers that figure prominently in the Gospels and their component episodes and speeches, then it may be possible to gain a fuller appreciation of Jesus' mission in its historical context. Considering how Jesus is dealing with the powers may enable us, among other things, to appreciate how his proclamation of the kingdom of God and his actions in manifestation of God's direct rule were inseparably political-economic-religious. Proceeding in this way will entail consideration of key aspects of power/the powers.

People's lives in the ancient world involved a plethora of powers. The heavens and sometimes the earth as well were alive with spiritual beings. Some of these, referred to variously as "spirits," "messengers (angels)," "demons" (originally a neutral or ambivalent term), or *numina*, were of lesser, sometimes local importance. The importance of the powers in ancient civilizations, however, is more readily discerned in the major powers that are usually named in sources such as ancient myths and historiography.

The significance of the major powers of Mesopotamian civilization, for example, is indicated in surviving texts such as the myth of origins *Enuma Elish* ("When on high . . ."), although this is often obscured when scholarly translators transliterate rather than translate their names. *Anu* was Sky (not "the god of the sky" or "the sky god," which are modern concepts); *Ea/Nudimmud* was Irrigation (not "the god of . . ."); *Enlil* was Storm. In Mesopotamian myths, these powers are personified superhuman forces for which we might use the abstract general concept "gods" (although the Mesopotamians evidently did not yet have such a concept). In the first stage of *Enuma Elish*, Sky has connotations of authority, and Irrigation also means something like the wisdom of rational planning and technology, as they guide the course of what appears to have been an early stage of Mesopotamian civilization. When they can no longer hold civilization together, they generate a new power, Storm, both born as king and then acclaimed by the other major powers as king; he imposes order by massive military violence. Storm is thus obviously also military King(ship). It is thus not surprising that the role and functions of Storm-Kingship are taken over by *Marduk*, the principal power of the city of Babylon in versions that reflect events in the early second millennium, when Babylon became the controlling imperial city. In Mesopotamian myths and culture, Sky(-Authority) and Storm(-Kingship) are clearly fearsome superhuman *natural* powers (but not "supernatural," a modern concept). As illustrated by Irrigation, Sky-Authority, and Storm-Kingship, however, the powers of Mesopotamian civilization were also *civilizational* powers, with their political-economic and cultural dimensions being or having become inseparable from their function in the "natural" environment of the Tigris and Euphrates rivers and the developing "high" civilization of Mesopotamia.

The importance of the powers was paralleled in other ancient civilizations, such as that of the Greeks, again as discerned from their names. *Ouranos* was Sky; *Gaia* was Earth, but also Mother/Fertility; and *Kronos* was Time; these were the mysterious origins from which the major powers were generated and, by implication, from which civilization developed. From their roles and functions in Greek and Roman myths, we can see that many of the principal "gods" were natural-civilizational powers (another example would be Poseidon, closely identified with Sea but also associated with seafaring).

The people of Israelite heritage were no exception in antiquity; they also dealt with multiple powers, a fact often obscured by the theological emphasis on "monotheism." For many if not most books in the Hebrew Bible, YHWH or "the Most High (God)" is not the only god, but the God of Israel, believed to have ultimate sovereignty over history. Indeed, in some texts YHWH/the Most High is not even the only heavenly power attending to the people of Judea/Israel. In the visions of Daniel (7:1-18; 10:2-21), for example, "the holy ones of the Most High" and the heavenly "princes" Gabriel and Michael, in particular, represent, protect, and fight for the Judeans against the "princes" of Persia and Greece as well as against the beastly Persian and Greek emperors.

By analyzing the roles and functions of the major powers of ancient civilizations, we can begin to discern some key aspects of power of various kinds, or the various interrelated powers.

1. Most fundamental, these examples may be sufficient to suggest that the principal powers of the ancient civilizations that we think of as their gods were the forces that most affected or determined their lives. However, in contrast to the term *gods/God* in modern Western society, associated mainly with a separate religious sphere of life, the powers of ancient civilizations were usually inseparably political-economic and religious-cultural and environmental-natural.

2. Insofar as the ancient world involved changing "international" affairs, the powers were not static but changing and dynamic for particular societies. Ancient societies cannot be understood as if they were

closed and constant cultures, such as "Judaism" or "Hellenism." The rapid development of elaborate honors to the Roman emperor in the cities of Greece and Asia Minor shortly after Augustus consolidated his power in the Roman Empire is a vivid example of how a civilization could encounter and enshrine a major new power. That temples dedicated to Caesar and statues of Caesar were erected side by side with those of the other "gods" in the Greek cities indicates that the Roman emperor had become one of the great powers (gods!), perhaps the principal power for those cities.

3. The reality of the powers was not a matter of whether the people chose them or believed in them. The powers were aspects or elements in the overall environment of people's lives, including any and all dimensions, often interrelated, whether natural-environmental, political-economic, or cultural-religious. Irrigation-Wisdom and Storm-Kingship were the most determinative powers in the lives of ancient Mesopotamians. The Sun, identified with pharaoh, and the annual fertilizing floodwaters of the Nile were principal powers determining the lives of ancient Egyptians. Similarly, in the Second-Temple period, the Judeans had no choice about the power of Persian imperial rule or the even more invasive power of "Greek" imperial rule. The impact of the powers, the way they were experienced, however, was mediated and shaped by culture-religion in various ways. Mesopotamians' and Egyptians' anxiety about whether the powers would send productivity or destruction each year was shaped by developing culture into fear of the powers. The intellectuals ("the wise") who produced the book of Daniel, for example, evidently experienced or knew, at least through dream-visions, that "the holy ones of the Most High" and Michael and Gabriel were defending them against the heavenly "princes" of Persia and the Greeks, heavenly powers behind or connected with the invasive Persian and Greek rule of Judea.

4. The people who held the political-religious power to mediate and manage the people's relationship with the great powers in ancient civilizations insisted that they required not just worship but service. This service took two forms in the ancient agrarian civilizations. The people were expected (required) to yield up a percentage of their crops, the produce of their labor on the land, as tithes and offerings (taxes in kind) to the powers. And the people were expected (required) to devote some of their

labor, often in construction of the "houses" of the great powers and/or great monuments to the gods and kings (e.g., the pyramids in Egypt).

But this leads to the recognition of another fundamental aspect of the operation of the powers. The powers "worked," that is, they influenced and even determined important aspects of people's lives, because the people collectively yielded up the produce of their labor to the control of the political-economic-religious authorities. This was thus relational power, dependent on the people's handing over a significant portion of their labor-energy and food-energy to centralized control. The people were usually induced to this by a well-cultivated fear and/or physical coercion (or at least the threat of it).

5. Theoretically, however, people could fail or refuse to yield their crops and/or labor; they could cooperate in using resources to generate their own collective power, in direct or indirect opposition to centralized power. This is precisely what happened in the formation of the people of Israel, according to the exodus stories and the stories of early Israel led by Joshua and Deborah and other "liberators" (the *shofetim*). Led by Moses, the Hebrews, a sizable section of Pharaoh's labor force, had withdrawn or escaped from their hard bondage (service) in Egypt. Led by Joshua and Deborah and others, the Israelites asserted their independence of the kings of the Canaanite city-states. And, if the Mosaic covenant in some form goes back to the formative period, the people of Israel established an alternative society in the hill country, guided by more cooperative and egalitarian principles. Most to the point of political-economic-religious power relations are the first and second commandments. According to the first ("you shall have no other gods"), of all the powers operative in the world, Israel is to maintain exclusive loyalty to the power that delivered them from service in Egypt. What that means more concretely is the burden of the second commandment, the scope of which has been narrowed in translations of the Bible (NRSV) to "worship," that is, to "religion" as separate from political-economic life:

> You shall not make for yourself an idol, whether in the form of anything that is in heaven above, or that is on the earth beneath, or that is in the water underneath the earth. You shall not bow down to them or worship them; for I the LORD your God am a jealous God. (Exod 20:4-5)

The meaning in Israel and the ancient Near Eastern context was "you shall not bow down and *serve* them!" "Idols" were not merely carved stone or wooden statues but representations of heavenly or earthly powers that the people served with their labor and produce. The people of Israel were thus commanded by their God not to yield produce and labor to (other) powers.

At the outset, we noted three prominent features of the Gospel stories: a dominant conflict that is inseparably political as well as religious, Jesus' renewal of Israel as the main agenda of the stories, and a struggle between opposing powers in the life of the people. Insofar as the Gospels are our principal sources for the historical Jesus and the traditions of Jesus cannot be understood apart from the Gospel stories of which they are components, it seems necessary to consider the conflict, the renewal of Israel, and the powers in investigating the mission of Jesus in its historical context. From the discussion above, it appears that the tradition of Israel, political-religious conflict in ancient Judea, and the broader historical context under Roman rule can all be approached and understood through analysis of the many powers that were operative.

Focusing on the powers and power relations enables us to move beyond the separation of religion and politics in standard biblical studies, which limits our understanding. It also moves beyond the simplistic alternatives of imagining that if Jesus did not foment a revolt, he was therefore politically acquiescent or innocuous. And it enables us to conceive of ways in which Jesus and those who responded to him generated power to form creative alternatives to the dominant order determined by Roman power in its various faces. When power becomes largely monopolized by a sole superpower such as imperial Rome, it seems overwhelming, and most people understandably simply acquiesce. Jesus' mission shows that for those rooted in a tradition of independence and power sharing, it may still be possible to (re)generate sufficient empowerment to formulate movements of resistance and alternatives to that superpower.

Chapter 1

The Powers of Empire

Jesus worked among people subject to the Roman Empire. His renewal of Israel, moreover, was a response to the longings of those people, who had lived under the domination of one empire after another for centuries, to be free of imperial rule. Israelite tradition from which Jesus worked in his mission bore the marks of a prolonged struggle of the people both to adjust to and to resist the effects of the powers of empire.

Ancient empires were all about power, or rather, a whole network of interrelated powers. While some of those powers were relatively more natural, others more political, others more economic, and others more religious in their operation, there was no separation between these aspects, as is often assumed in modern Western society. The principal powers were superhuman, far beyond the control of humans, but they were usually not "supernatural" or "otherworldly," as is often assumed by modern "scientifically" minded people. Indeed, the powers of ancient empire, mysterious in their operation, were thought of as divine, as gods. Modern science, including the academic field of biblical studies, has tended to misunderstand or to demythologize these superhuman Powers, imagining that they were "just" vestiges of a prerational worldview or even "just" a certain premodern mode of language. But biblical and other ancient Near Eastern sources do not share Enlightenment theology of sophisticated intellectuals (ancient and modern).

IN THE "CRADLE OF CIVILIZATION"

The most accessible example of how the powers of empire operated as a cosmic-political-economic-religious system is that of ancient Babylon.

17

It also happens to be the empire from which the ancient Hebrew Bible and the subsequent Abrahamic traditions of Christianity and Islam made their decisive departure. A fuller examination of the civilization of ancient Mesopotamia, and especially its main myth of origins, can illuminate the powers in response to which Israel established an alternative society and Jesus strove to renew Israel.[1]

The great civilization that developed in the land "Between the Rivers" was a truly remarkable achievement. In the area that is now modern-day Iraq, the ancient Mesopotamians built many large cities along the Tigris and Euphrates Rivers. The burgeoning population built an extensive irrigation system to sustain the agriculture that supported the "great ones" and their armies as well as the people themselves. The construction of the cities, with their massive monuments (ziggurats, like "the tower of Babel"), as well as the vast system of irrigation canals, required sophisticated organization of the people's labor. And that required a complex hierarchical administration, from the (district) commanders at the top to the foremen in command of gangs of laborers at the bottom, all under the autocratic command of the principal "great one." The construction of the massive monuments to the glory of the gods and the rulers, the ziggurats in Mesopotamia, like the pyramids of Egypt, also required the commandeering (by "trade") and transport of stone and timber from upriver. The whole imperial system of powers, great ones, administration, and construction was supported by the agricultural produce of the people who worked the irrigated fields.[2]

But what motivated those people to toil in the fields in the stifling heat and humidity day after day? What led them to submit to the forced labor necessary to construct the extensive irrigation system and palaces for the great ones and for the Powers who communicated with them? Apparently it was an intense fear of the terrifying superhuman Powers that determined their lives. They lived in constant fear, for example, that River, the Power that supplied water to the fields, would overflow his banks in a fit of rage, destroying both the irrigation ditches and the crops to which they brought water. They were terrified lest that even greater Power, Storm-Kingship, would suddenly swoop down upon the cities so laboriously built along the banks of River and topple buildings and fill the irrigation canals with sand from the desert. So, to appease the terrible wrath of these forces, at whose whim their collective life might be devastated (a tsunami, or a Katrina), the people rendered up tithes and offerings to the Powers. They surrendered a certain percentage of their crops to the chief servants of the Powers in their "houses" (the priests-managers in the palaces-temples-storehouses), who tended to the care and feeding of the Powers.

As in any ancient society, religion was inseparable from political and economic life. In Mesopotamian civilizations, a single term, "the great ones," could refer to people we would distinguish as "king," or "high priest," or "manager." More obviously than in Rome centuries later, the annual cycle of festivals celebrated the annual cycle of productivity. Planting and harvesting were surrounded with special prayers, sacrifices, and fertility rituals. In ancient Babylon, the climax of the annual natural-economic-political-religious cycle was the New Year festival (*Akitu*). This week-long festival celebrated both the end and the beginning, both the completion and the regeneration of the cyclical political-economic-natural divine order, the delicate balance among the great Powers that determined the people's lives.

The renewal of order against (the threat of) chaos was focused in the great ritual drama enacted in the grand temple-palace of Marduk, principal Power of Babylon, who as Storm King stood at the head of the divine forces of order. This ritual drama offers fascinating glimpses of the relationships among the divine Powers and of the people's relationship to them. The "text" of this ritual drama, the Babylonian epic of origins, *Enuma Elish* ("When on high . . . ," its opening phrase in Akkadian), even provides a sense of the two major stages in which this imperial civilization developed.

In the first act of the drama, River and Sea, intermingling their waters, "begat" Silt and Sediment, who in turn "begat" Horizon of Sky and Horizon of Earth. The latter generated Sky-Authority, who generated Irrigation-Wisdom and other offspring. It is clear from their names and roles in the drama that they were the principal Powers of nascent civilization in the land Between the Rivers. Annoyed by the noise that the forces of civilization were making, Father River threatened to destroy them all. But the enterprising Irrigation-Intelligence, drawing a map of the (Mesopotamian) universe and casting a spell, put River to sleep ("killed" him).

In this first act of the drama we discern that the Mesopotamians' sense of the origins of their civilization centered on the "houses" of the divine forces, presided over by high-ranking specialists (priests-managers) in communicating with those forces. At this still relatively simple stage of irrigation civilization, the temple-communities were held together by authority (Sky) and intelligence (Irrigation), no coercion by military force yet being necessary to maintain order.

As the nascent civilization became more complex, however, with the emergence of larger cities up and down the rivers, the system experienced chronic conflict. In the next "act" of the ritual drama, Sea (Chaos) went on a violent rampage to avenge her consort's defeat. Sky-Authority and Irrigation-Wisdom, the older forces of social cohesion, were unable to withstand the assault. To cope with the desperate situation of civilization in chaos, Irrigation generated a new force, Storm, who was acclaimed King by the forces struggling to reassert order over chaos. In a scene of horrifying violence that disturbingly juxtaposes domestic relations with the order of the universe, Marduk (god of Babylon) as Storm-King slaughtered (his ever-so-great grand-) Mother Sea. He then butchered her body to produce both the heavenly order, symbolized by the zodiac, and the earthly order in the land of the two rivers (Mesopotamia), which flowed through her eye sockets. After the victory of the forces of order over the forces of chaos, palaces had to be built for Storm-King/Marduk and the other victorious Powers. But it would have been unseemly for the vanquished forces, who were also divine, to be subjected to physical labor. So Marduk created people to be slaves of the gods, to build palaces for the divine Powers. In the final scene, Marduk (= Storm-Kingship) is celebrated as eternal King of the universe.

The climax of the ritual drama both reflects and models the establishment of empire by military violence in Mesopotamian civilization. After a period of chronic warfare between the city-states that developed along the Tigris and the Euphrates, one city-state finally imposed its rule by conquering the others. The imperial order, achieved by Babylon's military conquest in the land of the two rivers, was understood as the earthly counterpart of the imperial order achieved in the violent victory of Marduk and his forces of order over the disrupting forces of chaos.

Regularly reminded by the annual New Year ritual drama of the precarious order established by the violence of the great Powers, and reminded also of their own origin as the slaves of the Powers, the people acquiesced not just in worship of but in concrete economic service to the Powers. The great ones of Babylon, such as Hammurabi, in the role of the chief servant of Marduk and the other Powers, maintained the cosmic-political-economic order with the threat of military violence against any who might act as agents of Sea and her forces of chaos. And, of course, also being in control of the produce and labor of the masses of "slaves of the gods," the great ones lived in wealth and privilege. Agricultural surplus was transformed into the wealth of conspicuous display for the glory of the gods, products of high civilization such as gold inlay in the gods' palaces, artistically designed plates and goblets of precious metals for the gods' dining pleasure. And they hired intellectuals, who developed writing, initially to keep records of payment of tithes and offerings, and studied the heavenly powers of sun, moon, and the stars (astronomy) in order to determine the right time for planting and harvest, along with the timing of the rituals that synchronized the agrarian political economy with the annual cycle of the heavenly powers.

What powered the Babylonian Empire or the similar imperial system in ancient Egypt was the labor and produce of the people as the servants of the Powers. But the way the system worked was that when the people rendered up their labor to build the ziggurats and their agricultural produce to feed the Powers, their labor and produce became power in the control of the great ones who managed the religious ceremonies, the administrative organization of labor, and the military forces. The imperial civilizations of the ancient Near East were thus systems in which the labor-power of the people, yielded up as offering to the Powers, was transformed into power wielded *over* the people by their rulers, the great ones.

One of the many stories of Joseph's exploits at the court of Pharaoh (Genesis 41, continued in Genesis 47) offers a vivid illustration of how, in the parallel imperial system of Egypt, the (labor-) power of the people was expropriated by the central rulers and transformed into power over the people. Pharaoh dreamed of "seven sleek and fat cows," followed by seven ugly and thin cows, who "ate up the seven sleek cows." Joseph interpreted the dream to mean that there would be seven years of abundant harvests followed by seven years of drought and famine. Joseph advised Pharaoh to appoint additional managers, presumably with strong-arm backup, to expropriate one-fifth of the produce during the years of plentiful harvests to be stored under the authority of the pharaoh. As Pharaoh's newly appointed CEO, Joseph thus built up a huge surplus.

What ensued would be called extortion on a grand scale were it not so familiar from the practices of contemporary megacorporations that manipulate supply and demand while ostensibly operating under the sacred impersonal "law" of supply and demand. When the famine became severe and the people clamored for grain, Joseph demanded in exchange all their "goods" or "possessions," presumably meaning (since money had not been invented yet) precious metals, jewelry, and other such movable goods of value. When the starving people again clamored for grain, Joseph further demanded all the livestock (draft animals, flocks, herds). Finally, when the desperate people again came begging for relief, they had nothing left as collateral for loans but their land and labor. "We with our land will become servants of Pharaoh; just give us grain, so that we may live and not die." All the land became Pharaoh's and the people themselves became slaves—or more like sharecroppers or serfs—who no longer controlled their land and labor. By manipulating the people, who were utterly vulnerable to drought and famine, the rulers, who had extracted and now controlled huge reserves of grain and other produce, used their power over the peasants to escalate their now permanent share to one-fifth of the harvest (GDP). The story in Genesis leaves out the religious dimension of the people's slavery in the Egyptian system. As in Babylon, however, what motivated people to render up their labor and produce was the fear of the powers that determined their lives.

THE "SHOCK AND AWE" OF THE "SOLE SUPERPOWER"

The Roman Empire was more complicated than its Near Eastern counterparts but displayed many of the same features and the corresponding powers. The Romans, like the Greeks, feared and honored, many of the same powers that determined their societal life with temples, sacrifices, and festivals. Here we are interested in reviewing various aspects of power in the historical working of the Roman Empire, particularly as it affected the eastern Mediterranean and the Middle East, the context of Jesus' mission and the earliest Jesus movements.

Rome built its empire by military conquests, which it pretended were necessary to defend its own territory, interests, and "allies." Rome's destruction of both Carthage and the classical Greek city of Corinth (146 B.C.E.) signaled to the rest of the world that it would brook no rival for power in the Mediterranean. After the Hellenistic empires that succeeded the conquest by Alexander the Great had collapsed from making war on one another, the Romans sent large military expeditions to conquer the lands and peoples on the eastern shores of the Mediterranean. As the sole superpower, Rome was the dominant military power of its time. Overwhelming military force, however, supplied the necessary but not the sufficient power to invade and control subject peoples who resisted in serious and persistent ways, such as the Judeans and Galileans. Only after repeatedly sending in huge military forces to conquer and reconquer them over a period of two centuries were the Romans finally successful in effectively "pacifying" the populace.

The Roman warlords practiced an ancient equivalent of "shock and awe," that is, the use of overwhelming destructive force to terrorize the targeted populations into submission. The ancient Romans' version of "shock and awe" was extremely low-tech, but intentionally and systematically executed. They devastated the countryside, burned villages, and either slaughtered or enslaved the people. For good measure they then rounded up those who had put up the greatest resistance and hung them on crosses along the roadways as a public warning to any who had survived the conquest.

For centuries, Roman warlords relied on this means of expanding their *imperium,* conquering one people after another. The Greek historian Polybius, who identified with the Roman advance, was nevertheless candid about their "scorched-earth" practices. He personally witnessed the Roman devastation of a city that left in its wake a horrific scene littered with animal as well as human corpses. "It seems to me that they do this for the sake of terror," he commented (10.15–17).[3] The Roman historian Tacitus minced no words about Germanicus's slaughter of the tribes across the Rhine: "for fifty miles around he wasted the country with sword and flame. Neither age nor sex inspired pity. Places sacred and profane were razed indifferently to the ground. . . . Only the destruction of the race would end the war" (*Ann.* 1.51.56; 2.21). A new generation of classical historians, no longer paying homage to "the glories of Rome," now recognizes that such brutality "was traditional, it was the Roman way." "The aim was to punish, to avenge, and to terrify."[4] The Romans, in building their empire, like the modern European colonial powers in the Middle East and Africa and the United States' administration in recent years, believed that uncivilized people were, virtually by nature, irrational, stubborn, and violent—that the only language they understood was that of force.

The Romans invaded the Middle East to secure its supply of needed resources in the "unstable" eastern Mediterranean, which was being disrupted by pirates or "bandits." The Roman Senate entrusted the great warlord Pompey with bringing the East under effective control. When Pompey finally invaded Palestine, he faced little resistance until he arrived at Jerusalem. There he stormed the Temple, in which the priests were fortified, and plundered the Temple treasury. He also laid the conquered people under tribute, a standard Roman punitive as well as revenue-generating measure (Josephus, *War* 1.7.6–7 §§153–56; *Ant.* 14.4.4 §§73–76).

The more serious Roman devastation of Galilee and Judea came in the aftermath of Pompey's initial invasion. The Roman invasion of the Middle East triggered decades of turmoil, including Arab raids against Roman interests and a civil war between rival claimants to the Jerusalem high priesthood (Josephus, *War* 1.8.2–7 §§160–78; *Ant.* 14.5.2–14.6.3 §§82–102). Crassus, another of the infamous Roman warlords of the period, in his quest for greater glory, invaded the Parthians across the Euphrates River and lost an entire Roman army. En route, he plundered the Jerusalem Temple of whatever Pompey had not taken (*War* 1.8.8 §179; *Ant.* 14.7.1, 3 §§105, 119). His arrogant behavior further aggravated anti-Roman sentiment among Judeans and Galileans. Shortly thereafter, Cassius, as Roman governor in Syria, ruthlessly exacted an extraordinary levy of tribute (*Ant.* 14.11.2 §272).

Our sources offer only occasional glimpses of what the Romans did to complete their conquest at certain times and places. Some of those times and places in Galilee and Judea, however, undoubtedly had a direct impact on Jesus and his movement. To regain control of the area in the aftermath of Crassus's debacle, Cassius presided over one of those typical Roman acts of terrorization. At Magdala, along the shore of the Sea of Galilee southwest of Capernaum, during what would have been the lifetime of Mary Magdalene's grandparents, he enslaved thousands of people (Josephus, *War* 1.8.9 §180; *Ant.* 14.7.3 §120). This same Cassius, when the Judeans were slow to render up the special levy of tribute, enslaved the people of the district towns of Gophna, Lydda, Thamma, and Emmaus, one of the sites of Jesus' later resurrection appearances (*War* 1.11.1–2 §§218–21; *Ant.* 14.11.2 §§271–76). And in western Galilee, only a few miles from the village of Nazareth at about the same time Jesus was born, Roman armies burned the town of Sepphoris and enslaved the inhabitants (*War* 2.5.1 §68).

MANIFEST DESTINY: THE POWER OF IDEALS

Military power in empires, however, does not operate by itself. In the case of Rome, as in the new American Rome, the aggressive use of military power was sometimes paired with and sometimes driven by the power of ideas or a sense of mission. What drove the ancient Romans to extend their control over more and more territories and to expand their power generally was a sense of what nineteenth-century Americans called "Manifest Destiny."[5] In its civilizing mission, the Romans set the example for their later American imitators. They believed that their empire had been willed by the gods, whose favor they had earned by practicing piety and justice. Cicero articulated the conviction, which can be traced to well over a century before, that "it was by our scrupulous attention to religion and by our grasp . . . that all things are ruled and directed by the gods that we have overcome all peoples and nations" (*Har. resp.* 18–21). In what became the foundational epic of Augustus's consolidation of the Roman *imperium,* Virgil has Jupiter, king of the gods, bestow on Rome a dominion without limits in space or time, over the whole *orbis terrarum* (Virgil, *Aeneid* 1.277–83; cf. Cicero, *De or.* 1.14). The limits of the latter, of course, were continually expanding, certainly at the time of its invasion of the Middle East.

In its sense of mission, Rome also claimed an exceptionalism and universalism similar to that of the later American Manifest Destiny. Romans thought of themselves as a special people that had learned from the woes of others and taken the best from history, which was now embodied in Rome's piety, justice, and institutions. And Rome, like America, claimed to be a universal example insofar as it represented the ideals and interests of humankind generally. This status conferred special international responsibilities and exceptional privileges in meeting those responsibilities.

Rome's stated purpose in extending its rule to other peoples was its civilizing mission. With its dominion, it brought law and order—although usually Rome simply imposed its own law and order. Rome practiced "civilized right" as its "great world duty," to eradicate instability by intervening in states that were already civilized as well as in unstable semi-states on the periphery of civilization. As Cicero, the great Roman teacher of law, said, just as masters had a duty to treat slaves with justice, so an imperial power was bound to protect the ruled. The expansion of civilization among the uncivilized, however, involved a considerable amount of brutality. Nevertheless, what the Roman "master organizers of the world" claimed to be doing was to bring about salvation, peace, and security—as they inscribed on monuments all over the empire.

THE "MILITARY-AGRIBUSINESS COMPLEX": THE CONSOLIDATION OF ECONOMIC POWER

What happened as a result of the Roman warlords' creation of Roman *imperium* was a concentration of economic and political power somewhat similar to the "military-industrial complex" that President Dwight D. Eisenhower warned the American people about in the late 1950s.[6] Roman warlords such as Pompey and Julius Caesar controlled the recruitment and deployment of the legions for the enhancement of their own and other patricians' wealth and power in Rome. Until recently, however, because of the modern Western glorification of ancient Rome and the tendency to focus on the elite and the military campaigns they led, historians glossed over what happened to the spoil the Romans took from conquered rulers, the people they enslaved, and the legionaries they exploited. The warlords and other patricians systematically siphoned away the remaining power of the peasantry in both Italy and the provinces. The result, in an ancient agrarian economy, was what might be called the Roman imperial "military-agribusiness complex."

Whatever their sense of mission in controlling other peoples, the Roman patricians also had economic motives. As in other ancient agrarian empires, the elite in Rome were looking to control additional land and the people who labored on it. Until modern industrialization, imperial civilizations were powered by the produce generated by human labor on arable land. Given the limited productivity of land and labor in antiquity, the powerful could extract only so much without killing the peasant sheep they were shearing. If they wanted to expand the resources they controlled, they had to expand the amount of land and labor that they ruled. The general effect was an increased flow of power, in the form of control of resources, from the peasantry to the rulers. In the Roman Empire, this happened both in conquered areas such as Judea and Galilee and in Rome and Italy itself, in parallel and interrelated processes.

In the Roman Republic, as in ancient Athens, the military was a people's militia. Citizens were expected to serve in the military, under the command of fellow citizens usually from the aristocracy. In the last two centuries of the Republic, however, this proved to be a boon for the patrician warlords and their officers and a disaster for the Roman and Italian peasants who served in the legions. The "system" of continuing conquests steadily transformed the peasants' power of subsistence into power exercised over them by the wealthy.

The perpetual military campaigns mounted by ambitious Roman warlords such as Julius Caesar and Pompey forced prolonged military service on tens of thousands of peasants.[7] During the last two centuries B.C.E., more than 10 percent of the estimated adult male population served in the army for years at a time. If their wives and children could not provide the labor to eke out a subsistence living, the families fell into rising debt. The creditors from whom they borrowed were wealthy patricians, often the warlords and the officers whose ambitions the recruits to the legions were serving.

The Roman warlords and their ranking officers from wealthy senatorial and equestrian families, meanwhile, were returning to Rome with huge amounts of treasure as the spoils of their conquests. The profits that a high-ranking governor or "publican" ("tax-farmer") could rake in during even a short stint in a given province were enormous, supplying a hereditary fortune for a family, if it was not already wealthy. According to the ideals of a traditional agrarian aristocracy, however, the only respectable investment was land and the only respectable pursuit was farming. These wealthy families built up large landed estates (*latifundia*) by foreclosing on indebted peasant families' land. With their surplus wealth from booty and interest on loans they then bought large numbers of slaves captured by the legionaries in the warlords' triumphant conquests and replaced the labor of the peasants they had displaced. Slave labor was probably not any less expensive than free labor (peasants had fed themselves). But the wealthy land- and slave-owners could control the labor of slaves far more than they could that of free laborers. What the wealthy families did not consume in their lavish households in Rome, also staffed by slaves, they could sell to the government for the food supply of Rome and other cities. The ancient biographer Plutarch sums up the process.

> The rich men in each neighborhood . . . contrived to transfer many of these holdings to themselves, and finally they openly took possession of the greater part of the land under their own names. The poor . . . found themselves forced off the land. . . . The result was a rapid decline of the class of free small-holders all over Italy, their place being taken by gangs of foreign slaves, whom the rich employed to cultivate the estates from which they had driven off the free citizens. (Plutarch, *Life of Tiberius Gracchus* 8; cf. Appian, *Civil War* 1.7)

Another key development in this process was an ominous shift from the traditional principle of the "commonwealth" of the Roman Republic. This process required changes in the laws governing the holding and use of land to allow the powerful to claim land as their *private* property. The patricians in the Roman Senate enacted a deregulation, to make possible the unlimited privatization of public resources (land) and the expropriation of citizen soldiers' inheritances of land.

It has been estimated that from 80 to 8 B.C.E. about 1.5 million people, roughly half the peasant families of Roman Italy, were forced off their ancestral lands. Many went to new lands in Italy, many were sent to Roman colonies in other lands, such as Corinth, and many simply migrated to the city of Rome and other towns in Italy.[8] It is estimated that between 45 and 8 B.C.E. more than 250,000 adult males from Italy, roughly one-fifth of the 1.2 million who had lived there, were displaced from the Italian countryside.[9] In a complementary flow, over the course of the first century B.C.E., more than two million peasants from conquered provinces such as Judea were taken as slaves to Italy. By the end of the first century B.C.E., slaves amounted to about 35 to 40 percent of the total estimated population, the same percentage as the slaves in the southern United States in the nineteenth century.[10]

The effects of the Roman conquests were similar on the peoples they subjugated, such as the Judeans and Galileans. The Roman warlords enslaved large numbers of peasants, as noted above. The Romans also laid subjugated peoples under tribute, which the peasants had to pay on top of the taxes due to their local rulers. With additional percentages of their crops expropriated by tax collectors, peasants found it necessary to borrow to feed their families, at unmercifully high rates of interest. Heavily indebted peasants were forced to become sharecroppers on their own land, or they were forced off the land to become wage laborers. Thus, in subjected areas as well as in Italy, the Roman conquests had set in motion a process in which increasing amounts of the peasants' produce were siphoned upward into the control of the wealthy, thus augmenting their political-economic power.

BREAD AND CIRCUSES:
THE CENTRALIZATION OF POWER IN ROME

The impoverishment of the Roman peasantry had further implications for the empire's exploitation of the peasantry in the provinces. With increasing numbers of peasants forced off their ancestral farms flooding into Rome, the population of the city expanded exponentially. By the time Augustus "restored" the Republic, it had reached a million, an unwieldy population for an agrarian economy. This created a number of interrelated problems. Since many, perhaps the majority of these people, had been displaced from their traditional source of livelihood and were un- or underemployed, they had to be fed. Since they had time on their hands, they needed entertainment or diversion. And since they were concentrated in the imperial capital, they were potentially volatile politically and a threat to imperial rule.

But Roman institutions evolved as they adjusted to the forces unleashed by imperial expansion so that the potential threat never effectively materialized. The key Roman institutions were "bread and circuses," made famous by the satirist Juvenal (*Sat.* 10.77–81).[11] As the second-century C.E. orator Fronto observed, "The Roman people are held fast by two things above all, the grain-dole [*annona*] and the shows. . . . The success of the *imperium* depends on entertainments as much as more serious things." As the people who had come to dominate the rest of the world, the Romans felt they had a right to enjoy the good life of bread and circuses. Juvenal's satire of the consumption and spectacle might seem to exaggerate their importance in Rome, but Augustus's official propaganda, which he ordered inscribed on monuments in Rome and elsewhere, confirms that the "bread and circuses" that he ("personally") provided for Roman citizens constituted fully half of the imperial program.

To preserve public order—and to preserve their own positions of honor, privilege, and power—the Roman elite had to provide the burgeoning populace of the imperial metropolis with adequate food. While half of the Roman plebs succumbed to the expanding patron-client system, the other half resisted the indignity of becoming personally as well as economically dependent on powerful figures. The need to feed the populace became so overwhelming that only state action could deal with the problem. Already by 123 B.C.E., the numbers of indebted or displaced peasants was so large that officials enacted sweeping economic "reform" measures. All of Rome's citizens would receive, at a low price, monthly quantities of grain. Another "reformer" with his eye on the Roman populace, Julius Caesar, made the distribution of grain free. Under Augustus, grain was doled out to an estimated 250,000 male citizens, affecting (if not completely feeding) around 670,000 people (not counting the 30 percent of the population who were slaves and resident aliens). Since the emperor had become the state, the populace of Rome became, in effect, the clients of their imperial patron.

Provision of food for the imperial metropolis became one of the major factors in the Roman Empire's expropriation of resources from subject peoples. It only compounded the seizure of spoil by the warlords in the initial conquests, the extortion of huge fortunes by governors and publicans (highest-level tax collectors), the produce taken to supply the other major imperial cities, and the continuing drain of resources needed to feed the army. The bulk of the grain (and other food) imported to Rome and taken for the army was extracted from subject peoples in the form of tribute and taxes in kind (Josephus, *War* 2.16.4 §383). The effect of the tribute levied on top of the local taxes, tithes, and rents gradually forced the provincial peasants into debt. Unable to feed their families after the multiple extractions from the piles of grain on their threshing floors, they had to borrow from creditors who controlled supplies of grain, probably officers and stewards of the provincial elites. For the peasant producers, the imperial drain on their resources meant increasing hunger and, with spiraling debt, potential loss of their family inheritance of land.

Hand in hand with the bread went the circuses.[12] The satisfaction of the people's material needs by the distribution of grain produced an abundance of leisure that required entertainment, stimulation, and excitement. Rome observed an annual cycle of celebrations and festivals in honor of its principal gods (the powers that provided fertility, security, and so on), called the public games. These religious festivals consisted mainly of chariot races in the circus and theatrical performances, organized and presided over by some of the magistrates of the year.[13] The games were entertainments that the city dedicated to the gods/powers, and public banquets in which they offered sacrifices to the divine powers of the imperial order. Religious devotion was thus inseparable from—indeed, took the form of—indulgence in merrymaking, revelry, and spectacular entertainments.[14]

The games were also a form of gift giving, not only to and from the powers/gods but from the warlords and other magnates to the people. The wealthy and powerful magnates were giving back to the people a portion of what they had gained from their positions of power in the state and army. The Roman people resented private luxury but heartily approved luxury shared with the public. Those in possession of wealth and power had to demonstrate that they were being devoted to the good of the populace. The imperial dimension of this can be seen most clearly in the display of military glory that was the popular face of imperial conquest. When the victorious warlords returned to Rome with their mountains of booty and enslaved prisoners of war, they celebrated *triumphs*. In these festivals and by building great monuments, they demonstrated that their victories had been manifestations of the divinely ordained destiny of the Roman people and signs of the gods' favor.

Beginning with Augustus, the emperor increasingly monopolized the role of gift giver (sponsor) as well as the roles of presider and commissioner. All games and gladiatorial shows in the Colosseum began with acclamations of homage to the emperor. Religion and politics were clearly inseparable in the power relations expressed in these elaborate spectacles.

The games and shows were official state ceremonies, developments of deeply rooted Roman custom, but also popular entertainment. In the annual calendar of state festivals, each of which lasted a few days, the games and shows filled the equivalent of four months—more than the total of weekends and holidays in American society. And for those spectacles *given* by the emperor, the people spent part of nearly a third of the days of the year with their patron being entertained in the stands of the arena. The people developed important forms of communication with their imperial sovereign, via approval or disapproval of the performances he sponsored. But most important was the continuing bond that these ceremonial spectacles forged between emperor, people, and even the now powerless Senate. The power centralized in the emperor thus took ceremonial form in the civil-religious festivals as well as economic form in the distribution of grain—bread and circuses.

PATRONAGE PYRAMIDS AND CLIENT KINGS: POLITICAL(-ECONOMIC) POWER

After the Romans created their empire by military power, they secured and maintained it by political power, although political power was hardly separable from economic and religious power, as we shall see. The forms taken by political(-economic-religious) power, however, depended on whether the subject peoples were already "civilized" or not. The basic division was between the "Greeks," who had long since established city-states, and the barbarians, who had not yet developed such a "civil" form.

To maintain order in the already "civilized" parts of the empire, the Romans adapted the pyramids of patronage developed in Rome itself into a mode of imperial political-economic power. Following their military conquests of city-states or smaller kingdoms, ancient Babylon and Assyria had established a giant pyramid of agriculture-based economic power, which in turn supported their political and military power. Somewhat similar pyramids of power developed in the Roman Empire, but focused on personal relations in a patron-client system.[15]

In Rome itself, as the peasantry was forced off the land and into the city, pyramids of patronage relations evolved in which wealthy and politically ambitious patricians promised to alleviate the hunger and poverty of the poor in return for personal political loyalty. The pyramids of patron-age that emerged were thus instruments both of social cohesion across the gulf dividing the poor and the wealthy and of social control by the wealthy patrons. As Seneca observed, the exchange of favors and services (*beneficia*) "most especially binds together human society" (*Ben.* 1.4.2). Patron-client relations also developed within the aristocracy between prominent politicians and their protégés—although considerate patrons thoughtfully avoided the demeaning term *cliens*. The most powerful fig-ures surrounded themselves with "friends"; and both those of lesser rank and aspiring younger politicians needed "friends" in high(er) places.

The institution and the model of patronage was readily developed into an empirewide system under Augustus.[16] He began running the empire as a vast network of power pyramids. In Rome itself, he set himself up as the patron of patrons, controlling the aristocracy by distributing *ben-eficia*, including senatorial offices, magistracies, and honors, as personal favors to senators and knights. In addition, in Rome itself he became the grand patron of the populace that was not already dependent on one of the great houses, as noted above.

Beyond Rome, Augustus established patron-client relations with the elite of the major cities and provinces. In the major cities of the empire, prominent provincials proudly publicized their gratitude to the emperor in public inscriptions and the shrines, temples, and games that they spon-sored in his honor. Paralleling the benefits that the emperor bestowed on urban and provincial elite in return for honors rendered, Roman gov-ernors cultivated a loyal clientele among local aristocrats by dispensing certain favors and benefits for them or their cities. As far as the provincial elite were concerned, they were no longer governed by foreign conquer-ors but by "friends" of "friends." In the cities and provinces, wealth was already consolidated in the hands of a few local families. The patron-client relations established between them and the imperial family thus consolidated political-economic power in a network of many pyramids of power, all unified at the top in the person of the emperor.

The pyramids of personal-economic power relations also had a unify-ing effect politically, at least at the top, among the wealthy and powerful, who dominated affairs in their respective cities, provinces, and petty king-doms. Many of those inscriptions that prominent provincials dedicated to their imperial patron articulated the imperial ideology: the Romans demonstrated their *fides* (= Gk *pistis*), loyalty in the sense of protection, while the friends of Rome showed their *fides*, that is, their loyalty to Rome. Many will find this language familiar from Paul's letters, where *pistis* is usually translated as "faith," which only points to the dominance of the imperial context in which Paul was working. Pliny (*Panegyricus* 2.21) declared that the good emperor was not so much an efficient administrator as a paternal protector and benefactor. Since subjects could not repay imperial benefactions in kind, the reciprocity ethic dictated that they make a return in the form of deference, respect, and loyalty. The emperor who played the role of a great patron well had no need of guards because he was "protected by his benefits" (Seneca, *De clementia* 1.13.5).

To maintain control of the less "civilized" peoples, on the other hand, the Romans relied on the more concretely coercive forms of client kings and military strongmen. As Tacitus commented, this was an "old and long-standing principle of Roman policy, [to] employ kings among the instruments of servitude" (*Agr.* 14.1).

After their initial conquest of Palestine, the Romans attempted to rule through the temple-state that had been established originally under the Persian Empire. By this arrangement, Judeans continued to serve "the god who is in Jerusalem" (Ezra 1:3) in the Temple with their tithes and offerings, thus supporting the priestly aristocracy that maintained order and collected tribute for the imperial regime. To put an end to the battles between rival Hasmonean pretenders to the high priesthood, however, in 40 B.C.E. the Romans appointed the energetic and ruthless young military strongman Herod as "king of the Judeans." "Antony and Caesar left the senate-house with Herod between them, preceded by the consuls and the other magistrates, as they went to offer sacrifices and to lay up the decree in the Capitol" (Josephus, *War* 1.14.4 §285). After subduing the reluctant Judeans, Samaritans, and Galileans with the help of Roman troops, Herod established a highly repressive regime that maintained relative stability in his realm from 37 to 4 B.C.E. To bolster his own security, he established an elaborate system of impregnable mountaintop fortresses around the countryside. Masada, overlooking the Dead Sea, is only the most famous of these. Herod ruled with an iron fist, required oaths of loyalty to his own and Roman rule, and used informants to spy out dissidents.

Well before the end of his reign, Herod had become paranoid in his tyranny. He executed his own elder sons for suspicion of disloyalty and ordered two distinguished scholars and their students burned alive for attacking the Roman eagle he had erected above the gate of the Temple as a symbol of his loyalty to Rome. We don't know that a "massacre of the innocents" such as recounted in the Gospel of Matthew ever took place. But it would have been very much in character for Rome's client king obsessed about security.[17]

With his westernizing policies of economic development, Herod became Augustus's favorite client king. To ensure that his sons were properly socialized into Roman imperial culture, they were sent to be raised at the imperial court in Rome. Herod mounted numerous building projects, some of them massive in scale. He built several Roman-style cultural institutions around his realm, such as amphitheaters and hippodromes, and several temples in honor of the emperor. Most impressive were whole new cities also in honor of Augustus. Partly to facilitate "trade" and the shipping of tribute and other goods to Rome, he built the seaport city of Caesarea on the coast, with huge statues of the goddess Roma and the god Caesar facing west across the Mediterranean and the appropriate Roman-Hellenistic installations of theater and stadium. On the site of the previously destroyed capital of Samaria, he built the city of Sebaste (Augustus) and settled a military colony there. To maintain favorable relations with the imperial regime and the elites of the great cities of the empire, Herod made lavish gifts to imperial family members and endowed the construction of temples and colonnades in several Greek cities. Meanwhile, he established a lavish court, and he and extended family members built up huge personal fortunes. The funding of all this "development" and "diplomacy," of course, came from taxation of his people and the produce of his royal estates worked by tenants.

Perhaps because of his own illegitimacy and unpopularity with his subjects, Herod kept the Temple and high priesthood intact as instruments of his own—and imperial—rule. As quickly as was expedient, he eliminated the last members of the incumbent high priestly family, the Hasmoneans, and installed high priestly families of his own choosing, some from Diaspora communities in Egypt and Babylon. Four of these families became the high priestly aristocracy after Herod's death. Besides offering the traditional sacrifices to God, the priests also performed sacrifices in honor of Rome and Caesar. Their dependence on Herod ensured that the Temple served as an instrument of his rule. The Temple itself

Herod rebuilt in grand Hellenistic fashion. "Herod's" Temple in Jerusalem, which took nearly eighty years to complete, became one of the great "wonders" of the Roman imperial world, a pilgrimage destination for prominent Romans and for wealthy Jews from the Diaspora communities in cities of the eastern Mediterranean. Since peasants almost never leave written records, we do not know exactly what the people thought about the huge new Temple with Hellenistic-style colonnades and travelers from abroad. The economic implications of the new structure of power, however, were clear. The Roman installation of Herod and his rebuilding of the Temple and expansion of the priestly aristocracy meant that the Galilean and Judean peasants now had not just one but three layers of rulers to support.

When Herod's son Archelaus proved unsatisfactory as a client ruler, the Romans resorted again to the priestly aristocracy to control Judea and Samaria and to collect the tribute. Now, however, they placed the high priesthood under the supervision, and military backup, of a Roman governor based in Caesarea. Since the governors usually exercised the power of appointment, it was incumbent on the four high priestly families from which the high priest might be appointed to maintain close collaboration with the governors. These high priestly families became increasingly wealthy during the first century. They maintained private gangs of strongmen, apparently for their own security as well as to implement their predatory appropriation of the people's crops. As Josephus reports,

> [The high priest] Ananias had servants who were utter rascals and who, rallying the most reckless men, would go to the threshing floors and take by force the tithes [meant for the regular] priests; nor did they refrain from beating those who refused to give. The [other] high priests were guilty of the same practices. (*Ant.* 20.9.2 §§206–7; cf. 20.8.8 §181)

The popular memory of these high priestly families left its mark in the Talmud.

> Woe unto me because of the house of Baithos;
> woe unto me because of their lances!
> Woe unto me because of the house of Hanin (Ananus); . . .

Woe unto me because of the house of Ishmael ben Phiabi,
woe unto me because of their fists.
For they are high priests and their sons are treasurers
and their sons-in-law are Temple overseers,
and their servants smite the people with sticks! (*b. Pesaḥ.* 57a)

Roman rule through the priestly aristocracy in Judea proved increasingly less capable of controlling the growing turbulence toward mid-first century.

In Galilee, after Herod's death, the Romans imposed his son Antipas. As a second-generation client ruler who had been raised at the imperial court, Antipas came to power already integrated into Roman imperial political culture. He continued the "development" of his father. Within twenty years, he had built two new cities in the tiny territory of Galilee. Besides the alien urban culture suddenly set down upon the landscape, this meant that for the first time in history the ruler of Galilee lived in Galilee, with clear implications for the efficiency of tax collection. Presumably the Jerusalem Temple and high priesthood no longer had jurisdiction over Galilee. Yet we must wonder whether they still attempted to keep at least some flow of tithes and offerings coming to the Temple and priesthood from Galilee, and what the implications were for the economic pressures on the Galilean peasantry.

In this system of indirect rule, the Herodian "kings" and the Jerusalem high priests based in Herod's massively reconstructed Temple became the face of Roman imperial rule in Galilee and Judea. Indirect rule may have been less objectionable to the subject people than direct rule, with an occupying army. It was effective, however, only so long as either the client rulers or the Romans themselves applied repressive coercive force. Herod maintained tight control with his police state. Roman governors periodically sent out the military to suppress protests and movements.

THE APOTHEOSIS OF IMPERIAL RULE: RELIGIOUS POWER

Just as Roman religion itself was transformed into one of the principal manifestations of imperial power, so too religion in cities and countries subject to Rome was transformed into a form of imperial power. The religious forms taken by Roman imperialism may be difficult for modern Westerners to understand, handicapped as we are by our assumption of the separation of religion from politics and power and our reduction of religion to mere individual belief. In attempting to understand how religion could become one of the principal forms of power by which the empire held together, it may help to review the principal religious institutions of the Greek cities (and the Judean temple-state) that were subjugated by Rome.

The ancient Greek city-state (*polis* in Greek, *civis* in Latin), like ancient Rome, had its "civil" or "political" religion: temples, statues, sacrifices, and other celebrations in honor of and devoted to its gods. The gods that the city-states served in these forms were the principal natural-civilizational powers that determined their lives, such as the forces of fertility (Demeter/Aphrodite, and so on), earth (Gaia), heaven (Uranus), the sea (Poseidon), and the personification of the power of the city-state itself that nurtured and protected it (e.g., Athena). As in Rome, sacrifices and games, such as the "Olympic" games, were celebrations of and communion with these life-giving and/or life-threatening powers. The survival, welfare, and general life of the city-state depended on the goodwill of these powers—hence their appeasement. In the Greek cities, religion had to do with power every bit as much as politics. Better stated, religion was inseparable from politics in representing and structuring the power relations of society.

When Rome picked a fight with the league of Greek cities and then utterly destroyed classical Corinth, it was evident that there was an overwhelming new power to reckon with. In Greek cities and elsewhere, temples and ceremonies were dedicated to Roma (the power of Rome). Far more decisive historically was the victory of Octavian, which ended ten years of utterly chaotic empirewide civil war. The victorious *princeps* of Rome had at last established peace and prosperity and brought salvation to the world. He was the Savior. Within decades, the elite of nearly every Greek city, all long since subject to the empire, began to transform the religion of their city.[18] They installed statues of Augustus in the city temples beside the statues of the deities to whom they were dedicated. In the space between the temples in the city center, they built shrines to the emperor. In many cases, the dominant oligarchies built temples to the emperor, even redesigning the city center to focus on the imperial temple. City or provincial elites also renamed or set up new games in honor of Caesar. The presence of the emperor thus came to pervade public space in the Greek cities.

The reorientation of religious-political life of Greek cities was still more pervasive. The magnates who sat on city or provincial councils even transformed their annual calendars. Public festivals now focused on imperial events such as birthdays of imperial family members, thus injecting the imperial presence further into the consciousness of the public. For example, in 9 B.C.E., the provincial council of the province of Asia decreed that, insofar as the emperor was central to world order and the welfare of humankind, Augustus's birthday would henceforth be observed as the beginning of the new year. "The birthday of the most divine emperor is the fount of every public and private good. Justly would one take this day to be the beginning of the Whole Universe. . . . Justly would one take this day to be the beginning of Life and Living for everyone."[19] The appearance of the emperor and his family on coins and shrines even became the model for clothing and hairstyles. The emperor was portrayed naked, like the gods, dressed in military garb, like the gods, represented in colossal size, like the gods, and overlaid with gold, like the gods. Greeks regularly identified Augustus with Zeus.

It seems clear that the highly civilized Greek city elites, when subjected to external imperial power, simply created a prominent place for that power within their traditional religion and in the forms of traditional religion. The power of imperial domination was so overwhelming that they could not represent the emperor merely as similar to a traditional local hero. They rather had to represent the new power that had established the peace and security of the world, including the order of their city life, in forms traditionally used for the gods. For the previously civilized areas, the Romans had no need of occupying armies or an elaborate bureaucracy. The Greek city elites represented and institutionalized imperial power in traditional indigenous religious forms.

Finally, with regard to the "civilized" areas of the empire, the religious form of imperial power relations was articulated closely with the pyramids of social-economic and political power.[20] We have no reason to believe that ordinary people in cities such as Corinth or Thessalonica or Ephesus were enthusiastic participants in the games and ceremonies that honored the emperor. But the presence of the emperor permeated public space, and the rhythm of public life revolved around imperial events. For the very poor, who made up the vast majority of the populace in any city, the imperial festivals were their only opportunities all year to eat meat, from the sacrifices sponsored by the wealthy patrons of the city. One suspects that most people simply went with the flow of urban life. Decisive for the cohesion of the empire was that those who sponsored the imperial shrines, temples, games, and festivals were the very families who, controlling the wealth in the Greek cities, were also the local magistrates and members of the city councils. For the obvious benefits that might accrue to them and their cities, these magnates cultivated the patronage of the imperial family and served as the priests of the imperial cult.

In the less "civilized" areas of the empire as well, honors to the emperor also played a significant role in holding the far-flung empire together, at least at the top. Herod's rule in Palestine provides an instructive case. Many of the major economic "development" projects he sponsored were religious forms and expressions of imperial power. With the exception of the Temple, however, he was not "building" on the forms of traditional religion. In constructing the temples to the emperor Augustus, Herod was copying forms from elsewhere in the empire, such as the Greek cities. It is difficult to discern how these temples might have been related to indigenous elite religion in Samaria or other towns in Palestine. The statues of Roma and Caesar looking out over the Mediterranean from Caesarea must have seemed garishly "over-the-top" to tradition-minded elites in the Hellenistic towns along the coast as well as to the priestly elite in Jerusalem.

The temple-state in Jerusalem was different from the Greek city-states in two major respects. On the one hand, the Jerusalem Temple had from the outset been established under the Persian Empire as an institution subject to and the local representative of imperial rule. On the other hand, the god served there was understood as transcending all of the gods (the divinized forces served by other peoples) and being ultimately responsible for all their functions.

Herod was somewhat more subtle and sensitive in his massive reconstruction of the Temple in Jerusalem than in his other major building projects—but not that subtle. Because the site was super-sacred, he agreed to have some of the priests qualified by lineage to serve in the Temple trained in masonry and other skills to carry out the most sensitive parts of the construction. The style of the buildings around the perimeter of the Temple Mount, however, was more Hellenistic-Roman than traditional Judean. The erection of the Roman eagle over the principal gate of the Temple, however, proclaimed the power of Rome. It was highly objectionable to those grounded in Israelite tradition, such as the teachers and their students who tore down the eagle as Herod lay dying and the populace who acclaimed them as martyrs.

In contrast to the development of the imperial cult in Greek cities, no statue of the emperor was erected inside the Temple, and no sacrifices were offered directly to the emperor as one of the gods. But sacrifices were offered daily for Caesar and Roma, the personified imperial city. Those were essential as well as required acts of loyalty to ("faith in") the emperor and empire. But they were objectionable to those deeply rooted in and committed to Israelite tradition. Seventy years after Herod's death, when the priests in charge of the daily sacrifices suddenly refused any longer to perform the sacrifices for the emperor, it was understood, evidently by both Jerusalemites and the Romans, as tantamount to a declaration of independence. The embodiment of imperial power in religious form, including injection into traditional religion, may have helped maintain the imperial order in Judea temporarily. But its roots were shallow and, if anything, helped alienate the priests, scribes, and people from Roman imperial rule.

Chapter 2

Israel's Covenant and Prophetic Protest

In contrast to the sustained empire building of Rome, the heritage of ancient Israel was more complex and ambiguous. The people of Israel cherished their origins as an independent people and an alternative society. They attributed their deliverance to a power that transcended the divinized natural-political-economic powers of the ancient imperial civilizations. Indeed, they referred to this power as the one who had brought them out of bondage in Egypt. Israel then received from their liberating power a covenant featuring principles of political-economic cooperation and justice, with power shared in community.

The ancient Romans could not understand and could not tolerate the Israelite people's exclusive loyalty to a transcendent power and the principles of political-economic justice that had become embodied in resilient "Mosaic" and prophetic tradition. The peoples of Israelite heritage whom the Romans conquered, then the nascent Christians who originated in reaction to Rome rule, and later the people of Islam all looked back to the stories of Abraham and Sarah and Moses and Joshua as the paradigmatic break with imperial rule. All of the "Abrahamic" traditions held to the principles of justice articulated by Moses and the Israelite prophets. The Gospels of the Christian tradition in particular portrayed Jesus as a new Moses and a new Elijah. Peoples whose traditional way of life was rooted in the Abrahamic-Mosaic-prophetic tradition found it difficult simply to acquiesce and compromise their commitments even in the face of invasion by imperial powers. To understand this, we need a sense of the heritage of ancient Israel.

STORIES OF STRUGGLES FOR INDEPENDENCE

The stories told by early Israelites focus on how their ancestors managed, step by step, to make a break with the imperial civilizations of Mesopotamia and Egypt, and to establish their independence as an alternative society. The books of Genesis, Exodus, Joshua, and Judges include story after story of people who fled from the cities of the empire, or who struggled to maintain their independence from the fortified cities in Palestine.[1]

Ironically, the eventual outcome of this early history was that Israel itself was transformed into a monarchy. Accordingly, the numerous stories of withdrawal from or rebellion against centralized hierarchical power were blunted in their effect by inclusion in an overarching history that climaxed in the imperial kingship of David and Solomon. The theme of that overarching history was (fulfillment of) the promise that the children of Abraham would become a prominent people. Stories of withdrawal or insurrection against kings were later framed into episodes in a history of conquest. Centuries later, in the hands of translators in the service of colonizing European monarchies, stories of guerrilla warfare against rulers in fortified cities were further transformed into stories of genocide against conquered peoples. Despite pointed criticism by biblical scholars, standard editions of the Bible (e.g., NRSV) persist in printing translations that legitimate the European conquest and colonial rule of Native Americans, Africans, and others, as we shall see below.

The biblical history of early Israel thus "speaks out of both sides of its mouth." As many subject peoples to whom the European colonizers read or handed the Bible realized, it speaks with different voices.[2] The dominant overarching narrative often has an imperial agenda. But by "reading between the lines," we can discern the editorial stitching and overwriting, in order to hear again the earlier versions of the stories.

The break with ancient Near Eastern empires is prepared for by God's condemnation and destruction of "the tower of Babel," symbolizing the arrogance of the imperial regimes who built those monumental ziggurats in Mesopotamia (Gen 11:1-9). God calls Abram and Sarah to leave Babylon, to become refugees, and to start a new life in a land beyond the control of the empire (Gen 12:1). The decisive break with ancient Near Eastern imperial civilization is the exodus of the Hebrews from bondage under Pharaoh in Egypt, which became the historical prototype of subsequent liberation movements. The larger-than-life figure of Moses is the paradigmatic prophet who hears the voice of God and patiently cajoles and organizes the people to make their daring escape. Making the break with the oppressive imperial system is a prolonged struggle to summon the courage to leave behind the security of servitude to the system and to risk the insecurity entailed in establishing an alternative society.

In the exodus story, the crucial first step is for the prophet and the people to hear the voice that comes from beyond the imperial system, a force that, far from being one of the recognized divine powers of the civilization that keeps the Hebrews in bondage, calls them to escape. It is surely significant that the story that sets up this breakthrough portrays the people as Hebrews, and not yet the people of Israel, who were the eventual result of the exodus. Nor is it by accident that these people, who groan under servitude to the powers of the Egyptian empire and eventually generate the courage to make a break with the system of domination, have memories of ancestors who had not been subject to the empire, such as Abraham and Sarah. The story of resistance begins not with Moses but with the Hebrew midwives, who refused the pharaoh's command to kill the male babies at birth (Exod 1:15-22). But the Hebrews' prolonged bondage had resulted in their domestication into Egyptian culture. They "groaned under their bondage and cried out" (2:23). But they did not cry out to "the Kinsman of Abraham" or "the Shield of Isaac." Did they no longer remember the name(s) of the god of their ancestors?

It cannot be by accident that the voice of the outside force calling them to freedom comes through first to Moses. Born a Hebrew and then assimilated into Egyptian culture and the Egyptian imperial order, Moses finally identified with his Hebrew heritage and became a representative figure. Significantly, the voice of the outside force broke through to the fugitive "Hebrew-Egyptian" in a special location outside the imperial system. The story of the bush that burned but was not consumed (Exod 3:1-6) is subtle, clever, and cagey. It seems to play with us as if "we were there" with Moses and the other Hebrews. The "Hebrew-Egyptians" had become domesticated during their bondage in Egypt, so worn down by the routine of dependence on the system and stuck in their oppressive but secure niche that (so the narrative allows us to imagine) they could not even remember the name of the god of their ancestors when they cried out for help (2:23-25). They/Moses would have been able to recognize and be addressed by only the already familiar powers of their life-world, the cosmic-political-economic forces that determined and controlled their civilization. If the outlaw Hebrew-Egyptian Moses or anyone immersed in an ancient Near Eastern culture heard a voice coming from a flame in a bush, for example, he/they would immediately assume that the great force Fire was attempting to communicate.

The narrative, however, says "a messenger of YHWH appeared to him in a flame of fire out of a bush; he looked and the bush was blazing, yet it was not consumed." That is a considerable circumlocution—a lot of words to avoid saying simply that Fire appeared to Moses in a bush. There are multiple actors in the scene: the *messenger* appeared, then *YHWH* saw . . . , and then *God* called to Moses. Any teacher of composition worth her salt would ask the writer to be clearer about who is appearing and speaking to Moses. But perhaps the narrator is purposely speaking in a puzzling way. For how would a voice that Moses had never heard before and could not even imagine cut through his Egyptian cultural assumptions and conceptualizations? The narrator is purposely trying to avoid representing the liberator-force as one of the powers of the Egyptian empire, since those are the gods and the way of thinking about gods from which Moses and his people must make a break. And sure enough, the power addressing Moses is not one of the gods of the empire of abundance, security, and slavery; this power summons them to leave their bondage in Egypt (3:7-12) to serve itself, the force of freedom.

Moses, however, still thinks like an ancient Near Easterner, and he knows that the people he is instructed to lead do so as well. The gods with which they had become familiar in Egyptian bondage were particular powers whose identity was indicated in their names: Sun, Moisture, Fire, Isis, Osiris. After all, as indicated several episodes later in the narrative (6:2), though God had appeared to the ancestors as "Mighty God," s/he had never before revealed her/his identity as the force calling them to gain their freedom. What should Moses say is the name/identity of this force that is summoning them in such a vague and indefinite way to flee into such an uncertain future? Who are you, Force? Or, what force are you, Voice? (3:13). And the Force/Voice gives what is obviously a non-answer, or rather two nonanswers to the question (3:14-15). First, with regard to the future: "I will (cause to) be what I will (cause to) be." This nonanswer suggests something like: "Not to worry; I'll be there, I'll do what's necessary when the time comes." The Force/Voice promises to do what is necessary as they summon the courage to break with the system of slavery. Second, with regard to the past: I am "the God of your ancestors, the God of Abraham, the God of Isaac, and the God of Jacob." They are summoned to remember the power of their ancestors in their semi-independent lives in the hill country prior to their incorporation into the imperial system of Egypt. Memory of life before bondage will also motivate them to risk freedom despite the insecurity.

Hearing the call of the power of freedom, however, leads nowhere until and unless leaders and followers can organize themselves into a movement that can mount resistance to the oppressive system and its relentless measures of repression. Pharaoh is utterly unprepared to relinquish control over the slaves of the gods who provide the economic base of his imperial power. He insists that his managers and supervisors, even while skimping on materials, extract even greater productivity from the Hebrews' hard labor (5:1-21). And the repressive measures are effective. The people, suffering all the more for daring to challenge the system, would no longer listen to Moses, "because of their broken spirit and their cruel slavery" (6:9).

The sequence of stories of the plagues that God visits upon Pharaoh and the Egyptians is usually deemed a later addition to the basic exodus narrative, designed to heighten the drama into a contest of who can command the greater powers, the expert advisors and high-ranking officers of Pharaoh or God acting through the hand of Moses. In its political-economic effects, however, the series of plagues displays how Pharaoh's desperate repressive measures to keep the Hebrews in his labor force result in serious damage to the economic resources and productivity of the imperial system. The pollution of the Nile River, on which the whole agricultural system of Egypt depended, would have meant a complete failure of the crops. The decimation of the livestock, including draft animals necessary for plowing, would have hamstrung agriculture for years, until livestock could be replenished. And the destruction of the crops by storms or a plague of locusts that devoured the grain would have utterly ruined yet another year's crop. Pharaoh's stubborn determination to maintain control by ratcheting up the repression was, in effect, resulting in the implosion of his economic power.

The Hebrews, along with a larger "mixed multitude" (12:38), eventually summon the courage to flee across the frontier to freedom. The three different images by which their miraculous escape is represented—God dividing the waters of the Reed Sea (14:21-22, 26, 29), the wind driving the water back in a shallow lake (14:21), and a storm at sea that capsizes the barges ferrying the war chariots (15:1-10)—all seem fantastic, although the latter two could be seen as a coincidence of timing, attributed to the agency of God.

Often missed are the clear indications in the biblical text of the remarkable break in theology that is involved in the Hebrews' break away from the ancient Near Eastern imperial system. The victory song included in the exodus narrative (Exod 15:1-18) is the earliest example of Hebrew poetry retained in the Bible—hence an early understanding of YHWH as the force of freedom that motivated and inspired the people's break with the dominant political-economic-cultural system of the ancient Near East.

How starkly the nascent Hebrew "theology" contrasted with that of the dominant culture appears most dramatically in how the same words and seemingly the same phenomena express such utterly different views of the world and its dominant powers. As noted in chapter 1, in the climax of *Enuma Elish*, the Mesopotamian ritual drama of the origin of Order, Storm-Kingship defeats and slaughters Sea and from her body forms the firmaments of heaven and earth (and then creates humans as slaves of the powers to supply the labor required to build the great houses of the Powers in the imperial metropolis of Babylon). In a parallel Canaanite myth, Storm-Kingship kills Sea, thus establishing order over threatening chaos.

In the Song of the Sea in Exodus 15, however, YHWH defeats Pharaoh's armies, sent out to enforce forced labor on the Hebrews, by causing a storm at sea in order to free the Hebrews and bring them to the "sanctuary" that YHWH had established. Storm and sea are no longer divinized cosmic powers before whom the people cower and whom they serve with their labor and the produce of their labor. They are now simply some among the natural forces of the stage on which the struggle between rulers and subject peoples is acted out. The enemy, Pharaoh and his troops, is now historical-imperial, the head and enforcer of the imperial system of forced labor. And YHWH is the liberating force that defeats the cultural-religious and military powers of empire. This is not "monotheism." There are still other divine powers out there, other powers that affect lives of other peoples, and possibly also the lives of the Hebrews. But for the Hebrews, those powers of nature and/or civilization are no longer gods whom they serve.

The early chapters of the book of Joshua also feature several stories of independence and even insurrection. The editorial framing and modern translation of these stories, however, have made them read like integral components of a longer story of conquest and genocide by the early Israelites against "the inhabitants" of the land of Canaan (Josh 10:40-43; 11:16-23). According to the themes of the Deuteronomic history that leads up to the Davidic monarchy, this is the land that God promised the Israelites, who were charged to "take possession of the land" under the leadership of Joshua. Most fateful and tragic for the way this history of early Israel was used by European colonizers to take over other peoples' lands and "slaughter the inhabitants" has been the translation of the Hebrew construct, "those who sit in X (city or town)" as "the inhabitants." In later prophetic oracles, translators recognized that "those who sit in" a fortified city, in a line parallel to "the king of" another city, meant "the rulers of." In the victory song in Exod 15:1-18, celebrating YHWH's defeat of Pharaoh's armies, however, the NRSV (and other translations) missed that the phrase "those who sit in Philistia/Canaan" in 15:14-15 is parallel to "the chiefs of Edom" and "the rulers of Moab." The reference is thus not to the "inhabitants" but to "the rulers of" the fortified cities of Philistia and Canaan. The ordinary people of the land, from whom "those who sat" in positions of power in the fortified cities extracted taxes and tithes, lived in villages.[3]

It is striking how most of the struggles narrated in the early chapters of Joshua are against kings. Even the editorial summaries (10:40-43; 11:16-23) that represent the taking of the land as a "blitzkrieg" state explicitly that Joshua and the Israelites were fighting against kings. "Those who sit in X city" in these same stories, therefore, are almost certainly not "the inhabitants" but "the rulers," including the professional military by means of which the kings maintained their positions of wealth and privilege. The details of several of these stories, moreover, indicate that the struggles are what in other times and places would be called "peasant revolts." The Israelites, having only simple weapons, have no alternative but to use guerrilla warfare, such as trickery, ambush, and hamstringing the horses, against the professional military of the kings of Ai or Hazor and their war chariots (Josh 8:1-29; 11:1-15). In the story of the taking of Jericho (Joshua 2 and 6), members of the lower class who service the rulers of the city, symbolized by Rahab, make common cause with the insurgents from outside the city walls. Once we know that Rahab (like other servants of the rulers inside the walled city) had probably been taken as a debt-slave to work off her family's debts, we can better understand why the Israelite spies make contact with her.

The stories in the early chapters of Judges suggest that it was necessary for the Israelites to struggle for many generations against the kings and ruling aristocracies of the cities of Canaan to maintain their independence. The list of tribal territories in Judges 1 portrays the Israelites as having gained their independence only in the hill country. In the coastal plain and the other rich agricultural areas, they could not have held their own against the military power of heavily armed horse-drawn chariots. The Song of Deborah (Judges 5) portrays a poorly armed independent peasantry (5:7-8) braving battle against the chariot forces of "the kings of Canaan" near the fortified town of Megiddo (5:19, 22). They succeed only when a timely thunderstorm gets the chariot wheels bogged down in mud and the professional warriors are forced to flee on foot.

It may not be possible satisfactorily to reconstruct a credible history of Israel's origins from these stories. But the stories tell of a struggle of the people of Israel to establish their independence from the centralized hierarchical power of the ancient Near East.

COVENANT COMMUNITY

The messenger of YHWH's call in the Song of Deborah to "Curse Meroz" (Judg 5:23) presupposes that the various social units ("tribes") of the people of early Israel (Ephraim, Zebulun, Issachar, Reuben, Gilead, and so on) stood in a covenant with YHWH and with one another. In this covenant, they had undertaken the obligation to come to one another's defense when one or another tribe was threatened with subordination by one of the kings or city-states. Similarly, when the charismatic "liberator" (shofet, often translated as "judge") Gideon, who has led the people in one of these struggles to reestablish their independence, refuses the people's demand that he become "king" over them, it is another indication of the covenant: he cannot become their king since, according to their covenant, YHWH is literally their king. Israel lives under the direct rule (kingdom) of God.

The covenant with YHWH on Sinai (Exodus 20) was far more than the Ten Commandments to which it is often reduced.[4] Comparisons of core covenantal texts in Exodus 20, Joshua 24, and the book of Deuteronomy with Assyrian treaties and earlier Hittite treaties suggest that the covenant was shaped according to a particular pattern. The covenant given through Moses on Sinai and renewed under Joshua at Shechem has three main interrelated steps or parts.

First, the "historical prologue" was a summary of YHWH's great acts of deliverance, particularly the liberation from bondage in Egypt. This served as a reminder of and warning about what life is like under centralized power. YHWH having rescued them, the people are obligated to observe the "ten words" or commandments of their transcendent liberator.

Second, at the core of the covenant were the commandments of exclusive loyalty to the force of freedom as their transcendent ruler and further commandments prohibiting exploitative social-economic practices in the people's relations with one another. In the first two commandments, Israel swore exclusive loyalty to YHWH. Israel was to have "no other god." This meant also, since YHWH was the king giving the covenant, that Israel was to have no king apart from YHWH, including no human king. Gideon could not agree to be their king, since YHWH was their exclusive king (Judges 8:23). The Israelites, moreover, were not to bow down and serve any other gods, as represented by their images ("idols"). This was only fitting for a people who had only recently managed to become free of Pharaoh and other oppressive kings. Although represented as literally the king of Israel, YHWH was not an imperial king who demanded tribute from the people but the power of freedom who insisted that the people maintain their independence of centralized power.

Corresponding to the exclusive loyalty in the first few commandments were the prohibitions of exploitative social-economic relations between Israelite families in the rest of the commandments. Again, appropriate for people who had just become free of circumstances where the powerful expropriated a hefty portion of the crops produced by each peasant family, Israelites agreed to YHWH's demands that they not covet or steal one another's goods and produce and not cheat or kill one another. These commandments were far more than rules of morality. They were also more than laws. They were too general to be laws. They pertained very concretely to basic economic livelihood. In today's terms, they were principles of social-economic policy. Each one covers a certain broad area of social-economic interaction among persons or families in the society. They in fact protect the people's rights in each of those general areas: "you shall not commit adultery" protects the integrity of marriage and family; "you shall not kill" protects each person's right to life; "you shall not covet" and "you shall not steal" protect the right to property; "honor father and mother" protects the right of the less productive elderly to food and shelter.

It may not be by accident that John Locke, who wrote in the seventeenth century about the natural rights of "life, liberty, and property," was a Scottish Presbyterian thoroughly imbued with the covenant and covenantal teaching of the Pentateuch. The same covenantal background underlies Thomas Jefferson's paraphrase of Locke in the Declaration of Independence: We are all endowed by our creator "with certain unalienable rights, that among these are Life, Liberty, and the pursuit of Happiness."

The covenantal principles of social-economic policy designed to protect the basis of each family's livelihood in a simple agrarian society were then implemented in further economic measures. Each family, in its transgenerational lineage, was understood to have inalienable rights to its ancestral inheritance of land, which had been given by YHWH. Israel accordingly devised certain mechanisms to help protect the economic rights and viability of each component family in a village community. At the most basic level, Israelites were to lend liberally to those in need (for example, Deut 15:10-11). But charging interest to a neighbor in need was strictly forbidden (Exod 22:25-27; Lev 25:36-37). As an economic safety net or a "sharing of the risk" that individual families might fall on hard times, all families were to leave their field unsown every seventh year, so that the poor could harvest the crops that would have grown anyhow from the seed that fell on the ground during the previous harvest (Exod 23:10-11; Lev 25:1-7).

For those who fell seriously into debt due to bad harvests or bad luck, debts were to be canceled every seven years (Deut 15:1-5). Moreover, debt-slaves were to be released every seven years (Exod 21:1-6; Deut 15:12-18). Permanent enslavement of Israelite by Israelite was strictly forbidden (Lev 25:39-55). For those families who lost control of their land, there was always the provision that the next of kin could purchase the land to bring it back into the family (Lev 25:25-28). In addition, supposedly, in the fiftieth or "jubilee" year, all were to be able to return to their original family land (Lev 25:8-24). The jubilee year, however, may have been more of an ideal than a concrete practice. But later sources indicate that the other mechanisms—the sabbatical year for the land and the sabbatical cancellation of debts—were to a degree actually practiced in Israel and later in Judean society up to the time of Jesus. That many of these mechanisms are grounded specifically in YHWH's deliverance of Israel from bondage in Egypt is a clear indication that they are designed to avoid a reversion to such an exploitative system. Because Israelites had been resident aliens in Egypt suffering hard bondage, there was a concern for the rights of the resident alien living among the Israelites (Exod 22:21; 23:9).

All of these covenantal commandments were principles to guide interaction of people in a covenantal community. This meant that community members would not take advantage of another family's bad harvests or other misfortune to enrich themselves or gain power over a neighbor. Ideally, the fortunate could not become wealthy or powerful at someone else's expense, since debts were to be canceled and debt-slaves released every seven years. The covenantal principles meant also that the members of local village communities would share risks, providing "welfare" for the poor, who could glean what was left in the fields, and coming to one another's aid with noninterest loans in times of difficulty. The community as a whole had a responsibility to see that all of its constituent families had a sufficient living.

Third, what made the covenant "work" was its religious-cultural dimension as an agreement between YHWH and the people (and among the people). Since God was the only king of the society, Israel had no human king able to enforce the principles of the covenant with legitimate use of force. Israel was, with regard to YHWH, a theocracy, but with regard to concrete social practice, it was what might be called a cooperative anarchy. Observance of the principles meant to guide social-economic relations depended on several interrelated structural and cultural-ritual features of the overall covenant. Frequent covenant renewal ceremonies activated these, as in the prototype recounted in Joshua 24. Recitation of the historical prologue reminded Israelites of their ancestors' slavery in Egypt and of YHWH's deliverance—hence of their obligation to observe the principles of freedom. It is significant that Mosaic covenantal discourse uses the same root word for both God's having done justice for the Hebrews (*shofet*) and for the principles of justice that they were to observe (*mishpatim*). In those covenant renewal ceremonies the people also recommitted themselves to their divine king and to one another. Further, not believing that the powers of high civilization were (their) gods, they looked to the inscription of the covenant on monumental stones and witnessed against themselves (Josh 24:22, 26-27) and called down detailed blessings and curses on themselves for the observance or non-observance of the principles (Deuteronomy 28).

The Mosaic covenant given on Sinai was thus, in effect, a "constitution" for ancient Israelite society that attempted to keep power with the people in mutuality and cooperation. The covenantal principles of social-economic policy were designed to keep particular people or families from gaining economic power over others by taking advantage of their economic difficulties and from gaining political power by such maneuvering. But certain historical developments and political-military contingencies were not foreseen in the making of the Mosaic covenant.

IMPERIAL KINGSHIP

For a time, according to narratives in the Hebrew Bible, early Israel managed to maintain its independence as a network of village communities in the hill country, effectively out of reach of the chariot forces of the lowland cities. The Philistines, however, who had come to rule the lowland city-states, sent military expeditions into the hill villages of Hebrews to extract a portion of their crops as tribute. Israelite villages, clans, and tribes living in separate mountain valleys could not effectively resist the Philistines.

Panicked about their inability to maintain their independence as a loose association of villages and "tribes," the Israelites clamored for the centralization of their own peasant militias under a king. The "Deuteronomic history" (the books of Joshua, Judges, 1–2 Samuel, and 1–2 Kings) tells the story in two different versions that have been stitched together in 1 Samuel 8–12. The one, quite uncritical, exudes enthusiasm about the charismatic warrior Saul. The other, focusing on the role of Samuel as the last of the "liberators" and first of the "prophets" and representative of the covenant with YHWH, is sharply critical of kingship. Israel already has a king, YHWH (8:4-9). Samuel prophetically warns Israel that a king will become oppressive, taking their lands and pressing their sons and daughters into onerous service (8:10-18). Nevertheless, in a reluctant compromise in the face of the rising Philistine military power, Samuel, in consultation with YHWH, attempts to set up what, according to the Mosaic covenant, was a contradiction in terms, a "constitutional/covenantal monarchy." He wrote up "the rights and duties of kingship and laid it up before YHWH" (10:25).

Other stories incorporated into the biblical history of the rise of kingship indicate that the early Israelites understood kingship as a provisional and conditional means of regaining the people's independence from foreign domination. The popularly acclaimed and conditional kingships of Saul and David were very different from the imperial monarchy finally set up by the older David and Solomon after a prolonged power struggle. The great prototype of subsequent "anointed ones" (*messiahs*), David son of Jesse, was a shrewd political operator. Having become an outlaw as a result of the jealousy of Saul, the charismatic young warrior even served for a time as commander of a garrison for the enemy, the Philistines. He became head of the tribe of Judah, however, by popular acclamation: "the people of Judah anointed David king over the house of Judah" (2 Sam 2:1-4). Similarly, his recognition as king of all Israel involved negotiations and popular agreement. All the elders of Israel "made a covenant" with David, and "they anointed David king over Israel" (2 Sam 5:1-3).

Lack of archaeological evidence that attests Jerusalem as the capital of a large monarchy in the early Iron Age has led scholars to question the historical veracity of the biblical accounts of Solomon as a great imperial king. But this only makes the grandiose portrayal of Solomon's imperial kingship all the more interesting as the royal ideology of the later "Davidic" kings of the tiny monarchy of Judah.

The Deuteronomic history in 2 Samuel portrays David as having conquered not only most of the cities of Canaan but also the smaller surrounding kingships. Solomon then, according to the narrative in 1 Kings 1–10, consolidated power over these other cities and peoples as well as Israel, in an imperial kingship based in the Jebusite city of

Jerusalem that David had conquered. In the newly developed ideology of imperial kingship, the king was enthroned "at the right hand of God" by divine declaration as "the messiah," "the (only-begotten) son of YHWH" (like the Mesopotamian great ones), to whom God had subjected all other kings and peoples (Psalms 2; 110). The ideology of imperial kingship focused on another "covenant"—between YHWH and the Davidic dynasty—which effectively overrode and suppressed the Mosaic covenant between YHWH and all the people (2 Samuel 7). YHWH declared that the Davidic dynasty would rule over Israel forever, regardless of what it did, in return for which the dynasty (Solomon) would make YHWH a house, that is, a temple. Although the Temple was only half the size of his own palace, Solomon proceeded with construction of it, along with his own palace, palaces for his many wives, and military fortresses, by instituting forced labor (1 Kgs 5:13-18). The only way for the ruler of an "underdeveloped" country to fund these massive "development" projects (1 Kings 6–7; 9) was to tax the produce of the Israelite peasantry heavily to generate agricultural produce to trade for the building materials and technical building expertise (1 Kgs 5:7-12). When that did not suffice, the imperial king apparently had such power that he could simply cede to Hiram, king of Tyre, twenty villages along the frontier in Galilee, together with all their people and their ancestral land (1 Kgs 9:10-11). In story after story of the Davidic monarchy included in the Deuteronomic history, kings claimed to be above the principles of the Mosaic covenant, authorized by divine right to use their power in whatever way they saw fit. They were copying the ideology of imperial kingship.

PROPHETIC INDICTMENTS

The people of Israel, however, were not prepared simply to submit to imperial rule. In reaction to David's consolidation of his power in the non-Israelite capital city of Jerusalem, the people of Israel mounted two widespread revolts against their "messiah" (2 Samuel 13–19; 20). David managed to retain his power only by using his foreign mercenaries to suppress the revolts. Even after the further consolidation of power by Solomon, the ten northern tribes of Israel revolted again, against his son and successor, Rehoboam (1 Kings 12). The northern Israelites continued to mount insurrections when their own popularly acclaimed kings attempted to make their power more permanent by establishing dynasties (1 Kgs 15:25-30; 16:5-10). Instrumental in touching off these revolts were the actions of prophets such as Ahijah of Shiloh, who declared God's condemnation of the oppressive king and the divine designation, or "anointing," of a new king (1 Kgs 11:26-33). The most famous of these prophets were Elijah and his protégé Elisha, who along with other spirit-inspired prophets led popular resistance to the first successful attempt in the northern kingdom, Israel, to impose a typical ancient Near Eastern–style monarchy in service of the powers of productivity (Ba'al [Lord Storm] and Asherah, powers of fertility; 1 Kings 17–21; 2 Kings 1–9). The resistance led by Elijah and Elisha was also a locally based renewal of Israel, symbolized in its twelve tribes, in which the prophet(s) combined life-restoring acts of power, such as healing and multiplication of food, with opposition to centralized rule, which had become intolerably oppressive, in direct violation of the Mosaic covenantal principles.

By the eighth century, however, the kings of Judah and Israel had consolidated enough power that they were able to suppress effective resistance. Thereafter, protest and resistance took the form of individual prophets' "speaking truth to power" in the form of "the word of YHWH." Like the Israelite peasantry still solidly rooted in the Mosaic covenant, the prophets declared YHWH's indictment and punishment of kings and/ or their officers for breaking the covenantal commandments that prohibited exploitation of other Israelites.[5] Amos indicted the wealthy rulers and officers of Samaria for constructing mansions and dallying in luxury and conspicuous consumption, all funded by "trampling on the needy and bringing the poor to ruin" through heavy taxation and manipulation of weights and measures to bring peasants into debt (Amos 5:11; 6:1-3, 4-7; 8:4-6). Even more explicitly, Micah indicts the wealthy and powerful rulers for violations of covenantal principles "because it is in their power": "They covet fields and seize them; houses and take them away; they oppress the householder and house, people and their inheritance" (Mic 2:1-5; 3:1-3, 8-12). Isaiah gives the same sense that the ruling elite had systematically exploited the poor, getting them into debt and then taking over their lands and houses.

> YHWH enters into judgment with the elders and princes of his
>   people:
> It is you who have devoured the vineyard;
> the spoil of the poor is in your houses.
> What do you mean by crushing my people? (3:13-15)

> Woe to you who join house to house, who add field to field,
> until there is room for no one but you. . . .
> Surely many houses shall be desolate,
> large and beautiful houses without inhabitant [ruler?]. (5:8-10)

Such systematic exploitation and destruction of the peasantry by the wealthy and powerful rulers could not help but steadily weaken the very economic basis on which the rulers were dependent for their power. The prophets persistently articulated the decline and the reasons for it, the flouting of the covenantal principles of justice for the people. While the prophets of the eighth century pronounced YHWH's condemnation of rulers for violation of particular covenantal commandments, Jeremiah, at the end of the seventh century, just before the Babylonian conquest of Judah and Jerusalem, appeared to indict the whole monarchic and temple system. In his famous condemnation of the Jerusalem Temple (Jeremiah 7; 26), prefiguring that of his latter-day successor Jesus of Nazareth (Mark 11:15-18), Jeremiah pronounced that God was about to destroy the Temple. Why? Because the very institution and its practices violated the whole Mosaic covenant and its principles (7:5-20). Similarly, Jeremiah declared that the Davidic monarchy had condemned itself, as the kings continue to impose forced labor on the people to rebuild their luxurious palaces (Jeremiah 22). The prophetic pronouncements exposed just how oppressive the kings had become, ignoring the principles of the Mosaic covenant in their confidence that God had blessed and guaranteed their position of power and privilege.

AGAIN UNDER ANCIENT NEAR EASTERN EMPIRE

The rulers of Judah exhausted the very people who were their productive economic base, with the result that the severely weakened country was unable to resist imperial conquest. The Babylonian imperial army easily conquered Judah, destroyed Jerusalem and its temple, and deported the officials and other servants of the monarchy. They did leave most of the Judeans who survived the conquest on the land, but the populace had been reduced to a mere twenty-five thousand or so in a limited area near Jerusalem and Bethel.[6] Assyrian armies had similarly conquered the northern Israelites over a century earlier. After these conquests, the Israelite people remained under foreign rule until modern times, except for a period under the successors of the Maccabean leaders prior to conquest by the Romans.

Some years after Persian armies conquered Babylon, the Persian imperial regime sent some of the deported Jerusalem elite back to rebuild the Temple as the basis for a temple-state. The Jerusalem temple-state was the local representative of the Persian imperial regime, set up to control the area and to collect tribute for the emperor as well as tithes and offerings for support of the Temple and its priestly administration. In Christian biblical studies, what emerged in Judea has been anachronistically referred to as "Judaism." But Judea and Judeans under the Persian Empire were both more and less than what developed in late antiquity as what might be called a religion and a distinctive culture ("Judaism"). Judea was still a two-tiered society, with the Judean peasantry still raising the crops and supporting the Temple and priesthood with tithes and offerings as well as rendering tribute to the imperial regime. The Temple was the central political-economic as well as religious institution, having replaced the monarchy (with its temple). So Judea was far more than a religion. Judeans did not yet have a well-defined Bible or synagogue buildings or rabbis engaged in study of Torah. Judeans were a tiny people subject to the Persian Empire. Furthermore, corresponding to the Temple in Jerusalem becoming an instrument of the larger imperial administration, YHWH was now reduced in status to "the god who is in Jerusalem" for whom that "house" was built (Ezra 1:2-3).[7]

While they had no choice but to acquiesce in their subjection to the Persian Empire, given the power of the imperial regime, Judeans did not accept an identity as perpetual "slaves of the (imperial) gods/powers." More precisely, the elite Judeans who produced the texts from this period did not acquiesce (we have no sources for what Judean peasants were thinking). In contrast to the earlier prophets, who represented the interests of the ordinary people, the prophets of the Second-Temple period speak mainly for the Judean elite. The latter, whether still in exile or restored to positions of local power in Jerusalem, now themselves subordinate to imperial rule, identify strongly with the traditions of early Israel, in particular the exodus and the Mosaic covenant. Even in the book of Nehemiah, named after one of the principal governors sent by the Persians to reform the temple-state (by limiting the exploitation of the poor by powerful aristocrats), we find the lament:

> Here we are, slaves to this day—slaves in the land that you gave
> to our ancestors to enjoy its fruit and its good gifts. Its rich yield
> goes to the kings whom you have set over us because of our sins;
> they have power also over our bodies and over our livestock at
> their pleasure, and we are in great distress. (Neh 9:36-37)

Many Second-Temple Judean texts express a hope for the restoration not just of Judea but of all Israel, including the gathering of those deported and dispersed under imperial rule. Memory of the original exodus informed the yearning for a new exodus, only now not of Hebrews pressed into forced labor on building projects, but of the Judean elite deported to Babylon. Some eager prophetic advocates of rebuilding the Temple indulged in fantasies that the Jerusalem Temple itself would (again) be an imperial center, with the treasure of all peoples filling the house in tribute (Hag 2:6-9).

Other prophets had a more sobering sense about what "Israel" could be as a covenanted people even under imperial rule. As can be seen in a sustained prophetic vision included in the book of Isaiah (chapters 40–55), some descendants of the Jerusalem elite now thoroughly identified with the exodus story and the Mosaic covenant. In retrospect, given their mediating position in the Persian imperial structure, their identification with the exodus was somewhat self-serving. Even though they were responsible to the Persians for maintaining order in Judea, they viewed the Persian imperial permission for them to return to Jerusalem as the restored elite as a new exodus.[8] But they also made a virtue of the necessity of being only a humble and obedient local elite, with little or none of the glory of imperial power and wealth. They developed a distinctive ideology of Israel as called to be the servant of YHWH, not of the powers of empire. Thus called to be the servant of YHWH, the restored community under

Persian rule would faithfully embody covenantal justice. In so doing, in fact, the restored covenantal community would become a model of social-political justice for other peoples.

> Here is my servant, whom I uphold,
> I have put my spirit upon him;
> He will bring forth justice to the peoples. . . .
> He will not grow faint or be crushed
> until he has established justice in the earth;
> and the coastlands wait for his teaching. (Isa 42:1, 4)

> I have given you as a covenant to the people. (Isa 42:6)

Far from imposing justice on other peoples from a position of power over them, the servant of YHWH was to embody justice in a covenantal community in abject humility as an example to other peoples. Even in acquiescence to imperial rule, some had confidence that it was possible to establish a covenantal community as an alternative to replicating imperial power relations in Judean society itself.

Chapter 3

Heavenly Powers and People Power

THE DESTRUCTIVE AND
DEVOURING FOURTH BEAST

In what may be the most influential nightmare of all time, "Daniel" dreamed of a sequence of four great beasts. A lion with eagle's wings, a bear with three tusks in its mouth, and a leopard with four wings and four heads were followed by a fourth beast, which was by far the most ferocious of all: "[It] was terrifying and dreadful and exceedingly strong. It had great iron teeth and was devouring, breaking in pieces, and stamping what was left with its feet" (Dan 7:1-8, esp. v. 7). "One of the attendants" in the heavenly court of Daniel's vision explained that the beasts represent the sequence of the four great empires that had dominated the Judean people—the Babylonians, the Medes, the Persians, and the "Greeks." These last were the successors of Alexander the Great's conquest of the Middle East, the Ptolemies based in Egypt, who controlled Judea until 200 B.C.E., and the Seleucids based in Syria, who ruled Judea after 200 B.C.E. Later, after the Romans had conquered the area, the fourth beast was understood to represent Rome.

"Daniel" purportedly had this vision in the sixth century (under Babylonian rule). But critical analysis has established that the vision really pertains to the situation of Judeans under the most violent of the "Greek" emperors, Antiochus IV Epiphanes, right around 169–168 B.C.E., when the visionaries who received the vision of "Daniel" were living. The book of Daniel and other sources from the early second century B.C.E., moreover, indicate that certain scribal circles were engaged in active resistance to the Greek emperor.[1] Within a few years, moreover, a widespread revolt led by the Maccabees erupted against the imperial forces sent to control Judea.

Biblical scholars have previously interpreted this conflict that led to the Maccabean Revolt as a conflict between cultures, a "clash of civilizations" between "Judaism" and "Hellenism." This interpretation prefigured the recent oversimplification that the early-twenty-first century is experiencing a "clash of civilizations" between the West and Islam.[2] Both of these interpretations of conflict in the Middle East are rooted in the modern Western assumption that ideas drive history, and both are deeply rooted in an ideology that cultural critics have exposed as Orientalism. The latter is a stereotyped view of "Oriental" people and culture developed in travel literature, novels, Western European foreign affairs establishments, and studies of exotic "Oriental" languages by Western European biblical and religious scholars.[3]

The branch of Orientalism specific to Christian biblical studies was the construct of "Judaism" as a parochial and overly political religion. Western theological interpreters viewed Christianity as a universal and purely spiritual religion that had taken over the supposed universalism of ancient "Hellenism" and thus moved beyond the supposedly ethnocentric and legalistic Judaism from which it broke away. What happened in the Jewish "apocalypticism" of the book of Daniel and the Maccabean Revolt was supposedly a conservative reaction to the spirit of Hellenism by some Jews after other, more progressive Jews had responded more positively to its supposedly enlightened cosmopolitan spirit. The alternative interpretation shared the same assumptions but was far more sympathetic to the rebellious Jews: the emperor Antiochus Epiphanes imposed a program of hellenization enforced by religious persecution of faithful Jews who fought for their traditional Judaism in dedication to the Torah.

Recent critical review of historical sources, however, finds little evidence of a cultural program of hellenization sponsored by Antiochus Epiphanes or any other Seleucid emperor. More recent critical analysis of archaeological and other evidence suggests that Hellenism as a worldview and/or a commercialization of economic life had not made strong inroads into the villages of Judea. Clearly, we must take another look at why Judeans in particular (and other subject peoples, such as the Egyptians) came into such severe conflict with the Hellenistic empires and why they continued to resist so persistently when the Romans took over.[4] Why did Judeans see the fourth beast as so much more fearsome and ferocious than the previous beasts? It is important to consider how the cultural workings of power are related to, perhaps inseparable from, political-economic power relations.

It may be helpful at the outset to recognize whose view is represented by the literary sources. In Second-Temple Judea, as in the rest of the ancient Near East, literacy was limited to a class of scribes, intellectuals who served as advisors to the priestly aristocracy at the head of the temple-state.[5] The wise scribe Jesus Ben Sira, who worked in the service of the Oniad high priest Simon II, indicates in his instructional speeches collected in the book of Sirach that the learned scribes cultivated traditions of covenantal torah and of the prophets as well as of wisdom (39:1-4). Since the scribes were *the* specialists in the cultivation and production of texts, it is fairly clear that they were the ones who left us sources such as the books of Sirach and Daniel. Since they worked for the aristocracy who headed the temple-state, they also had a stake in its operations. But what if their high priestly patrons collaborated too closely with the imperial overlords, especially in ways that violated the traditions and laws of which they were the professional guardians? They were thus, potentially at least, caught in the middle between their loyalty to the Judean cultural heritage, which guided the traditional way of life, on the one hand, and the priestly aristocracy, who were vulnerable to the imperial regime that kept them in power, on the other.

The Persian takeover of the Middle East had not involved a destructive conquest of Judea. In the original arrangement setting up the Jerusalem temple-state as the local representative of Persian imperial rule, moreover, the people of Judea sent offerings and tithes to the God of Israel and to the priests who served at the altar. In the context of the Persian Empire as a whole, of course, YHWH was demoted to "the god in Jerusalem" (Ezra 1:2-3). In Judea itself, however, the Temple, its sacrifices and rituals, and its constitutive texts were understood to be the continuation of Judean/Israelite tradition. However ambivalent the Judean peasants may have felt about tithes and offerings, they were still sending their offerings to the God of their ancestors. Scribes, Levites, and ordinary priests would presumably have been aware that their aristocratic superiors were responsible for collecting and rendering tribute to the Persians. Even if they sensed a conflict about their loyalty to the Most High God, however, the benefits that they received from of the tithes and offerings sent to the Temple surely motivated them to compromise.

Judging from our limited sources for the early Hellenistic period, however, the relations between imperial rule and the temple-state in Jerusalem began to change. Sources suggest that a number of interrelated factors and events resulted in tensions that came to a head in the early second century B.C.E. and eventually resulted in widespread revolts of Judeans and other Israelite peoples first against Hellenistic imperial rule and then against Roman domination.[6] We focus on three principal factors: (1) an escalation of violence and economic exploitation by the "western" (Hellenistic and Roman) empires that succeeded the Persian Empire; (2) opportunities that the new empires offered to the elite of subjected peoples for power, wealth, and position if they assimilated into the imperial political culture and economic opportunities; and (3) the imperial regimes' practice of backing the local elite, who controlled subject peoples when the latter rebelled. These three factors will be familiar to critical observers of modern Western imperialism insofar as British, French, and American governments have pursued a similar use of power to create and control their empires.

1. Alexander the Great's death shortly after he conquered the Middle East led to a long struggle between rival successor regimes, the Ptolemies and the Seleucids, for control of Syria-Palestine. Those who suffered most in every successive war were the people whose crops were taxed, whose fields and houses were devastated, and whose families were killed and enslaved. In 200 B.C.E., the war between the two Hellenistic empires was waged in Jerusalem itself, resulting in great destruction before the Seleucids finally took control. No wonder "Daniel's" dream image of the most violent beast of all was "devouring, breaking in pieces, and stamping what was left with its feet." Thirty-some years later, the Seleucid regime repeatedly sent imperial armies, including war elephants, into Judea to suppress the Maccabean Revolt. After the Romans conquered the area in 63 B.C.E., "civil war" between great Roman warlords and rival Hasmonean priest-kings brought repeated devastation to Judea and Galilee. The Romans wrought further devastation of the land and its people in vengeful retaliation against the stubborn Judean and Galilean peasants who repeatedly mounted insurrections, in 4 B.C.E., in 66–70 C.E., and again in 132–135 C.E.

2. The Hellenistic empires offered the elite of subject peoples opportunities for power, position, and wealth, as well as compelling reasons to

assimilate into the dominant imperial culture. Just as religion was an integral instrument of imperial power in the ancient Near East, so culture was an integral aspect of power and power relations in the Hellenistic empires. Biblical and classics scholars have often thought of Hellenism as a realm of culture separate from political power relations. They have also projected the structures of early modern commercial relations onto the Hellenistic period, imagining that merchants, trade, and a monetary economy were somehow the vehicles by which Hellenistic culture was spread into "backward" barbarian areas such as Judea. To counteract such anachronistic projection, we should recognize that Hellenism was an imperial political culture instrumental to power relations. The Greek language and adaptations of Greek political forms (the *polis* or city-state) were the political institutions of the privileged and, in varying degrees, wealthy "citizens" of the cities who controlled the indigenous peoples of the countryside and exploited them economically. In many cases, indigenous elites of subject peoples joined Macedonian soldiers as citizens of such "political" foundations, their adopted "Greek" culture now distinguishing them from the natives in the countryside. Many such cities were established in Syria and Palestine not far from Judea. The Romans simply continued these arrangements in their rule of the peoples in the Near East.

Where such new cities were not yet established, as in Judea itself, the administration and tax collection of the empire offered opportunities for enterprising local magnates to seek fame and fortune, power and position. But this required assimilation into the dominant imperial culture. The first-century C.E. Judean historian Josephus incorporates into his coverage of the Hellenistic period a salacious "romance" about a Transjordanian potentate who eagerly acted on such an opportunity (*Ant.* 12.4.1– 11 §§154–236). The Ptolemaic regime in Egypt that ruled Palestine in the third century, in order to secure maximum revenues, "privatized" the collection of taxes. The Ptolemies authorized the highest bidder to collect whatever he could from the principalities of Palestine, so long as he remitted the required amount to the imperial treasury. This meant a higher rate and a more rigorous collection of revenues, to the detriment of peasant subsistence. The highest bidder for the area that included Judea was Joseph the Tobiad, whose family in the Transjordan had long intermarried with the Jerusalem high priestly family. He was a skillful "operator" at the Ptolemaic court, having learned key Hellenistic cultural touches such as lavish gift giving, courtly charm, and clever repartee. Appropriate to the prominence of his position, he displayed the accoutrements of cosmopolitan culture, including hiring the best-known teachers to educate his children in Greek literature.

Joseph's gain in political-economic power and prominence diminished the power of the high priesthood and its incumbent(s) and aroused the ambition of rival factions in the aristocracy. Joseph set an example of how one could rise to wealth and prominence for aspiring young Jerusalem aristocrats, who became strongly attracted by the imperial political culture of the Greeks.

It was a small step for the next generation of ambitious young aristocrats to maneuver at the Seleucid court. Only now, Jason, the brother of the incumbent high priest, offered the new emperor, Antiochus Epiphanes, higher tribute in payment for the office of high priest itself. He was, in turn, "outbid" for the office by Menelaus. Meanwhile, the ambitious Judean aristocratic agenda had broadened from personal power and position to a more general drive finally to gain respectability in the Hellenistic world by transforming Jerusalem from a hill-country temple-town into a proper Hellenistic city. Accordingly, they established a *gymnasion* (school of physical fitness) and other institutions to properly train the "citizen body" of the newly established *polis* of "Antioch" in Jerusalem.

Joseph and Jason are both illustrations of how the elite of subjected peoples, such as the Judeans, seized the opportunities offered by the new imperial order to enhance their power and wealth while also assimilating to the new imperial political culture, all supported by increased economic exploitation of their people.

3. Since they depended on local aristocracies and urban elites for the maintenance of local and regional order and income, the Hellenistic imperial regimes sent in their military forces to suppress local insurrection and to bolster the local power holders. As opposition escalated to the aristocratic transformation of Jerusalem into the Hellenistic city of Antioch, named after its sponsor, Antiochus Epiphanes, the emperor sent in his troops to suppress resistance. When insurrection spread, he attacked the city again and left a garrison of troops to enforce the transformation of the city by the "reforming" aristocratic faction. And when insurrection arose in the countryside, he sent in imperial armies, a seemingly

overwhelming force including war elephants, to suppress the revolt. Having upset the delicate balance of political-cultural ("soft") power in the relations between imperial regime and subject people in their misguided attempt to maximize revenues for the imperial rulers and their clients, the imperial regime resorted to blatant use of overwhelming military ("hard") power to regain control of Judea.

REVELATION AND RESISTANCE

The terrifying fourth beast devouring and breaking in pieces was a key image in attempts by Judean intellectuals to understand the escalation of violence by Antiochus Epiphanes. With imperial armies visiting gratuitous destruction on their country, in no particular relationship to what the Judeans themselves were doing, history seemed "out of control." Resorting to the prophetic role they were familiar with from their cultural tradition, scribes received visions, along with interpretations by heavenly figures, that illuminated their desperate situation.[7]

Learned scribes, professional intellectuals in the service of ancient rulers, were among other things experts in the relations among the heavenly powers and how those powers affected historical affairs. The ancient Israelites, having rebelled against the service of the divine powers, had covenantal principles prohibiting the service of these powers, and to a degree denied their divinity but did not deny their existence. These powers survived in Israelite culture as "the children of the gods" surrounding YHWH in the heavenly court. Prophets such as Micaiah ben Imlah and Second Isaiah, caught up to the heavenly court in ecstatic experiences, overheard the voices of some of these heavenly powers/spirits (1 Kings 22; cf. Isaiah 40). They believed that such spirits even served as agents who implemented YHWH's will regarding historical affairs. (In 1 Kgs 22:19-23, Micaiah hears one who becomes "a lying spirit in the mouths of the prophets" advising King Ahab.) Second-Temple Judean scribes were thoroughly acquainted with this cultural tradition of the many forces active in the heavenly court of the Most High.

When violence and destruction escalated under the Hellenistic empires, visionary Judean scribes understandably sought explanation and reassurance about a history seemingly out of control in what had been happening among the heavenly forces that participated in the divine governance of the universe. In the long penitential prayer in Neh 9:26-31, at least some Judeans interpreted their subjection to the Persian Empire as punishment for their sins. The Judean scribes who composed the Book of the Watchers (*1 Enoch* 1–36), however, explained Hellenistic imperial violence against the Judeans and the expropriation of their crops as the result of a rebellion by some of the superhuman heavenly forces against the divine governance of earthly affairs. Some of "the watchers" had descended from heaven, coupled with the daughters of humans, and produced a generation of giants. The latter "devoured the labor of all the humans, who were unable to supply them; and the giants began to kill humans and to devour them . . . and to devour one another" (*1 Enoch* 7:3). Other rebel heavenly forces had taught humans to make "swords of iron and weapons and shields and breastplates," the standard equipment of the Hellenistic armies, and to fashion precious metals and stones into jewelry for the imperial elite (8:1-2). It is not difficult to see that this "mythic" explanation of the primordial origins of violence is a reflection of the Judean experience of the violence of the Hellenistic empires.

In the continuation of the vision of the beasts in Daniel 7, violence escalates after ten horns come forth from the fearsome fourth beast and finally a little horn, making war directly on "the holy ones of the Most High," prevails against them. As the heavenly interpreter explains, this symbolizes the attempt by the latest king "to change the sacred seasons and the law," that is, to force the transformation of Jerusalem and the traditional practices of the temple-state. In other visions in Daniel 8 and 10–12, some of the heavenly forces are engaged in attacking "the holy ones" who have special care for and charge of Judea, while Michael, the semidivine heavenly power, is busily engaged in fighting against the hostile heavenly forces on behalf of the Judeans.[8]

In key texts from the Dead Sea Scrolls that were central to the life of the scribal-priestly community at Qumran, the conflict among the heavenly spiritual powers is much more severe. In a grand explanation of earthly affairs toward the beginning of the *Community Rule* (1QS cols. 3–4), historical life generally as well as the situation of particular people is now determined by the all-controlling struggle between "the spirit of light" and "the spirit of darkness." It is clear in the *War Scroll* (1QM) that this dramatic escalation of conflict at the heavenly spiritual level reflects the escalation of imperial domination in Judea by the Romans.

Besides offering an explanation of imperial oppression, Judean scribal visionary texts offer reassurance that the Most High, despite having become a remote heavenly emperor, is ultimately in control. The Most High has delegated certain heavenly forces to bind and punish the rebel heavenly forces and will eventually control or destroy them so that a good life can be restored for the faithful in a renewed Judean society (*1 Enoch* 1–36; Dan 7:27; 12:1). In the grand scheme of history in the Qumran *Community Rule,* God had fixed a time of deliverance for the covenant community when the domination of the spirit of darkness would end. And in the *War Scroll,* in the anticipated final battle between the forces of light and the forces of darkness, in which community members antici-pated doing battle with the *Kittim* (code name for the Romans), the forces of darkness would be defeated.

Modern Western biblical interpreters have dismissed these ancient scribal visionary explanations of a history seemingly out of control as mere myth and/or an utterly unrealistic otherworldliness. This dismissal, however, is an expression of an unwarranted universalization of Enlight-enment reason, which was ironically the cultural counterpart to Western imperial subordination of peoples still supposedly embedded in mythi-cal cultures. Given the Hellenistic and Roman empires' overwhelming military power, subject peoples such as the Judeans had no choice but to accommodate themselves to imperial domination. The Judean scribes' visionary explanation of western imperial violence and exploitation, how-ever, was a way of resisting complete submission and possible assimilation to Hellenistic and Roman (western) political culture as well as military power. Explaining imperial violence as the result of rebel heavenly forces enabled them not simply to blame themselves as hopeless sinners.

From a modern rationalist viewpoint, explanation of imperial domi-nation as due to heavenly spiritual forces is a mystification of the real, concrete source of violence and exploitation, the imperial armies and tax collectors. But with regard to the real situation of power relations, the visionary explanation at least recognizes the reality of superhuman powers that control the life of subject peoples, which modern rational-ism, embedded as it is in imperial power relations, cannot discern. In this sense, the scribal visions were in effect demystifying. Not only was the dominant imperial order not inevitable and eternal and the emperor not divine, but particular invasions and exploitations were embedded in a much larger superhuman system of power. The visions also gave the scribes and others the confidence to resist imperial measures to control their lives in the conviction that God was not only ultimately in control but would eventually take action to end imperial violence and to establish a humane and just society.[9] Such conviction empowered "the wise among the people" (the *maskilim;* Dan 11:33) to remain faithful to the Judean covenantal way of life when the Seleucid emperor Antiochus Epiphanes attacked Jerusalem to enforce the reform by the high priestly rulers (Dan 11:20-35; 12:1-3). It enabled them "to stand firm and take action" even though the inevitable result would be to suffer martyrdom at the hands of the imperial political-military power (11:32-33).

ALIENATION OF THE INTELLECTUALS

Roman imperial rule in Palestine quickly became far more disruptive than that of any previous empire. While Rome did not attempt to suppress the traditional Israelite/Judean way of life as Antiochus Epiphanes had done a century earlier, its disruptive rule eventually escalated into the destruction of Jerusalem and the Temple. Rome worked initially through military conquest and a repressive security system. But Roman imperial power became embodied also in new urban construction, imperial temples, theaters, and amphitheaters, and even in Herod's reconstruction of the Jerusalem Temple complex, which became one of the wonders of the Roman world. Imperial power now impinged from every direction on the traditional Israelite way of life in Judea and Galilee, including in Jerusalem and the Temple.

Intellectuals in Jerusalem may have been the ones who felt the conflict most acutely on a daily basis. In the structure of imperial power relations, they were literally caught in the middle, as noted above. As retainers in the service of the temple-state, scribes and teachers such as the Pharisees, like earlier scribes, were economically dependent on the priestly aristocracy, who owed their position of power and privilege to Herod and then to the Roman officials. But as intellectual retainers of the temple-state, the scribes and teachers were also the designated guardians and interpreters of the authoritative Judean laws and traditions. In that capacity, they knew very well that Roman imperial rule ran counter to Israelite tradition, particularly the Mosaic covenantal commandments. There was to be no god or king other than God, no service of other gods. God's demands on the people were comprehensive, and the people's loyalty was to be complete and exclusive. Scribal intellectuals' commitment to the sacred traditions thus conflicted directly with the realities of imperial politics, in which they were implicated in their high priestly patrons' collaboration in Roman rule.

The Pharisees and other scribal retainers of the Jerusalem temple-state thus could not have been happy about the incursions of imperial power into the traditional way of life. In any number of ways, Roman rule and Herod's "westernizing" development projects posed direct challenges to and violations of "the laws of the Judeans" (presumably including Mosaic covenantal torah). Judging from Josephus's brief accounts, the main body of the Pharisees, while refusing to sign the loyalty oath, agreed to serve in Herod's extensive governance apparatus, albeit demoted from their previous position of influence under the last of the Hasmoneans. Only as Herod lay dying do we hear of the first of three significant protests by intellectuals.[10]

In *the first protest*, Josephus relates that two highly regarded teachers of covenantal torah conspired with their students to tear down the golden Roman eagle that Herod had erected above the great gate of the Temple complex (*War* 1.33.2–4 §§648–55; *Ant.* 17.6.2–4 §§149–67). Their action, moreover, reverberated with wide "demonstration value" in Jerusalem into the chaotic period of Herod's death and its aftermath. Judas son of Sariphaeus and Matthias son of Margalothus, says Josephus, were "the most learned of the Judeans and unrivalled interpreters of the ancestral laws," engaged in the instruction of the youth. Their interpretation included a blunt condemnation of Herod's many building projects as a violation of the ancestral laws. They had apparently reproached Herod in public before. Viewing Herod's demise as an opportune time for bolder action, they challenged their students to cut down the Roman eagle, a blatant violation of the covenantal prohibition of images (representations of other gods). Although Josephus appears to downplay it, the eagle was also an optimally positioned symbol of Judean subjection to Rome that evoked widespread resentment at all the other ways that Roman power had come to invade the people's traditional way of life.

The youth, surely aware that they would be captured and executed, climbed up to the roof of the temple colonnade at midday, when a crowd would quickly gather, let themselves down to the gate, pulled down the eagle, and chopped it up with axes. The symbolic strike at Roman rule could not have been more obvious. Herod's commander, with a considerable force, dispersed the crowd and captured the demonstrators and their distinguished teachers, who courageously awaited their fate. Josephus portrays their arraignment before the king as a typical scene of martyrs speaking truth to a tyrant. Herod, outraged at their defiance, asked them who had ordered them to cut down the golden eagle. They replied, "The law of our ancestors!" (*War* 1.33.3 §653).[11]

Further, like the earlier Judean martyrs (2 Maccabees 7), these distinguished scholars and their students took bold action in defiance of imperial rulers in the confidence that God would vindicate them. Charging the perpetrators, ironically, with gross impiety for destroying the dedicatory offering he had erected over the temple gate, Herod had them burned alive at a public assembly.

The act of the scholars and their students dramatizes the power that martyrdom can have as it reverberates ever more widely among a subjected people deeply rooted in the Israelite heritage of resistance to oppressive kings and liberation from foreign rulers. After Herod died a few weeks later, the martyrdom of the heroes became the rallying point for a large crowd of outraged Jerusalemites. They clamored to Herod's son and heir apparent, Archaelaus, not just for a reduction of taxes and release of political prisoners, but for removal of the high priest and other key Herodian officers. The crisis escalated at the Passover festival, with pilgrims in from the countryside and a much larger multitude again clamoring that the martyrs be avenged. In typical fashion for petty kings, Archaelaus panicked and sent in the troops, which made the people furious, to which the soldiers reacted with a massacre of thousands (*War* 2.1.2–3 §§4–13; *Ant.* 17.8.4–17.9.2 §§204–12). With popular anger already intense against both Herodian and Roman rule, the protest and martyrdom of the intellectuals became the spark that led to the widespread popular revolt in Judea, Galilee, and the Transjordan.

Although the Romans and their client kings commanded the political-military power to execute dissidents and to crush public protests and revolts, they lacked legitimacy in scribal circles as well as among the general populace. Herod lacked *authority*, or legitimate power, as did the high priests he had appointed. The bold defiance by the scholars and their students exposed the illegitimacy of Herod's power. They protested his violation of the very ancestral laws of the Judeans to which they appealed as the higher authority under which they acted. Their act, moreover, emboldened the people to risk acting on the basis of that higher authority, with the collective force of their common outcry further empowered by their commemorative celebration of the liberation from bondage in Egypt at the Passover festival. Touched off by the spark of the martyrdom, the people generated considerable collective power in common action based on the authority of their sacred tradition.

The second protest involved what Josephus calls the "Fourth Philosophy." If Judas and Matthias made a direct attack on a central symbol of Roman power in 4 B.C.E., ten years later the "Fourth Philosophy" aimed to cut off Caesar's economic base in Judea (*Ant.* 18.1.1, 6 §§4–5, 23; *War* 2.8.1; 2.17.8 §§118, 433). Again, two intellectuals provided the leadership: Judas, a teacher originally from the town of Gamala in Gaulanitis, east of the Sea of Galilee, and Saddok, a Pharisee. As the Romans were setting up direct rule through a Roman governor, Judas and Saddok organized resistance to the tribute.[12] Since the Romans viewed failure to pay the tribute as tantamount to rebellion, however, refusal to render to Caesar was a very serious offense. But these Judean intellectuals were caught in a conflict between Roman imperial demands and their loyalty to God as their exclusive Lord and King, as traditionally affirmed in the Mosaic covenant.

From Josephus's accounts it appears that Judas, Saddok, and their compatriots were insisting that Judeans act on the basis of the first two commandments and in hope for independence of the people under the direct rule of God.

> [Judas and Saddok] said that the tax assessment amounted to slavery and urged the people to claim its freedom. If successful the Judeans would have paved the way for good fortune; if defeated, they would at least have honor and glory for their high

ideals. Furthermore, God would eagerly join in promoting the success of their plans. . . . They agree with the views of the Pharisees in everything except in their unconquerable passion for freedom, since they take God as their only ruler and master. They shrug off submitting to unusual forms of death and stand firm in the face of torture of relatives and friends, all for refusing to call any man master. (*Ant.* 18.1.1, 6 §§4–5, 23)

God was literally the king of Israel, according to the Mosaic covenant, and Israel owed exclusive loyalty to God. Having been delivered from the slavery of forced labor in Egypt and obtained their freedom, they were not to serve a human lord such as Caesar by paying tribute. If they were successful in resistance to the tribute, they would have actualized the kingdom of God. But if not, God would vindicate them, presumably like the *maskilim* at the end of the book of Daniel. God, moreover, would be working actively with them in their struggle for independence under God's rule, as suggested in any number of traditions of God's deliverance, such as the Song of the Sea (Exodus 15) or the Song of Deborah (Judges 5).

That they agreed generally with the Pharisees, except for their more intense passion for freedom, suggests that they were basically an association of activist Pharisees. Their commitment to acting on covenantal principles as demands of radical obedience and their passion for freedom meant that they themselves and their family members were prepared to suffer torture and martyrdom for their cause. The high priests, however, and probably other retainers, pressured them to compromise their principles and back away from confrontation with the Romans. Perhaps they realized that failure to pay the tribute would only have brought another brutal war of retaliation by the Roman military.

The third protest by intellectuals was a more desperate response to a more desperate situation under Roman rule. Although after 6 C.E. the Romans appointed governors to rule Judea and Samaria, they left the temple-state intact. From their headquarters in Caesarea the Roman governors ruled Judea through the priestly aristocracy, appointing occupants of the high priesthood from one or another of the four high priestly families previously elevated by Herod. Insofar as their position of power and privilege depended on the Romans, there was no effective restraint on their exploitation of the people. They expanded their wealth by charging desperate peasants excessive interest on loans, eventually making many into mere tenants or pushing them off their ancestral land into the ranks of day laborers.[13] In all the accounts of governors' excessive brutality against Judean peasants or urban protests, never do we hear of the high priests speaking out on behalf of their people.[14] Instead, Josephus and later rabbinic writings report the high priests' predatory practices of sending armed thugs and goon squads to the village threshing floors to seize the tithes intended for the ordinary priests and to intimidate the peasants in other ways (*Ant.* 20.9.2 §§206–7). After the severe drought and famine of the late 40s, the already desperate economic situation of the people deteriorated steadily. An increase in banditry by hungry peasants was met with severe repression by the Roman governors. Provocations by Roman governors prompted popular protests, which were suppressed by Roman military violence.[15]

In these circumstances, a circle of scribal teachers evidently decided that the situation was no longer tolerable and that there was no point in trying any longer to use their influence to mitigate the oppressive treatment by both Roman governors and the priestly aristocracy. As has happened in many other colonial or imperial situations, when all ordinary channels seem blocked and leave people such as intellectuals or artisans feeling powerless, the people may resort to terrorism. A number of Judeans, led by descendants of Judas of Gamala, who had led the Fourth Philosophy, formed a group called the Sicarii, or "dagger-men," named after their weapons of choice. These were daggers that resembled Persian scimitars, curved and similar to what the Romans called *sicae* (*Ant.* 20.8.10 §186). Not having the modern term "terrorist," Josephus calls them "a different type of brigand," operating surreptitiously in the city instead of openly in the countryside. Starting in the late 50s C.E., the Sicarii carried out a series of daring assassinations.

> [They] murdered men in broad daylight in the heart of the city. Especially during the festivals they would mingle with the crowd, carrying short daggers concealed in their clothing, with which they stabbed their enemies. Then when they fell, the murderers would join in the cries of indignation and, through this plausible behavior, avoided discovery. The first to be assassinated was

Jonathan the High Priest. After his death, there were numerous daily murders. (*War* 2.13.3 §§254–56)

Their targets seem to have been almost exclusively prominent members of the high priestly aristocracy, who had maximum political-religious symbolic value as power holders engaged in close collaboration in Roman rule. They began with *the* symbol of the high priestly families' collaboration, the former high priest Jonathan, who continued to wield considerable power in Judea. Like modern anticolonial terrorist groups, they appear to have carried out selective assassinations for their "demonstration" effect. These assassinations were warnings to the aristocracy about future collaboration with Rome and exploitation of the people as well as punishment for past actions. And they signaled to the people generally that the aristocrats were vulnerable.

Modern anticolonial terrorist groups, relying on rapid communications media, aim the "demonstration" effect of their strikes at convincing the government and people of the imperial power that the costs of maintaining their domination by violent repression will be unacceptable. Facing the very different situation of a remote imperial regime, the Sicarii had a different strategy. Their ultimate goal may well have been the removal of Roman rule from Judea, but Rome ruled through the local aristocracy. The logical, "rational" strategy was to focus on the local high priestly collaborators with Rome, and the obvious tactics were to focus on the "soft" targets of leading high priestly figures under the cover of large crowds at festival time and to nab indispensable members of their staff.

THE GENERATION OF PEOPLE POWER

Despite their dramatic and disruptive protests against Roman rule, Judean intellectuals, dependent on—hence vulnerable to—the Herodian and high priestly client rulers, had no way of generating the wider countervailing power necessary to sustain resistance. The Judean and Galilean peasantry did. Until recently, however, nobody noticed.

Previously, historians and social scientists alike assumed that history was made at the highest levels of national and international politics. Like their counterparts among ancient historians, they concentrated on the actions and affairs of the elite ("kings and wars"). Nineteenth-century European intellectuals and would-be leaders of revolutions became disillusioned with the peasantry, who seemed inert, like potatoes in a sack, oblivious to their own economic conditions as well as to historical events. Not until the many earthshaking "peasant revolts" of the twentieth century did a few historians and anthropologists take note.[16] The scholarly dogma that peasants do not really participate in politics, however, persisted.[17] Moreover, biblical interpreters were focused on religion to the virtual exclusion of politics.

In Judea and Galilee around the time of Jesus of Nazareth, however, it was the people who were driving history. The Roman conquest and imposition of Herod the Great as king of the Judeans had created new conditions of imperial rule. But from the end of Herod's reign in 4 B.C.E. through the Bar Kokhba Revolt in 132–135 C.E., it was the peasantry who acted, while the Romans and their Herodian and high priestly client rulers reacted.

At the death of Herod in 4 B.C.E., revolts occurred in Galilee and the Transjordan as well as in Judea. It took the Roman armies three years to reconquer the countryside and ferret out the rebels, thousands of whom they crucified beside the main routes of travel to intimidate the populace. Again in 66 C.E., revolt erupted throughout the countryside and even in Jerusalem itself. As Josephus admits, the high priests and leading Pharisees who did not flee could only pretend to go along (*Life* 4–5 §§17–23). It took the Romans four years before they could take Jerusalem and the Temple, which they destroyed. In the decades between the revolts of 4 B.C.E. and 66 C.E., the Judean and Galilean peasantry generated many movements of renewal and resistance as well as periodic protests—including a widespread and well-coordinated peasant "strike" in which the peasants refused to sow seed so that there would be no tribute from the harvest.[18]

Like peasant movements and revolts in other times and places, these ancient Galilean and Judean movements and revolts were rooted in the fundamental social forms and traditional customs and culture of peasant life in relation to those who determined the conditions under which they lived.[19] These fundamental social forms were the transgenerational family working its ancestral land and the village community composed of many such families. Village communities were semi-independent and self-governing, their rulers leaving them alone as long as they rendered up their taxes, tithes, and offerings. The form of local governance was the village assembly (*knesset* in Hebrew/Aramaic; *synagōgē* in Greek), whose activities ranged from collective prayers to repair of the local water system. Communication and organization were thus built into the village community, although more difficult between villages and from valley to valley.

The communication and organization of the village community were rooted in the popular culture, which differed appreciably from the elite culture known from written sources.[20] Since literacy was limited largely to scribal circles and high-level administrators, nonliterate peasants would not have known the Mosaic law in the version that was inscribed in the scrolls of the Pentateuch laid up in the Temple. This does not mean that peasants were ignorant of Israelite traditions. Just the opposite. They actively cultivated traditions of the exodus and covenant, of Moses and Joshua, of Elijah and Elisha, and of prophetic condemnation of injustice. Villagers' lives were deeply rooted in the *popular* Israelite tradition. In many respects, it ran parallel to the elite tradition enshrined in written scrolls. But villagers had their own special sense of the significance of Israelite tradition, just as the high priests and scribal intellectuals had theirs. An obvious example would be their different attitudes toward tithes and offerings. Priests, temple officials, and scribes who lived from the tithes and offerings viewed them as essential to the operations of the Temple and, of course, part of the people's obligation to God. Peasants who were having a difficult time feeding their families, on the other hand, might appeal to the basic covenantal principle of "honor your father and mother" as an expression of God's will that feeding one's family took priority over offerings to the Temple (Mark 7:1-13).

The principal reason that the popular tradition has not previously been recognized is that it has usually been hidden.[21] Unlike scribal intellectuals, peasants did not usually leave written texts as sources for their cultural tradition. Moreover, because peasants lived under various forms of controlling power, when they were interacting with local or imperial rulers or their representatives, they masked their real attitudes behind apparent acceptance of the prevailing power relations. They were in somewhat the same position as slaves in U.S. history, only under less complete physical and psychological domination. The indignities to which they were subjected, however, produced resentment. Again like slaves in their slave quarters, when peasants were "offstage," in their villages, out of earshot of the rulers, they could articulate their indignation and carry on a discourse of dignity in their own popular tradition.

The village communities in which the Galilean and Judean peasants lived provided the sequestered sites in which they could cultivate their popular tradition and develop their "raw" resentment into a "cooked" discourse of their desire for dignity and hopes for new deliverance. It was in the "hidden transcript" of the continuing cultivation of popular Israelite tradition in the village communities that past deliverance was remembered, anger given intelligible articulation, and hopes for a better life nurtured. This was the fertile soil from which movements could grow, as peasants transformed their resentment into the collective power of resistance and renewal.

PROPHETIC AND MESSIANIC MOVEMENTS

Among the many movements and revolts mounted by the Judean and Galilean peasants were two types that were distinctively Israelite.[22] Although peasants themselves usually leave no written sources, the literate elite often complain in hostile harangues about their activities that disrupt the established order. Josephus, the wealthy Judean priest who became a client of the Flavian emperors, provides our principal sources for popular movements in Judea and Galilee around the time of Jesus. His accounts make clear that several different movements took one or another of two forms distinctive to Israelite tradition. This in turn enables us to discern how large numbers of people could be mobilized on the basis of the popular tradition cultivated in village communities. These distinctively Israelite popular movements generated sufficient countervailing power that the Romans could suppress them only with substantial military force.

The revolts in Galilee, Judea, and the Transjordan in 4 B.C.E. all took the form of popular messianic movements. The largest force of people from the countryside that fought against the Roman armies in the great revolt of 66–70 took the same form (*War* 2.4.1–2.5.3 §§55–79; *Ant.* 17.10.5–9 §§271–94). In his accounts of these movements, Josephus says that groups of people from the country "acclaimed" one of their number "king" and that the leaders "aspired to the kingship" or "donned the diadem" or acted "like a king" (for example, *War* 2.4.1, 2 §§55, 61–62; *Ant.* 17.10.6, 7 §§273–74, 278). If we translate those terms directed to a Hellenistic readership back into traditional Israelite terms, the Galilean or Judean peasants in these movements acclaimed their leaders as *messiahs*. Just as the ancient hill-country Israelites "anointed" the young shepherd-warrior David to lead them against the Philistines (2 Sam 2:1-4; 5:1-3), so now their descendants were acclaiming popular figures as kings (messiahs) to lead the struggle against the Romans. In Galilee, they looked to Judas, son of the Hezekiah who had been a prominent brigand chief whose murder by Herod a generation earlier was long remembered. In the hill country of Judea, the peasants acclaimed a strapping shepherd named Athronges. Sixty years later, in southern Judea around Hebron, where the young David was first popularly "anointed," the people acclaimed Simon bar Giora their king.

All of these movements not only took control of their immediate area but managed to maintain their independence of Roman and Jerusalem rule and run their own affairs for months or even years. In Galilee and the Jordan Valley, they attacked the royal fortresses and took back the goods that had been seized and stored there and attacked royal palaces and the mansions of the wealthy (*War* 2.4.1–2 §§56–58; *Ant.* 17.10.5–6 §§271–77). In Judea, the movement attacked both Romans and Herodian officers, who had treated the people with arrogance and violence. At one point, rebel Judeans raided a Roman convoy transporting grain and arms near the village of Emmaus. Although it is unclear from Josephus's account whether the rebels were the followers of Athronges, a popular force was even threatening to take over Jerusalem. Seventy years later, Simon bar Giora and his movement, after gaining great strength in the countryside, not only took control of central and southern Judea but also became the principal fighting force that resisted the Roman siege of Jerusalem, having effective control of most of the city except for the Temple itself.

To suppress the messianic revolts in 4 b.c.e., the Romans mobilized a large expeditionary force of legions and auxiliary troops supplied by client kings to reconquer the country. Advancing from the north, the army attacked Galilee first, burned the town of Sepphoris, and enslaved the inhabitants (*War* 2.5.1 §§66–68; *Ant.* 17.10.9 §§286–88)—leaving devastation and collective trauma in the area right around the time Jesus was born. As they advanced into Judea, says Josephus, "the whole district became a scene of fire and blood" (*War* 2.5.1 §70). Emmaus, whose inhabitants had fled, they burned to the ground in revenge for the audacious attack on the Roman convoy. As the Romans rounded up the rebels, they crucified hundreds of them alongside the roads to terrorize the populace. Despite the size and brutality of the Roman military forces, however, Athronges and his movement managed to control parts of Judea for years. They held councils to discuss policies and plans. It took the Romans three years before they could capture Athronges and his brothers and pacify the area, which had established its effective independence.

Similarly, in the middle of the revolt of 66–70, Simon bar Giora and his movement were effectively independent in the area they controlled. Simon declared cancellation of debts and release for debt-slaves and evidently had no trouble enforcing such measures. Once they moved into Jerusalem, Simon and his movement maneuvered for control of the city before cooperating against the Roman attack with the other fighting groups, all from the countryside. As a mark of how important Simon's movement was in the Romans' eyes, Simon was taken to Rome and executed as "the king of the Jews" in the great Roman ceremonial triumph.

These movements illustrate the workings of Israelite popular tradition in the sequestered sites of village communities. Memory of the ancient Israelites' "anointing" of the young David as king to lead them against Philistine forces had been cultivated in the "hidden transcript" of Judean and Galilean villages. This memory of the hero who led Israel's liberation from foreign invaders would have become all the more powerful under the intense economic exploitation and political repression of Herod, installed by the Roman conquerors as "king of the Judeans." The protests that erupted in Jerusalem following Herod's death provided the opening for the people's resentment and yearning for a better life to surge into expression. Those emotions, however, had already been "cooked" into a "script" of a messianic movement. The popular memory of the movement led by the "anointed" young David thus *informed* the insurrections in the countryside, which accordingly took the distinctive Israelite form of a popular messianic movement.

The second distinctive Israelite form in which large numbers of peasants were mobilized can be seen in the popular prophetic movements that arose in the mid-first century C.E. Josephus offers accounts of two such movements among the Judeans as well as one among the Samaritans. He also makes a reference to several such movements in which prophets led masses of people out into the wilderness "where God would show them signs of imminent liberation" (*War* 2.13.4 §259; cf. *Ant.* 20.8.6 §168). This passing general account also indicates that the Roman governors (and wealthy elite such as himself) viewed these movements as serious "revolutionary actions" that required timely military action.

The prophet Theudas persuaded a large crowd to take their possessions and follow him out to the Jordan River, where "at his command the water would be divided to allow them an easy crossing." Fadus, however, "sent out the cavalry, which killed many in a surprise attack, took many alive, and cut off Theudas's head and carried it off to Jerusalem" (*Ant.* 20.5.1 §§97–98). Theudas's movement must have been a significant event in mid-first-century Judea, since it is remembered in Acts 5:36 alongside the "Fourth Philosophy" led by Judas as one of the two most significant movements that in some way resembled the nascent Jesus movement in their challenge to the established order.[23] Large numbers of people had left their lands, homes, and villages, taking their goods with them. Josephus's account suggests that the historical analogy was probably the Israelites' exodus into the wilderness, with the waters parting to liberate them from bondage. But the parting of the waters of the Jordan also suggests an analogy with Joshua's leadership of the entry into the land of promise, or even an analogy with Elijah and Elisha and the other prophets' dividing of the waters as a symbol of the renewal of Israel (2 Kgs 2:6-8).

A decade later a prophet, recently arrived in Judea from Egypt, rallied thousands of people from the countryside to follow him in a route through the wilderness up to the Mount of Olives, opposite Jerusalem. He said that the walls of the city would fall so that they could make an entry into the city. Felix sent heavily armed troops and cavalry, who killed or captured most of the people, while the prophet escaped with some of his followers (*War* 2.13.5 §§261–63; *Ant.* 20.8.6 §§169–71).[24] The action promised by the prophet from Egypt, presumably an act of God, was also conceived by analogy with a story from early Israel. That the walls of Jerusalem would fall down clearly alludes to "the battle of Jericho."

In these movements led by prophets, we can discern yet another distinctively Israelite common pattern. Each of these prophets led thousands of people from Judean villages out to experience some new act of deliverance by God. The prophets and their followers believed that God was about to perform a new act of liberation similar to one of the great acts of liberation in the origins of Israel, such as the exodus or the battle of Jericho. The participants were so caught up in their expectation of a new act of deliverance that they proceeded to act it out, to realize the new deliverance they were anticipating. Memory of the great events of deliverance of old informed the movements in which the people went out to experience new events of deliverance. When the people formed a movement led by a prophet, both people and prophet already knew the "script" for the renewal of Israel free of imperial domination.

The prophetic and messianic movements of resistance to Roman domination and renewal of their own societal life were the principal ways in which the people of Judea and Galilee made history. The Roman authorities and their client Herodian and high priestly client rulers were perpetually in the awkward position of scrambling to regain control. In 4 B.C.E. after Herod's death, it took the Roman army three years to retake control of the countryside. In the mid-first century, the Roman governors' military actions to suppress banditry in the countryside and protests in Jerusalem or to slaughter followers of the popular prophets only created deeper resentment among the people, which generated further protest and more movements. Meanwhile, the assassinations by the Sicarii in Jerusalem served notice to the high priestly families that their predatory practices against the people and their collaboration with the Romans would not go unchecked.

People's action and Roman governors' overreaction eventually escalated into widespread popular revolt in 66 C.E. The people generated a remarkable degree of countervailing power to drive out the Romans and to hold the ad hoc priestly regime in Jerusalem at bay for over three years. Like later Western armies attempting to regain control of subject peoples, the Romans repeatedly generated their own opposition by their brutal slaughter and destruction. Peasants quickly learned to flee to the hills and fight back with guerrilla tactics.[25] Roman armies devastated Galilee and

Judea and slaughtered and enslaved the people in order to regain control. Among the casualties of the Roman reconquest were the Temple and high priestly aristocracy. Overwhelming Roman military power had prevailed, but the people had shown how they could generate considerable countervailing power in highly creative resistance and renewal.

Chapter 4

The Power of Hope

Like the popular messiahs and popular prophets of the time, Jesus of Nazareth was also involved in the generation of people power. This is how he is portrayed in the Gospel sources read as whole stories. Like the popular messiahs, Jesus develops a following of villagers. Like the popular prophets, he announces new deliverance in the renewal of Israel under the direct rule of God. The Gospels refer to the sea crossings, healings, and feedings in the wilderness, reminiscent as they were of Moses, the prophetic founder of Israel, and Elijah, the prophetic renewer of Israel, as *dynameis*, "acts of power." Warning his followers that participation in the movement he is leading may result in their crucifixion as a threat to Roman rule, he reassures them that the kingdom of God that is already manifest in his teaching and healing will soon be established "with power."

From the beginning of his work in village communities until the climax of the Gospel story in Jerusalem, moreover, Jesus' renewal of Israel is set over against and is threatening to the Jerusalem rulers and their representatives. The people who witness his powerful exorcism of the demon in the village assembly at Capernaum acclaim in astonishment, "What is this? A new teaching—with authority!" That is, Jesus acts for the people with (*legimate*) *power*, as opposed to the scribal representatives of the Jerusalem "authorities" who lacked authority among the people, presumably because they wielded their power against the interests of the people. In Jesus' sustained confrontation with the Jerusalem rulers at the climax of the story, in response to their challenge to his authority (power), he answers indirectly with a counterquestion about whether John the Baptist's authority was of heavenly or merely human origin. The Jerusalem "authorities" cannot answer. They know very well that the people in the crowd following Jesus view them as devoid of authority but have responded to both John and Jesus as having authority (power) from God.

If we view Jesus' mission relationally, corresponding to the way Mark and the other Gospels present the story, we can see that the (divine) power channeled through John and Jesus becomes power among the people who respond to them. In the Gospel story, Jesus not only mediates divine power to the people but also generates power among the people, power of renewal in familial and village life and power in opposition to the rulers who had been draining away their strength.

MOVING BEYOND THE UNHISTORICAL QUEST FOR AN APOLITICAL JESUS

Standard interpretations of Jesus imagine a peculiar relationship, or rather *non*-relationship between Jesus and his first followers. As sketched briefly in chapter 1, modern interpreters who are limited by Western assumptions of individualism and the separation of religion and politics pay little attention to the conflict and power struggle evident in the Gospel sources. They also impose a standard Christian theological scheme of Christian origins in which Jesus' followers formed a community or movement only after Jesus' resurrection. They imagine that Jesus, as an individual teacher of individuals, spoke isolated individual sayings. Only some of them were remembered. His sayings thus apparently did not resonate with people; evidently the sayings were inconsequential when uttered. Rather, individual sayings were remembered by individuals and transmitted to other individuals as precious artifacts, nuggets of wisdom and/or apocalyptic predictions. Interpreters thus imagine a Jesus who did not communicate with people in the usual give-and-take, who was strangely isolated from his society and its culture.

Ironically, therefore, the "quest for the historical Jesus" has been seeking and finding a Jesus who could not possibly have been historical. In order to have become historically influential and significant, a person has to communicate and otherwise interact with others. But genuine communication cannot take place "one way" and in isolated sayings (separate proverbs or aphorisms). Communication, moreover, takes place in particular historical circumstances of the lives of leaders and followers. In order to understand the Jesus who became historically significant, it will thus be necessary to work from assumptions appropriate to the contours of life in ancient Galilee, Judea, and the Roman Empire and to assess our sources critically.

In ancient Galilean and Judean society, as in the Roman Empire generally, there was no individualism and no separation of religion from political-economic life, as noted in the introduction. Personal life was embedded in the social (-political-economic-religious) forms of family and village community, which were subject to the control and economic exploitation of local and imperial rulers. In order to understand the historical Jesus, therefore, it will be necessary to broaden our focus from Jesus as an individual figure to Jesus in interaction with his contemporaries in their common historical context. The previous chapters provide information on important features of life in Galilee and Judea under Roman rule as well as on the Israelite cultural traditions in which Galileans and Judean were rooted. The following chapters will include other information pertinent to particular aspects of Jesus in context.

The first task—and responsibility—of historians is to assess the sources critically. Once it is recognized that the Gospels are sustained narratives, complete stories about Jesus, they can no longer be treated as mere containers of sayings and brief separate anecdotal stories. There is no particular reason to believe that Jesus' teachings and prophecies consisted of and were transmitted as separate individual sayings. Jesus' teachings appear in the Gospels in the form of shorter or longer speeches on particular issues, such as mission, prayer, anxiety about food and shelter, and exorcism. In the Synoptic Gospels (Matthew, Mark, and Luke), these speeches and all of the brief stories about Jesus appear as integral episodes of a sustained narrative with multiple characters, a main plot, and subplots. The focus is always on Jesus as the main speaker and actor, but always in relation to and in interaction with others. Mark, Matthew, Luke, and John (and some noncanonical Gospels) tell stories of multiple conflicts, mainly between Jesus and the Jerusalem high priestly rulers and their representatives, the scribes and Pharisees. In all of the Gospels a movement forms around Jesus as leader and spokesperson. The principal guide to the significance of particular episodes in the Gospels is the overall story of which they are components. Particular episodes and speeches must therefore be considered in relation to the overall Gospel story.

To make our task simpler, there is reason to concentrate on what most interpreters consider the earliest Gospel sources. The Gospel of Mark is usually considered the earliest narrative source, commonly dated to the decade before or the decade after the great revolt of 66–70 C.E., about thirty to fifty years after Jesus' mission. The strikingly parallel (often verbatim) speech materials in Matthew and Luke, but not in Mark, are thought to have been derived from a common source "Q" (short for *Quelle,* German for "source") that may have been used by a Jesus movement within two or three decades of Jesus' mission. Previously thought of as a mere collection of separate sayings, this "source" can now be seen as a sequence of speeches on key issues important to the Jesus movement that developed and repeatedly recited them.

Matthew's and Luke's adaptations and developments of Mark's narrative and the sequence of speeches of Jesus and their additional materials about Jesus offer further portrayals for comparison with the depictions and emphases in the earliest sources. Gospels that were not included in the New Testament, most of them appreciably later than the canonical Gospels, also often offer significant comparisons of how traditions of Jesus were understood in subsequent generations and new circumstances. The *Gospel of Thomas,* for example, a development of Jesus' teachings in a more mystical direction, offers helpful comparative parallels to teachings in Mark and Q.

Again, to simplify the presentation, while sometimes including critical analysis of the sources in the discussion, I will depend on the fuller discussion of Mark and the parallel speeches of Jesus in Matthew and Luke (in Q) in my own and others' earlier investigations.[1]

RENEWAL OF ISRAEL OVER AGAINST THE RULERS OF ISRAEL

That the Gospel of Mark is a story about the renewal of the people of Israel catalyzed by a prophet like Moses and Elijah is evident in episode after episode. After being designated at his baptism as the chosen agent of God who is leading a new exodus and then spending forty days in the wilderness (like Elijah), Jesus immediately calls protégés (as Elijah had Elisha; 1:2-20). Jesus commissions the twelve disciples, representative of the twelve tribes of Israel, to continue and extend his own mission work, just as Elisha continued Elijah's (3:13-19; 6:7-13). The woman who has been hemorrhaging for twelve years and the twelve-year-old girl who is almost dead are representatives not just of Israel but of an Israel hemorrhaging and almost dead, but given new life through Jesus (5:21-43).

In addition to carrying out sea crossings and feedings reminiscent of Moses leading the exodus and performing Elijah-like healings (4:35—8:26), Jesus teaches about a renewal of the covenant for the families and village communities of the nascent movement. He declares in clearly covenantal terms that the "brothers and sisters and mothers" of the movement are those who do the (covenantal) will of God (3:31-35). Later, in a sequence of four dialogues (10:2-45), two of which explicitly cite covenantal commandments, he renews Mosaic covenantal teaching about the integrity of marriage and family, community membership, economic relations, and political leadership . On the eve of his arrest and crucifixion, finally, Jesus enacts a renewal of the covenant at the "Last Supper" at Passover, the festival in which Israel celebrated the exodus (14:12-25, especially "my blood of the covenant").

Jesus, moreover, is leading the renewal of Israel in opposition to the rulers of Israel, and he is opposed by them. Several aspects of the program of renewal pose direct challenges to the Jerusalem temple-state. Local healing and forgiveness of sin seem to make the Temple superfluous (for example, 2:1-12). Jesus insists that the basic commandment of God requires local families to use their resources to support needy family members ("honor your father and mother"). Local needs thus preclude devices in "the traditions of the elders" to induce peasants to "devote" (*korban*) further support to the Temple (7:1-13). Throughout Jesus' work in Galilee and then Judea, the (scribes and) Pharisees, representatives of the temple-state who "come down from Jerusalem" (3:22; 7:1), challenge what he is doing, and they "conspire with the Herodians . . . to destroy him" (3:6). Undeterred, Jesus and his followers march up to Jerusalem and the Temple, where Jesus engages the high priests, scribes, and elders in a series of confrontations, beginning with a demonstration of God's condemnation of the Temple (11:15-19). In response to the Pharisees' and Herodians' attempted entrapment, he declares, in coded language, that rendering tribute to Caesar is indeed counter to the (Mosaic covenantal) law. The high priests have Jesus arrested and turn him over to the

Roman governor, who orders him beaten and executed by crucifixion as a rebel "king of the Judeans."

The series of parallel speeches in Matthew and Luke (derived from Q), while different in form from the narrative in Mark, are also focused on the renewal of Israel, with many of the same themes and allusions. The first and longest speech by Jesus is a covenant renewal speech (Luke/Q 6:20-49). Next comes a dialogue (Luke/Q 7:18-35) in which Jesus declares that he has brought the fulfillment of the deep longings of the people for healing and good news for the poor, longings long ago articulated by Isaiah. In the mission speech (Luke/Q 9:57—10:16; cf. Mark 6:6-13), Jesus sends out disciples to expand his mission of preaching the kingdom of God and healing. In the last short speech (Luke/Q 22:28-30), it turns out that Jesus had appointed twelve disciples as representative heads of the people who were sharing in the program of effecting justice for Israel. Other speeches represent the exorcisms as manifestations of a new exodus (Luke/Q 11:14-20) and teach the prayer for the kingdom in which the covenantal principle of cancellation of debts will be realized (Luke/Q 11:2-4).

The parallel speeches of Jesus in Matthew and Luke (derived from Q), like the Markan story, also present the renewal of Israel as directly opposed to the rulers. In traditional Israelite prophetic forms, Jesus pronounces divine judgment against the ruling house of Jerusalem (Luke/Q 13:34-35). Similarly, in a series of prophetic woes, he declares God's condemnation of the Pharisees and scribes who advocate the interests of the temple-state to the detriment of the people (Luke/Q 11:39-52).

The two earliest Gospel sources thus present Jesus not as an isolated sage uttering pithy aphorisms or as an apocalyptic visionary, but as the leader of a movement directly engaged with the people, whose family and village community life has been disintegrating in serious ways. The presentations in both Mark's Gospel story and the Q speeches, moreover, portray the same fundamental conflict that we find in other historical sources such as the histories of Josephus. There is a sharp opposition between the people of Judea and Galilee and their rulers, the Herodian kings and high priestly aristocracy in Palestine as well as the Roman overlords. Matthew and Luke, who combine the Markan narrative with the Q speeches, and the Gospel of John, moreover, also present Jesus as leader of an expanding movement over against the Jerusalem and Roman power holders. The Gospel sources thus consistently present Jesus as the leader of a movement of renewal and resistance that resembles the other, contemporary movements among the Galilean and Judean people, especially those led by prophets. In this presentation of Jesus-in-movement, the Gospel sources also indicate clearly the political context in which Jesus, as the leader of a movement, must be understood.

Yet there was a significant difference between Jesus and his movement and the (other) popular prophetic movements. Both drew on the popular memory of Moses (and Joshua or Elijah). But, whereas the other prophets led their followers out of their villages and into the wilderness or up to the Mount of Olives in anticipation of God's new acts of deliverance, Jesus focused his mission on village communities and their concerns. Throughout Mark's narrative of Jesus' mission in Galilee and beyond, Jesus works in villages and synagogues (which were village assemblies, not buildings). In the parallel "mission" speeches in both Mark and Q, Jesus sends his envoys to work in village communities, proclaiming the kingdom of God and healing the people (Mark 6:6-13; Luke/Q 10:2-16). Some of the episodes in Mark and some speeches in Q, moreover, indicate that Jesus often addressed issues of social-economic interaction in village communities. Our earliest sources thus indicate that Jesus catalyzed a movement in the village communities of Galilee and nearby areas. What Jesus is represented as saying and doing must thus be understood in connection with those village communities. For it was their response that resulted in the Jesus movement(s), whose remarkable expansion made Jesus a significant historical figure.

Recognition of village communities, the fundamental social form of virtually any agrarian society, as the context of Jesus' mission enables us to appreciate how Jesus was speaking and acting politically in a new way, previously unrecognized. New Testament scholars, like modern Western political scientists and government advisors, have usually understood politics in the relatively narrow terms of public affairs on the public stage. They assume that for Jesus to have engaged in political activity, he would have to have led a revolt. But since the Gospel sources give no indication of Jesus leading a revolt, he must therefore have engaged only in religious-cultural activity.

The limitations of this modern Western understanding are illustrated by any number of recent popular movements based in villages. British imperial officials, who dismissed popular movements as merely religious, did not know how to respond to the anticolonial campaigns led by Gandhi and previous movements among the "subaltern" Indian peasants.[2] The "intelligence" of the British Foreign Service, like that of many historians and political scientists, was not attuned to two important realities. Village communities, the fundamental social form in traditional agrarian societies, are centers of communication and potential cooperation against the power of their rulers. And popular movements that are defined by modern Western intellectuals as "religious" can generate power in opposition to colonial rule that is political-economic as well as religious.

Learning from these somewhat analogous examples, perhaps researchers into Jesus and his movement can expand their "intelligence" to recognize these two important realities. This will enable us to appreciate that even though Jesus did not foment an armed revolt, he did engage in political activity and did catalyze movements that generated power, however local and temporary, over against the invasive forces of the Roman imperial order.

As in many agrarian societies, so in ancient Galilee and Judea, village communities were the sites of at least local political activity and were potentially the base of political activities directed against the established order, whether hidden or more overt. Villages were self-governing semi-independent communities. The form of local self-governance as well as of community cohesion was the village assembly (*synagōgē* in Greek, as in the Gospels; *knesset* in Hebrew and Aramaic, as in rabbinic texts). Besides holding common prayers and discussions, the village assembly would delegate members to repair the local water system and appoint elders of the community to serve as a court to deal with local conflicts.[3]

Village communities were thus also the safe places where, beyond the effective reach of the eyes and ears of the dominant, the always exploited peasants vented their resentment (as discussed in chapter 3).[4] These villages, moreover, were hardly cultural vacuums. People in Galilean and Judean villages had for generations cultivated the Israelite popular tradition. The latter included many stable cultural forms such as the stories of the foundational deliverance from Egyptian bondage in the exodus led by Moses and the heroic acts of the prophet Elijah to heal a suffering people and oppose the oppressive King Ahab. The villagers' Israelite tradition also included earlier prophetic articulations of the people's longing for independence from oppressive rulers and imperial armies who expropriated and sometimes even destroyed their harvests and houses (Isa 65:18-25). Their memory of past acts of deliverance and the great prophets and messiahs of old informed their yearnings for new deliverance. Current instances of indignity and hopes for a life free of violence and exploitation were thus experienced in the cultural forms of the Israelite tradition of resistance to and deliverance from oppressive rulers.

This is the context in which Jesus carried out his mission in Galilee. The attempt to comb his individual sayings for words that are unique, different from the culture in which he was operating, produces a Jesus irrelevant to the people he supposedly addressed. The appropriate procedure, rather, would be to appreciate how he creatively tapped into the Israelite popular tradition in which Galilean villagers were experiencing and discussing the disintegration of their traditional way of life and their longings for deliverance and justice. The Gospel sources offer several key ways in which Jesus' message resonated with Galilean villagers embedded in the memories and longings of Israelite tradition.

LONGINGS OF THE PEOPLE REALIZED

Both the Gospel of Matthew and the Gospel of Luke present many of Jesus' actions as the fulfillment of prophecy in explicit terms. After Jesus heals on the Sabbath and heals many in the gathering crowds, for example, Matthew comments that "this was to fulfill what had been spoken through the prophet Isaiah" (12:17-21) and recites the first of the servant of YHWH songs from Isaiah (42:1-4). As the first episode of Jesus' mission in Galilee, Luke (4:14-21) has Jesus read from the Isaiah scroll (a combination of lines from 61:1-2 and 58:6) in a village assembly and then declare that the prophecy was fulfilled in the people's hearing.

That Jesus' actions were the fulfillment of the Israelite tradition and expectations was not new in Matthew and Luke. They merely made explicit in quotations what was already central to the earliest Jesus movement and almost certainly to Jesus' interaction with Galileans, who were rooted in Israelite tradition. This is evident in the Markan series of episodes representing Jesus as a new Moses and Elijah. This same understanding of Jesus' mission as fulfillment of the people's hopes was expressed already in the two pre-Markan series of stories of sea crossings, healings, and wilderness feedings that were incorporated into Mark's Gospel (4:34—8:26).[5]

The most important indication of Jesus' fulfillment of the longings of the people is the parallel speech in Matthew and Luke (derived from Luke/Q 7:18-35) that alludes to some of those traditional longings without quoting a specific passage of Scripture. To John the Baptist's inquiry whether Jesus is "the coming one," he answers:

> Go tell John what you have seen and heard: The blind recover their sight and the lame walk, lepers are cleansed and the deaf hear, and the dead are raised and the poor receive good news. (Luke/Q 7:22)

Many biblical scholars, still working on the basis of the assumption of print culture, not yet aware of the limits of literacy, have mistaken these lines for "quotations" from the book of Isaiah.[6] But these scholars have difficulty making up their minds exactly which passage in Isaiah Jesus' speech is "quoting": Isa 29:18-19? 35:5-6? 42:6-7? or 61:1? One or another of the phrases in Jesus' speech corresponds roughly to a phrase in one or another of the Isaiah passages. But most of the phrases in Jesus' speech cannot be said to be a quotation of any one of the Isaiah passages.

Once we recognize that Israelite popular tradition was being cultivated orally we can explain the situation that baffles scholars who work on the assumptions of modern print culture. All of those passages in Isaiah that have similar and somewhat overlapping phrases that anticipate the future healing and deliverance of a suffering people are reflections of typical images of longings in the popular Israelite tradition. They were included in the late sections of the book of Isaiah, in which scribally formulated prophecies generally reflect popular hopes for the future. These standard images of hope for future deliverance, however, continued to be cultivated in the popular tradition into the time of Jesus. And Jesus and/ or the people who responded to his actions in Galilean villages found that he was fulfilling those longings: the blind were recovering their sight, the lame were walking again, and the poor were receiving good news. The fulfillment of popular tradition in Luke/Q 7:22 can be detected by comparison with the more sophisticated explicit quotation of Isa 61:1-2 in Luke 4:18-19. Only the later and literate Luke presented Jesus' actions as fulfillment of the particular passage in Isa 61:1-2. The earlier Q speech, much closer to the oral communication of Galilean village communities and an early stage of the Jesus movement, presents Jesus' actions as fulfillment of the age-old longings of the people.

The next step in the speech shows how directly the actions of Jesus address the resentment as well as the longings of the people. The speech draws a pointed contrast between the prophet that "the people went out into the wilderness to see" and "a man clothed in luxurious robes" who "lives in a royal palace." The reference is obviously to the Rome-appointed "king" Herod Antipas, who had built two cities during the previous thirty years, presumably funded largely by rigorous expropriation of taxes from the crops of Galilean villagers. The next lines, returning to the theme of the fulfillment present in Jesus' mission, present John the Baptist as the greatest in the long line of prophets, whose role is nevertheless preparatory to the program of Jesus, which is nothing less than a new exodus or a renewal by a new Elijah. John and, by implication, Jesus are the fulfillment of an eagerly anticipated prophecy, "what is written." The ostensible citation, however, (again) does not clearly quote a particular biblical text (at least in any version known to us). Instead, it alludes to both the "messenger" of the (exodus) way leading to the people's land (Exod 23:20) and the "messenger" of the covenant who is to restore Israel, Elijah (Mal 3:1). Again, Jesus (as received by his followers) is working from Israelite popular tradition as he declares his mission to be the fulfillment of the people's longings for deliverance.

We can appreciate the speech in Luke/Q 7:18-35 about fulfillment of the longings previously articulated by prophets of old and the (pre-) Markan representation of Jesus' actions as those of a new Moses and Elijah only if we view them as the result of Jesus' interaction with people in Galilean village communities where the popular tradition was cultivated. Jesus knew the indignities and yearnings of the people as articulated in Israelite tradition and addressed them in his message and actions. Galilean and other villagers eagerly responded to his initiatives and resonated with his actions. To ask whether a particular episode of healing "really happened" is a reductionist modern question. The speeches and stories of Jesus simply assume that he was engaged in healing. The message of the speeches and stories is about the revitalizing power of life that was happening in the actions of Jesus and his interactions with responsive people.

This is perhaps nowhere more vividly expressed than in the two inter-woven episodes of the twelve-year-old woman and the woman who had been hemorrhaging for twelve years (Mark 5:21-43).[7] Both women are representative of the people, as symbolized by the "twelve." In both, the power of life is ebbing away. The lifeblood of the older woman had been steadily drained from her. The younger woman, just at the age when she should be married and begin reproducing life in Israel, was "at the point of death." These are the representative figures of Israel in the Galilean villages where crowds eagerly greet Jesus. It is not Jesus but the people, moreover, who take the initiative. The young woman's father, "one of the leaders of the village assembly," asks Jesus to attend to his daughter, and the hemorrhaging woman herself, who knows that life-giving power is flowing through Jesus, reaches out and secretly touches his garment. And indeed power flows through Jesus whether he wills it or not, as the woman, confident that she will be made well if she but touches his clothes, feels her hemorrhaging stop. As Jesus confirms, it was her trust ("faith," NRSV) that made her well. Finally, at Jesus' command, the twelve-year-old comes back to life, presumably empowered to bear new life in Israel. The interaction between Jesus and the people yearning for new life gener-ates the power of restoration and renewal.

NEW HOPE: THE KINGDOM OF GOD AT HAND

Jesus' declarations that accompanied his actions must have been as aston-ishing as they were empowering to villagers in despair about their disin-tegrating families and communities. "The kingdom of God is at hand!" (Mark 1:14). "Blessed are you poor, for yours is the kingdom of God!" (Luke/Q 6:20). Just as God had heard the cries of their ancestors sub-ject to heavy bondage under Pharaoh, so God was responding to their increasingly difficult life under Caesar and Herod. The people could now boldly petition their heavenly Father to "establish your kingdom" (Luke/Q 11:2-4). They could eagerly anticipate that the people of Israel would "come from east and west and sit at table with Abraham, Isaac, and Jacob in the kingdom of God" (Luke/Q 13:28-29).

In declaring that the kingdom of God was at hand, Jesus was not uttering some pithy aphorisms or provocative proverbs that might be remembered and pondered later by his followers. Such an understanding does not take into account the character of Jesus' speech in his declarations about the kingdom, the role in which he spoke, and the social interaction in which both speech and roles are embedded. Statements such as "blessed are you poor, for yours is the kingdom of God" are what is called "performative speech," speech-acts that effect what they pronounce. The minister's statement "I pronounce you husband and wife" makes it so. A judge's pronouncement of innocence or guilt makes it so. As Jesus' pronouncement of the kingdom resonated with listening villagers, it effected God's blessing upon them.

In his declarations of the kingdom, moreover, Jesus was speaking as a prophet. He was speaking with divine authority, and both the performative speech and speaking in the role of a prophet happen in interaction with those hearing and responding to the speech. The minister's pronouncement of marriage is effective in the relationship with the couple being married and in their community of supporters. The minister speaks with the authority of the state, as recognized by the citizens. Jesus' pronouncements of the kingdom resonated with listeners in village communities—or they would not have been repeated, remembered, and included in the Gospels—and he spoke with the authority of "heaven," as recognized by the peasant listeners (cf. Mark 11:27-33). This whole relationship and its importance for Jesus' delivery of performative speech with authority in the role of a prophet are attested in one of the episodes of Jesus' confrontation with the ostensible "authorities" in Jerusalem. The high priests' and scribes' challenge to Jesus about the source of his authority leads them into a trap of their own making: like John the Baptist, Jesus speaks with divine authority as determined by the people's response.

Recent generations of scholarly interpreters have misunderstood not only the mode in which Jesus spoke but also the significance of his proclamation of "the kingdom of God." This may be principally because their own academic life situation is so far removed from the life situation of the peasants Jesus was addressing. Since the time of Albert Schweitzer, the dominant view has been that Jesus pronounced that the world was about to end in a cosmic cataclysm. More recently, members of the Jesus Seminar have concluded that Jesus was a sage who spoke of a personal spiritual kingdom to be gained from knowing his wisdom teaching. Both views are based on the interpretation of individual sayings, without recognizing that those sayings are integral components of larger speeches and without considering the overall Gospel narratives, as noted above. More determinatively, the debate about whether "the kingdom of God" Jesus preached was "apocalyptic" or "sapiential" is conducted in modern scholarly constructs. Interpreters have given little attention to the concrete circumstances of the ancient Galilean village life that Jesus addressed and how "the kingdom of God" may have resonated in that context.

"The kingdom of God" was a central symbol, deeply rooted in Israelite tradition, of the life that the people were supposed to have under the direct rule of their God as king, hence independent of exploitative human kingship. "The kingdom of God" was thus a political, or rather more comprehensively a political-economic, as well as religious symbol. It was rooted in the exodus withdrawal from the imperial system of servitude to the divine powers that determined the Egyptian political economy. God's direct rule of Israel, which excluded human kingship, was articulated and structured as a functioning polity by the Mosaic covenant. After the rise of the monarchy and subjection to later empires, the direct rule of God remained the ideal for the Israelite people as a whole and for village communities whose local interaction was still governed by the principles of the Mosaic covenant.

Because nonliterate peasants rarely leave literary remains, we have no direct sources (apart from the Gospels) for the continuing resonance of the kingdom of God ideal in villages. Scribal circles, however, also aspired to an independent life for Israel directly under the rule of God. The scribal tales in the first six chapters of Daniel insist that God retains the ultimate sovereignty in historical life and will take action to terminate arrogant and intolerable imperial rulers. The often-cited *Psalms of Solomon* 17, close to the time of Jesus, insists that "the kingdom of God is forever over the nations in judgment" and that God, through an "anointed one" as regent, will restore the tribes of Israel on their land. The scribal leaders of the Fourth Philosophy took the direct and exclusive rule of God so seriously that they organized resistance to payment of the tribute to Caesar (see chapter 3 above).

In utter contrast to the ideal and the expectation, however, the concrete life of the peasantry ground along under Herodian kings and Jerusalem high priests as well as their imperial sponsors and guarantors. Under the cumulative impact of Roman reconquests, a generation of repressive rule by Herod, and another generation of efficient collection of taxes by Antipas from his new cities, which commanded a view of nearly every Galilean village, family, and community, life had become difficult. Even in normal circumstances, peasant families struggle simply to maintain a subsistence living. When the tax collectors do not leave enough grain for families to make it through to the next harvest, they must borrow. Since their neighbors are usually also struggling, they become indebted to the government officers who, like Joseph in the story of the seven fat and seven lean cows, have control of the grain storage facilities. Before long in the reign of Antipas in Galilee, villagers would have been heavily in debt, chronically hungry, and distressed about the future.

To just such villagers Jesus spoke strong words of hope. "The kingdom of God is at hand." "Blessed are you who are poor, (. . . hungry, . . . and mourning), for yours is the kingdom of God." The ideal of life no longer subject to the invasive and oppressive powers of empire but directly under the rule of God is now happening. Informed by the deep memory of early Israel's independent life under their divine ruler, the long-hoped-for renewal of Israel is now at hand. Far from being an individual spiritual reality, the kingdom of God that Jesus proclaims to Galilean and other villagers is social and economic as well as political. Jesus speaks of people "entering" the kingdom. Indeed, the disciples' and others' qualifications for entering include attention to and concern for other people (Mark 9:42-49; 10:13-16). The coming of the kingdom means sufficient food and a cancellation of debts, even a mutual cancellation of debts in village communities, as articulated in the Lord's Prayer (Luke/Q 11:2-4). Those who are hungry now will be filled, while those who are full now will go hungry (Luke/Q 6:20-22). Another qualification for entry into the kingdom of God is observance of the covenantal principle against economic exploitation (coveting, leading to fraud in lending); it will be impossible for the exploitative wealthy to enter (Mark 10:17-25).

The kingdom of God, moreover, means the renewal of the people of Israel, which Jesus symbolizes to the hungry people as a great banquet of plenty. The scattered people will come from east and west and sit at table with Abraham, Isaac, and Jacob in the kingdom of God (Luke 13:29-28// Matt 8:11-12). At the commemorative celebration of the exodus, the Passover meal that is Jesus' "Last Supper," he anticipates resuming his ceremonial meal of covenant renewal in the kingdom of God (Mark 14:12-25).

The concluding speech in Q has a similar anticipation of the covenanted renewal of Israel with the representative twelve sitting at table in the kingdom "doing justice for the twelve tribes of Israel" (Luke/Q 22:28-30).

In all those same passages and others as well, it is also clear that far from being the apocalyptic end of the world in a cosmic cataclysm, the kingdom of God is happening in the people's response to Jesus' mission. John the Baptist, whom the people went out to see in the wilderness, was the greatest in the long line of prophets, but something greater is here in the fulfillment of the people's longings (Luke/Q 7:18-28, 31-35). In the more measured images of the parables, Jesus compares the kingdom of God to a small mustard seed that grew and developed into a tree in which the birds of the sky nested and to a bit of yeast that caused the dough to expand into large loaves of bread (Luke/Q 13:18-19, 20-21; cf. Mark 4:30-32; *Gos. Thom.* 20, 96). Mark has Jesus deliver a longer speech of several such parables that emphasize the abundant harvest that results from seed that is sown, despite the great obstacles that it must overcome (Mark 4:2-32).

Resonating with Jesus' declaration that God was taking action to restore Israel directly under divine rule, Galilean villagers had grounds for hope that the seeds being sown would produce an abundant harvest despite continuing difficulties. No longer debilitated by despair over their impoverishment, they were now empowered by the hope generated by Jesus' proclamation of the kingdom. They could thus rise to the challenge reassured that if they single-mindedly sought the realization of the kingdom of God, then in the solidarity of the common commitment, subsistence and shelter would take care of themselves (Luke/Q 12:22-31).

EQUITABLE ECONOMY

What the coming of the kingdom of God meant to Galilean and other villagers is most vividly seen in the "Lord's Prayer." What has become the most commonly spoken and deeply felt expression of personal piety in modern Christianity reveals just how concrete the kingdom of God was in Jesus' mission.

While Luke (11:2-4) reproduces the shorter, less developed version of the Lord's Prayer, Matthew (6:9-13) has the more concrete, down-to-earth reference to "debts" instead of "sins." The prayer has four petitions:

May your kingdom come!
The bread we need each day
　　give us today.
And cancel our debts for us,
　　as we too have canceled for those indebted to us.
And do not lead us to the trial.

Even through the various English translations of the Greek versions, we can almost feel the simple but profound poetry of the prayer in the original Aramaic. The first and last petitions frame the second and third. As is standard in Hebrew and Aramaic poetry, the petitions are parallel and make parallel, almost synonymous statements. The first states the overall plea for God to rule the people directly. The rest of the petitions then specify key aspects of why the people petition so desperately and what the kingdom would mean for them. These petitions could not be more concretely economic and political. And these compact lines with the simplest and most basic references are loaded with information and implications, including how the overwhelming power of Caesar and his clients, generated by their expropriation of the produce of peasant labor, relentlessly drains away the peasants' ability simply to survive.

That the people desperately petition their heavenly Father for bread indicates that they are desperately hungry. To put the matter in basic terms of energy, it takes a minimum of 1,800 calories per day to sustain human life. Peasants perpetually live close to the margin of subsistence, barely scraping together the calories of energy for their families to live on from harvest to harvest. Bad weather and especially drought means famine (the "seven lean cows" of Pharaoh's dream). Similarly, when their overlords demand too much of their crops, families starve. Having limited parcels of land, they cannot increase production. The heavy demands for tribute to Caesar and taxes to support the building programs and lavish lifestyle of Herod and Antipas took their toll on Galilean villagers.

Israelite covenantal tradition encouraged villagers to lend liberally to their needy neighbors, and without interest (Exod 22:25). But the meager surpluses of villagers were quickly exhausted, and the hungry were forced to borrow from officers of the regime, who did charge interest: 25 percent on grain and 100 percent on oil, according to Jesus' parable of the dishonest steward (Luke 16:1-8). Unable to feed themselves after meeting the demands of the Romans and their client rulers, hungry peasant families fell ever more hopelessly into debt with every passing year. Families and village communities began to disintegrate as families lost control of their land to outside creditors and were forced to send out a daughter or son as a debt-slave.

Jesus' teaching villagers to petition their Father for subsistence bread and cancellation of debts induced them to anticipate an economic life that would finally be equitable. Not only would they have sufficient food, enough calories—hence enough energy (power)—to sustain individual and family life. They would be out from under their debilitating indebtedness so that they would once again have a chance to produce enough to live on. The equitable economics anticipated in the Lord's Prayer, moreover, was not a matter of demanding that the heavenly Father do everything for them. In the third petition, the people, in pleading for cancellation of debts, declare that they are cancelling one another's debts, as expected in the economic principles of Mosaic covenantal tradition. Clearly, the petition about debts presupposes and belongs in the context of village communities involved in a movement in which, empowered by the hope of the kingdom's coming, the people are able to revive covenantal cooperation.

Episodes in Mark's Gospel also attest that Jesus was insisting on these same equitable economic relations in the renewal of Israel under the direct rule of God. In several episodes, challenges by the Pharisees (and scribes) function as foils for the renewal of Israel that Jesus is catalyzing. Previous interpretation usually took these episodes as Jesus' condemnation of the (supposed) legalism of "Judaism," especially purity codes. Underneath the criticism of the Pharisees' supposed obsession with purity in Mark, however, is a condemnation of the effects of their role as representatives of the temple-state on the economic subsistence of the people. In his condemnation of the Pharisees for pressing villagers to "devote" (*korban*) a portion of their land or its produce to the Temple (as "an offering to God," Mark 7:1-13), Jesus is objecting to the expropriation of peasant produce needed locally, for example, to feed elderly parents. In Mark, Jesus also indicts the Pharisees for "devouring widows' houses" (Mark 12:38-40), a poignant illustration of how the Pharisees' encouraging the people to give their resources to the Temple leaves them destitute, deprived of the "houses" (including fields) that had provided their livelihood (see the fuller discussion of these passages in chapter 6).

The series of woes that Jesus pronounced against the scribes and Pharisees (Luke/Q 11:39-52) parallels this sharp condemnation of the Pharisees for the effects of the measures they took as representatives of the temple-state.[8] Again, modern Christian interpreters have misunderstood the woes as mainly a criticism of Jewish emphasis on "legalism." The woes do indeed mock the Pharisees for their concerns about purity. The substantive charge Jesus levels, however, is that, while the Pharisees "clean the outside of the cup," inside they themselves "are full of extortion and rapacity" (Luke 11:39//Matt 23:25). Jesus is condemning the scribes and Pharisees for "loading the people with heavy burdens," while they themselves, in their role as the interpreters of the laws of tithing and taxes, "do not touch the burdens with one of [their scribal] fingers." By urging the peasants to pay tithes and devising additional ways, such as the *korban* ("devotion"), to siphon people's produce to support the Temple and priesthood, they in effect exacerbate the economic pressures on the people imposed by the multiple layers of rulers in the imperial system. Jesus' condemnation of the power holders' expropriation of the people's produce that they need for their own subsistence serves also to convince the people that the coming kingdom of God means a more equitable economic life for them.

THE EMPOWERING SPREAD OF "GOOD NEWS"

The Gospel of Mark clearly plays up how Jesus' "fame began to spread throughout the surrounding region of Galilee" (1:28) right from the start of his mission. In episode after episode, the news spreads and anticipations rise even before Jesus comes on the scene. The story of the Syro-Phoenician woman suggests that reports of Jesus' activity had even spread into villages across the lines of political jurisdictions. Toward the beginning of Mark's story, Jesus' mission appears to be "headquartered" in the village of Capernaum, at the northern end of the Sea of Galilee, along the frontier with Herod Philip's territory to the east. From this base, the mission and communication spread into surrounding villages. Mark's Gospel thus paints a picture different from the normally limited communication from village to village in agrarian societies: the interaction among Jesus, the disciples, and the responsive people generated an expanding network of communication around the countryside.

The parallel mission discourses in Mark and the sequence of speeches parallel in Matthew and Luke (Mark 6:6-13; Luke/Q 10:2-16) show that the expanding flow of excitement from village to village cannot be dismissed as a mere fictional artifice of Mark. In these early accounts of the mission, Jesus delegates disciples to spread the proclamation and manifestation of the kingdom into other villages, where they are to work closely and stay with the people. Jesus' mission thus involved an intentional orchestration of communication across village lines. Though exaggerated, Mark's representations of rapidly expanding communication at least partially reflect what was happening in Jesus' mission itself. This spread of excitement across the village communities of Galilee was a major factor in how Jesus' action and proclamation generated power among the people.

Studies of people's movements in other times and places suggest that rapid spread of "good news" is what often happens among desperate peasants longing for a better life independent of overlords and a restoration of their traditional rights to sufficient livelihood on their ancestral lands. In his highly suggestive comparative and theoretical study *Domination and the Arts of Resistance*, James C. Scott discusses such movements as a form of peasant political resistance. These movements gather momentum and their own grassroots oppositional power from the rapid spread of "rumor." Upon hearing the news that a distant king or God had finally decreed that they were freed from onerous obligations, enforced by violent coercion by local power holders, peasants or slaves excitedly spread the news and eagerly anticipated their imminent liberation.

Just prior to the French Revolution, for example, when the king finally summoned the Estates General for the first time in well over a century, peasants were called to local assemblies to draw up their concerns and elect representatives. They went home thinking that the king wanted everyone to be equal, with no more lords and bishops, and that they had already been released from tithes and feudal dues.[9] Accordingly the people ceased paying feudal dues and tithes and sent their cows to graze on what the lord had claimed as his land but had previously been the village "common." In Caribbean slave rebellions in the late eighteenth and early nineteenth centuries, the participants believed that the British king had set them free and that their local masters were keeping the word from them.[10] Scott cites numerous striking parallels of Russian serfs, Indian untouchables, and cargo cults among Melanesian peoples overwhelmed by Western conquest, where such people become convinced that God/ gods or a distant authority figure had granted their dreams. Rapidly spreading rumor can thus empower the people. Such cultural excitement can have political and economic effects, as the people keep for themselves goods they produce that previously had provided the basis of their lords' power over them. Any number of historical cases show that politically charged rumor can generate widespread popular movements and even peasant insurrection.

Aware of the expansive power of rumor from their predecessors' regrettable experience, kings and emperors have often taken measures to repress or control rumor. Roman emperors were apprehensive enough to employ a whole cadre of officials—*delatores*—to investigate rumor.[11] In this connection, the final petition in the Lord's Prayer, along with Jesus' speeches in Luke/Q 12:2-12 and Mark 8:34-38, provides a telling indication of the sober awareness in Jesus' mission that involvement in the movement might well mean arrest and trial by local or imperial authorities.

The highly unusual spread of communications from village to village thus constituted one of the major factors in the "people power" generated by Jesus' mission in Galilee and adjacent territories. Just as Caribbean slaves believed that the distant British king had set them free, Jesus' proclamation that the kingdom of God was at hand and its manifestation in healings and exorcisms generated a movement of people who believed that God was liberating them from domination by the Romans and their client rulers. The political impulse provided by rumor became integral to the revolutionary process.[12] Just so, the spread of reports of Jesus fulfilling the age-old longings of the people in his healing and exorcisms and proclamation of the presence of the kingdom of God fed the gathering momentum: it increased the power flowing through Jesus to a desperate people and the power of the spreading movement. A similar rapid spread of "good news" was also surely a factor in the movements led by Theudas and the "Egyptian" prophet a decade or so later, when large numbers of Judean peasants followed these prophets out to the Jordan River or up to the Mount of Olives. In Jesus' mission, however, while the spread of the "good news" enabled the movement to gather momentum, the focus was solidly on the renewal of the village community. This fostered a longer-range basis for the generation of local people power by mutual cooperation and solidarity against the outside forces that were siphoning off their life energies.

Chapter 5

Jesus and the Struggle for Power

Most people today think of Jesus as primarily a teacher. The earliest Gospel, Mark, however, presents Jesus primarily as an exorcist and healer. Mark does have Jesus give some long speeches, telling parables (4:1-34) and foretelling the future (chapter 13), and a series of dialogues on covenantal relationships (10:2-45). But the first two narrative steps of the Gospel (1:16—3:35; 4:35—8:26) that deal with Jesus' mission in Galilee consist mainly of twelve episodes of exorcism and healing. The Gospel story also offers periodic summary statements of how many exorcisms and healings Jesus was performing. The third narrative step (8:27—10:52) is framed by two episodes of healing of blind people and includes a lengthy exorcism episode. Indeed, the renewal of the people of Israel on which Jesus' mission focuses consists mainly of exorcism and healing.

Healings and exorcisms are not as prominent in Matthew and Luke, but are still integral to Jesus' mission. While they include most of the exorcism and healing episodes in Mark's Gospel, Matthew and Luke incorporate many speeches of Jesus, which contribute to the impression that he was primarily a teacher. The parallel speeches in Matthew and Luke, thought to derive from the source Q, refer to only one episode of exorcism, in the introduction to the debate about whether Jesus casts out demons by Beelzebul, the ruler of demons (Luke/Q 11:14-20). But another speech indicates that an integral aspect of Jesus' program as a prophet of renewal was healing: "the blind receive their sight, the lame walk, the lepers are cleansed, the deaf hear, the dead are raised" (7:18-23). In the mission speech, moreover, Jesus commissions his envoys to heal as well as to preach (10:2-16). It seems clear that Jesus' mission featured healing and exorcism as well as prophetic teaching.[1]

ACTS OF POWER (NOT MIRACLES OR MAGIC)

Some conservative interpreters, accepting the healing and exorcism episodes in the Gospels at face value, take them as proofs of Jesus' divinity. More liberal interpreters of Jesus, however, have been skittish about the healings and exorcisms. It has been difficult if not impossible in the modern world to understand such bizarre phenomena in scientific terms. In the modern rational cultural milieu, theologians and biblical interpreters have classified the actions portrayed in the exorcism and healing stories as miracles or magic. Many interpreters committed to a modern scientific understanding of reality still believe that Jesus did indeed perform exorcisms and healings, but when they critically examine particular stories, they find in them few "authentic" elements of particular incidents in Jesus' ministry. Lacking evidence for particular cases, liberal interpreters have tended to avoid discussion of Jesus as healer and exorcist. It is ironic that while Bible translators (for example, of the NRSV and the Jerusalem Bible) were presenting Jesus' healings in the modern Western biomedical terms of "disease" and "cure" (for example, Mark 1:34; 3:10), critical Jesus scholars found the exorcism and healing stories unreliable and unreal when measured by the canons of modern science.

The concepts of *miracle, miracle stories,* and *magic* have taken deep root in studies of Jesus and the Gospels. Even the most "critical" scholars now argue that Jesus performed miracles or magic.[2] The Gospels, however, have no equivalent of the modern concept of "miracle/miraculous," and certainly no equivalent of the modern Western dichotomy between the natural and the miraculous or the "supernatural." They do not present Jesus as performing miracles. The concept of the miraculous imposes a distinctively modern Western viewpoint and valuation onto the world, culture, and activities of Jesus.

Antiquity did have a concept of *magic/magician.* It functioned mainly in polemics, as when the elite denigrated popular religion as "magic." By the mid-second century, opponents of the nascent "Christians" were charging that Jesus had been working magic. In the first-century Gospels, however, Jesus is castigated for healing on the Sabbath, accused of casting out demons by Beelzebul, and executed as the (rebel) "king of the Judeans," but he is not accused of practicing magic. In recent years, some leading scholars have insisted that in his healings and exorcisms Jesus was engaged in magic.[3] But this only perpetuates old arguments in Western cultural debates and obscures rather than opens the way toward historical analysis more sensitive to other cultures.

Modern psychology offered new possibilities for explaining—or perhaps rather for explaining away—the illnesses and spirit possession of the ancient Galileans and Jesus' healings and exorcisms. Cases of possession by an "unclean spirit" could be diagnosed as hysteria, neurosis, or schizophrenia. Recent psychological interpretation of Jesus' exorcisms has become more sophisticated. Anthropologists began to explain spirit possession in terms of multiple personality disorder.[4] Following their lead, recent interpreters of Jesus' exorcisms have explained demon possession in terms of the possessed person's projection of repressed emotions and inner conflicts onto an outside "unclean spirit."[5] This approach, however, projects onto ancient people the assumption of a modern Western concept of the self as a (normally) integrated person, for whom multiple forces and their conflicts are internal. The belief in spirit possession, on the other hand, is based on what is virtually the opposite assumption: that a person can be possessed by outside forces. Instead of "projection," therefore, the Gospel sources, like many peoples studied by anthropologists, believe not so much that alien forces have been "introjected" as that they have invaded certain persons, who become the "hosts" of the alien spirits.

A modern Western psychological approach simply does not take indigenous cultural beliefs and representations seriously. The result is not only that persons who experience a conflict of forces are anachronistically isolated as individuals, but that their experience of possession is pathologized as well. Even the explanation of spirit possession as an "altered state of consciousness" comes close to this modern presumption of an independent, normally "integrated" self.[6] Just as people's consciousness depends on their culture, so presumably would an "altered state of consciousness" depend on the same culture. It is highly unlikely that the culture in which Jesus operated shared the modern Western assumption of an independent integrated self.

While the concepts of magic and miracle are alien to the Gospel sources for Jesus' mission and the assumptions of modern psychology are anachronistic, the Gospels have their own conceptualization: Jesus' exorcisms and healings are "(acts of) power." This is evident in particular episodes of demon possession and exorcisms. An alien possessing force has been driving the possessed person into bizarre, often violent involuntary behavior. Exorcism is a power struggle, like a military battle engaged between Jesus and the possessing spirit, in which the demon is driven from the possessed person with violent effects. In the healing of the hemorrhaging woman, Jesus senses that "power" has gone forth from him" (Mark 5:30// Luke 8:46). Jesus does these acts of power because powers are at work in him (Mark 6:14 par.). Summaries and discussions of Jesus' activity refer to exorcisms and healings explicitly as *dynameis*, "acts of power" (Mark 6:2, 5 par.; Matt 7:22; Luke 19:37). This is a standard term in both Mark and the parallel speeches in Matthew and Luke, in which it is common knowledge that Jesus had done many acts of power (Luke/Q 10:13).

Luke conceptualizes the healings and exorcisms more fully. Jesus possesses "the power of the Lord to heal," so that it can happen that "power came forth from him and healed them all" (Luke 5:17; 6:17-19). He can then, in turn, give the envoys he sends out to widen his mission "power and authority over demons" (Luke 9:1), and authority over the opposing "power of the enemy" (Luke 10:19). The ultimate power or source of power, of course, is God, who can even be referred to as "Power" (as in Mark 13:62 par., where "the human one" is "sitting at the right hand of Power"). The powers at work in Jesus were thus presumably from God (Luke 5:17).

In the healings and exorcisms, Jesus is thus transmitting power to the people of Galilee and beyond that enables them to overcome debilitating illnesses and possession by "unclean spirits." The implication is that, in the circumstances of their lives, the people lacked power to overcome these on their own. That the name of one of the unclean spirits turns out to be "Legion," that is, a unit of Roman troops, is highly suggestive in just this connection. Might the people's lack of power and eager response to the power acting through Jesus' healings and exorcisms be related to the military conquests and other forms of Roman power that had had a serious impact on the people's lives for the previous three generations? Because of the standard modern Western separation between religion and politics, interpreters have simply not investigated how the power struggle between Jesus and the occupying alien spiritual forces might be related to the effects of Roman imperial power.[7] After the massacres in Bosnia and Kosovo in the 1990s, however, we are much more aware of the collective social trauma that results from brutal violence and related forms of oppression. Recent developments in medical anthropology and related ethnographic studies of spirit possession and exorcisms in other societies, moreover, suggest that there is a close connection between spirit possession and forms of imperial domination.

COLONIAL POWERS AND SPIRIT POSSESSION

Medical anthropology has developed a critical perspective on the ethnocentrism and reductionism of modern Western scientific biomedicine. Especially important is the recognition that illness is culturally constructed. Western biomedicine focuses on *disease,* "the malfunctioning of biological and/or psychological processes," which it then attempts to diagnose and *cure.* Medical anthropologists think more broadly in terms of *illness,* as "the [broader] psychosocial experience and meaning of perceived disease. Illness includes . . . processes of . . . affective response, cognition, and valuation, . . . communication and interpersonal interaction, particularly within the context of the family and social network."[8] The response that corresponds to *illness* is *healing,* which is also culturally constructed. If we want to understand spirit possession and exorcism in a given society, therefore, we cannot impose the concepts of modern biomedicine or psychology. Rather, we must investigate the portrayal of spirit possession and exorcism in its own cultural context.

More recently, "critical" medical anthropologists have expanded the scope of investigation of influences on illness and healing to include historical, social, structural, political, and economic forces. Realizing that these factors generally go unattended, they have begun to examine the lasting effects of colonialism, expanding capitalist enterprises, and a globalizing economic system on illness and healing. They attempt to understand "health issues in light of the larger political and economic forces that pattern interpersonal relationships, shape social behavior, generate social meanings, and condition collective experience."[9] Many of these "critical" anthropologists also point out, with psychiatrist Frantz Fanon, that where there is power, there is also resistance. And with political scientist James C. Scott, they recognize that subordinated people such as peasants have traditionally honed certain "arts of resistance" that may operate in culturally disguised forms.[10]

This "critical" perspective offers a more appropriate approach to the spirit possession that Jesus encountered and its possible relation to the political-economic forces that were impacting the people. From "meaning-centered" medical anthropology we can learn to look for how spirit possession and other illnesses were understood in ancient Galilean and Judean (Israelite) culture (as evident in the Gospels and other sources). From "critical" medical anthropology, we can learn to consider also how Galilean and Judean society at the time had been seriously impacted by military conquest and other pressures of Roman rule.

Since information on spirit possession in ancient Palestine is limited and fragmentary, however, it may be helpful to look first at spirit possession in modern Africa, which has been studied extensively. Information from African peoples provides many illustrations of how spirit possession is related to invasive outside forces.

A number of African peoples, before and after European incursions, represented strangers as indigenous aspects of their own culture in various rites in which the strangers' spirits played a role.[11] Swahili peoples, for example, took grief and illness as indications that spirits of strangers wished to embody themselves in the ill people and to demand sacrifices and worship. Possessed persons were understood to be hosting, variously, the spirits of the Arabs (*sheitani*) or the spirits of the people of Kilimanjaro (*Kilima*) or those of Europeans (*Kizungu*).[12]

Where the alien spirits were experienced as threatening, the possession appeared to be more defensive or self-protective. As a consequence of the Christian mission in the early twentieth century, many of the Kamba people were possessed by *Kijesu*. The alternative to conversion was possession by *Kijesu*, a spirit symbolic not just of Jesus but rather of the broader Christian mission, the whole alien culture that threatened the traditional way of life.[13]

The *zar* cult in Sudan offers an example of how a people, embodied in local village communities, dealt with the cumulative effect of domination by a sequence of outside powers. The various names of the spirits (*zayran*) reflected the successive outside forces that came to dominate many women's lives but were met by the women's resistance in village society.[14] The list of the many hostile *zayran* included the *Bashawat*, the spirits of the Pashas and Turkish conquerors, and British spirits such as "Lord Cromer," who had led a military expedition through Sudan.[15]

The *Khawajat* were spirits of the light-skinned Europeans and other Westerners, alternatively referred to as *nasarin* (Nazarenes, or Christians). These spirits demanded "clean" foods, such as bottled beverages, white bread, and tinned meats, that represented the power of the Western conquerors. Another aspect of the power of these spirits was their immeasurable wealth—or rather the wealth that they demanded from their hosts. Particularly striking among the Western spirits was "Dona Bey," an American doctor and big-game hunter who put away prodigious quantities of whisky and toted a huge elephant gun. Clearly he represented Western technological overkill, destroying what he hunted, along with the invasion of Western medical science, all framed in licentious indulgence.[16]

The peoples who had already established cults of possession could deal with the impact of European colonialism by expanding their range of alien spirits and adapting their already existing ceremonies of diagnosis, negotiation, and exorcism.[17] In the *zar* cult, for example, women of the village would gather for sustained drumming and dancing. The exorcist(s) would attempt to induce the possessing spirits to identify themselves. Then with more drumming and dancing and often considerable struggle, the exorcist might succeed in forcing the spirit(s) to leave the possessed person(s).[18]

For largely homogenous peoples previously less acquainted with possession by alien spirits such as the Zulu, however, the sudden European invasion and colonization were far more traumatic. A bewildering array of previously unknown alien spirits that could not be domesticated suddenly attacked people who would become possessed.[19] In desperate attempts to marshal their traditional cultural resources against the invasive spirits, traditional Zulu healers (*izangoma*), the possessed mediums of their ancestors, attempted exorcism.[20] To reinforce the exorcism of alien spirits the *izangoma* "inoculated" their subjects with "soldiers" (*amabutho*) to defend them against further attack.[21] The "soldiers" spoke through their hosts in foreign languages, such as English, or in railroad sounds. The hosts of the "soldiers" used alien objects such as machine oil or white men's hair to symbolize their protective new identity.[22] Here are fascinating cases of identifying with less threatening alien powers in order to resist and ward off the greater alien powers that were destroying traditional culture and identity.

As the invasive European colonization intensified, men began organizing possession dances as well. One of the most prominent of these was the *beni ngoma* ("band-dance"), which began in the 1890s, spread widely, and continued through the 1920s. Such dances emphasized colonial attire. Possessed participants in the *hauka* cult that spread in West Africa in the 1920s imitated Islamic authority figures, French and British colonial officers, and the flag, uniforms, and drill formations of the British army.[23]

More political in their implications and eventual effects were the charismatic possession cults led by prophets. These movements created a wider community of peoples in resistance to the effects of colonial invasion, moving from local focus and diverging interests to more common interests over against the colonizing forces. In an unprecedented move, these charismatic movements claimed exclusive and unlimited authority, an idea they appropriated from and used against the colonizing power and/or Christian mission. Like the latter, these African prophetic movements demanded unity and selfless devotion to a broader cause. It was hardly coincidental that these prophetic movements prepared the way for and were the precursors of more politically oriented anticolonial movements.

Well before the emergence of critical medical anthropology, Frantz Fanon had recognized and critically analyzed the effects of colonial domination on spirit possession. In his clinical practice as director of a mental hospital in Algeria during the anticolonial struggle against French rule in the 1960s, this Paris-trained psychiatrist found spirit possession and general fear of demons rampant among the native Algerians.[24]

According to his analysis, the natives' widespread anxiety about hostile spirits was a response to and a reflection of the way the (French) colonizers had defined colonial power relations. The colonial situation in Algeria and elsewhere had been created by violent military conquest, and it was maintained by (the threat of) military or police violence. The French colonial authorities declared that the only language the indigenous Islamic peoples could understand was the language of force. Accordingly, the local colonial commanders brought that force into the homes and minds of the natives. Not content with physical and social violence, moreover, the colonial power defined the natives not only as uncivilized but even as a threat to civilization.

In response to the powers arrayed against them, colonized people came to believe that their subjugation was impervious to any action they might take. Their destiny was being decided by higher, superhuman powers. Colonial violence could be opposed only by greater violence, which was hardly at their disposal. It was obvious that the dominant foreign civilization threatened their own traditional way of life. Corresponding to the colonizers' view of the natives as the personification of evil, the natives viewed the power of the colonizers as evil.

As Fanon recognized, however, where there is power there is resistance. While the people may have been overpowered, they were not tamed. Yet like Africans earlier in the twentieth century, the Algerians did not mount direct opposition to European colonial power. The colonists' invasion of their lives kept the natives' level of anger high and provoked fantasies of freedom. But colonial power kept the subject people "hemmed in," denied any outlet for their anger. The regular exhibitions of colonial violence reminded the natives that any resistance to the Europeans would only evoke an escalation of violence against them. Direct opposition would be suicidal.

The Algerians' response to the overwhelming power arrayed against them was to focus not on the French but on the numerous demons that harassed them in every aspect of their lives. In his remarkable insight into the "Manichaean" colonial situation constructed by European power, Fanon saw that this was both self-defensively creative and debilitatingly mystifying.[25] Spirits (*djinn*) that in traditional society might have either helped or harmed people became terrifying demons to the people. These maleficent spirits created "around the native a world of prohibitions, of barriers and of inhibitions. . . . The zombies [were] more terrifying than the settlers."[26] The people's fear of the demons thus strengthened the inhibitions that contained their potentially aggressive action. Their attention focused on the threatening world of spirits, not on the instruments of colonial control. The demonic powers, not the concrete powers of imperial domination, were the cause of their distress. Belief in demons was thus self-protective insofar as it enabled the subject people to avoid direct confrontation with their colonial masters, which would result in their destruction. But it was thus also an effective means of social control in a colonial situation and a mystification that disguised the concrete colonial situation and the powers that created it.

THE SPIRIT OF LIGHT AND
THE SPIRIT OF DARKNESS

Possession of people by hostile alien spirits does not appear in the early Judean books that were later included in the Hebrew Bible. "Angels" make cameo appearances from time to time when God needs to communicate with key figures. Satan operates as an agent provocateur on God's behalf, but is not a semidivine power of evil. In early Israel the *ruaḥ Yahweh,* the "wind/spirit of Yahweh," seizes hold of the people's militia to fight furiously for the independence of the people. The spirit of Yahweh also seizes control of the prophets, who then declare the word of Yahweh, often against the king and his officers. But hostile alien spirits are conspicuous by their absence.

The situation has changed dramatically in the Gospels. Belief in spirits is simply presupposed; many people have become possessed by alien spirits; and Satan, now "the prince of demons," is locked in a sustained struggle with God. In this context, one of the principal functions of Jesus and the disciples he commissions is to "cast out demons," as noted above.

Perhaps one of the reasons modern interpreters have avoided the issue of spirit possession and exorcism is that these bizarre phenomena were so baffling and unexplainable. One of the most important aspects of the discovery of the Dead Sea Scrolls in 1947 was that it suddenly brought to light the existence of a community of priests and scribes contemporary with Jesus who thought that their lives were subject to an elaborate system of beneficent and maleficent spirits. Indeed, they believed that all of history, not just their community life, was in the grip of a struggle between opposing armies of heavenly spiritual powers. One of the discovered scrolls, *The War of the Sons of Light against the Sons of Darkness,* states explicitly that the hostile spirits are in close collaboration with the invading Romans. Thus, some key Dead Sea Scrolls, along with some earlier Judean texts, indicate how Judean scribes and priests were incorporating the spirits of invasive imperial powers into their culture as they attempted to deal with imperial domination. Appreciation of how the priests and scribes understood changes in the spirit world as related to their life situation may help us understand how Jesus and his followers, ordinary people for whom we have no sources other than the Gospels, viewed spirit possession and exorcism in relation to invasive imperial powers. We must take a closer look at the heavenly forces related to earthly affairs in texts touched on already in chapter 4.

Beginning with the destruction of Jerusalem and the Temple by the Babylonian armies in the sixth century B.C.E., Judeans were subject to one empire after another. After Alexander the Great and his Macedonian armies conquered the Near East in the 330s B.C.E., Judeans began to experience more frequent imperial invasions and intense taxation.[27] The rival Hellenistic empires of Alexander's successors fought a series of wars for control of Palestine that were destructive for Judea. The Judean intellectuals who produced the "Book of the Watchers," later included in the book of *1 Enoch* (chapters 1–36), sought revelation about the repeated violent invasions of their society. At several points in the Book of the Watchers, we can discern significant changes in the Judean understanding of the divine world that reflect the ways imperial powers were impacting Judeans historically—changes that lead in the direction of the elaborate scheme of dominating spirits in the Dead Sea Scrolls.

In contrast to earlier representations, "the Most High" is now pictured as an imperial king far removed from the day-to-day workings of life, dealing with his subjects only through an elaborate imperial court with multiple ranks and layers of (divine) imperial officers. What had been "the sons of the gods," well-domesticated as passive attendants at the divine court of YHWH in the prophetic books of the Hebrew Bible, now became semi-independent divine powers with wills of their own. Their very names suggest their functions as the powers of the universe that affect human life in various ways: "star-god," "thunder-god," "lightning-god," "rain-god," "sun-god," "moon-god," "winter-god" (*1 Enoch* 6:7).[28] Some of those heavenly powers charged with governing the universe had rebelled against the divine order. "The Watchers," attracted by the beautiful daughters of men, descended to earth and conceived with them great giants (*1 Enoch* 6–11). It is clear from the imagery that this "myth" was a representation, and explanation, of the devastating effect of the Hellenistic imperial conquests and demand for tribute from subject peoples.

> They were devouring the labor of all the sons of men, and men were not able to supply them. And the giants conspired to kill men and to devour them. (6:1)

> Asael [a chieftain of the Watchers] taught men to make swords of
> iron and weapons and shields and breastplates and every instru-
> ment of war. (7:2)

The dream-visions in the book of Daniel were originally responses to
the violent invasion of Jerusalem by the Hellenistic emperor Antiochus
IV Epiphanes in 169–167 B.C.E. The vision in Daniel 7 represents the
whole series of empires that dominated Judea as great beasts that trample
and devour their prey, as noted in chapter 3. The series climaxes in the
extremely vicious and violent "little horn," which is transparently a symbol for Antiochus Epiphanes, who repeatedly attacked Jerusalem, defiled
the Temple, and sent armies to kill anyone who persisted in the traditional Judean way of life. The vision in Daniel 10–12 portrays Gabri-el
("warrior-god") and Micha-el ("one who is like god," the patron "officer/
prince" of Judea) as doing battle on behalf of the Judeans against the
heavenly power that represents the dominant empire. Also evident in
these Danielic visions is that the people of Judea stand in close relationship with the "the holy ones of the Most High," the heavenly forces that
represent and protect them.

The scribes and priests who formed the community at Qumran in the
wilderness by the Dead Sea believed that history under Roman domination was even more out of God's control.[29] The Qumran community
articulated a generalized grand scheme of two dominant divine spirits that control human affairs (*Community Rule* [1QS] cols. 3–4). The
Qumranites believed that, individually and communally, they themselves
were controlled and guided by the spirit of truth/light, while attacked
and tempted by the spirit of darkness. The rest of humanity, however, had
evidently come under the control of the spirit of darkness or Belial. By this
scheme of an ongoing power struggle between the two armies of spirits,
they explained why historical developments seemed so utterly beyond the
control of the God of Israel, while still affirming that God was ultimately
in charge and had ordained a termination for the spirit of darkness.

What is only implicit in the *Community Rule* (1QS) becomes abundantly explicit in the *War Rule* (1QM), which evidently dates from the
early decades of Roman domination. The *War Rule* consists of an elaborate announcement of and instructions for the final battle between "the
sons of light" and "the sons of darkness," between the "officer/prince of

light" and his spiritual forces and "Belial" and his "spirits of destruction." But the battle is also against the *Kittim*, the scriptural code term for the Romans, who camp together with the spiritual "host of Belial." Correspondingly, the God of Israel and the whole "congregation of holy ones," the divine spirits, would fight alongside the foot soldiers and cavalry of the redeemed of Israel (see especially 1QM 1:10-15; 10:6-9; 14:10-16; 15:15—16:1, 9). Clearly Belial and the company of darkness, malevolence, and destruction are the spiritual forces that correspond to the Romans on the historical level, just as the congregation of holy ones are the spiritual forces that will fight with the community in the final battle.

Much of the *War Rule* consists of instructions for ritual anticipation of the final battle against Belial and the Romans. The Qumranites rehearsed ritual warfare against the *Kittim*, both imitating military formations of the Romans and drawing on Israelite holy-war ideology. They marched in designated companies with trumpets and banners, evidently as a counterforce to the invasive Roman armies (1QM 1:3-4, 13-14; 17:5-8; 18:4-5). In their ritual military drills, the Qumran community resembled some of the possession cults among African peoples in the early twentieth century. In their possession by the spirit of light, which protected them from the officer/prince of darkness, they resembled the Zulu people, whose alien spirits had been exorcised and replaced by "soldiers." Possession by such protective spirits enabled the Qumranites, like the Zulus, to hold their own against the imperial domination that threatened destruction of their traditional way of life. Living under the guidance of "the messenger (angel) of truth" and in close interaction with the holy ones, they anticipated that the God of Israel would soon inaugurate the final battle, in which Belial and the Romans would be defeated. This enabled them to "despise kings [and] mock and scorn the mighty" (1QM 12:6-9).

"MY NAME IS LEGION"

When we shift focus from the Dead Sea Scrolls produced by the Qumran community to the mission of Jesus, we move from the wilderness of Judea to the villages of Galilee. More significantly, we also move from a community of priestly intellectuals to "the people of the land." We should not imagine that Galilean peasants thought in exactly the same terms as

Judean intellectuals. Like the latter, however, they were deeply rooted in Israelite tradition. So Galilean peasants were also struggling to come to grips with Roman imperial domination on the basis of Israelite tradition, even though they had their own popular version of that tradition. While their experience of "unclean spirits" was also closely related to the effects of Roman imperial domination, they understood those spirits in more of an ad hoc way, less systematic than the Judean intellectuals' scheme.

As in Algeria and in earlier colonial Africa, Roman imperial rule was established by military power. The Romans attempted to terrorize people into submission by destruction, slaughter, enslavement, and crucifixion, as noted in chapter 2. The effects of brutal Roman conquest and reconquest were particularly severe in Galilee. In the turbulent decades following the initial conquest by Pompey, Roman warlords continued to despoil the area. Cassius massacred thousands in the town of Magdala (Josephus, *Ant.* 14.7.3 §§119–20). Herod mounted three successive expeditions into Galilee to subdue the stubbornly independent Galileans, who resisted his takeover as Rome-appointed "king of the Judeans." Sepphoris, not far from the village of Nazareth, bore the brunt of the vengeful Roman suppression of the revolt led by the popular messiah Judas son of Hezekiah after the death of Herod in 4 B.C.E. Many families would have experienced such exhibitions of violence and the attendant social trauma directly, many others indirectly. After the Roman reconquest, the Roman client ruler Antipas imposed two newly (re-)built capital cities, Sepphoris and Tiberias, onto the landscape of Galilee, from which he extracted a portion of the crops the Galileans needed for subsistence livelihood.

Galileans and neighboring peoples, however, while thus overpowered, were not pacified. Galileans' and other Israelites' memories of God's historical acts of deliverance reinforced their dreams of regaining their freedom. The tradition of liberation remained strong, as evident in the periodic popular revolts and prophetic movements. Except for those outbursts, however, the power of intimidation was effective. The people focused on "unclean spirits" as the cause of their distress and suffering. As in Algeria and elsewhere in Africa, the fearsome spirits formed a spiritual world of inhibitions, keeping the people from suicidal attacks against the Romans and/or their client rulers, which would have drawn an escalation of repressive violence. As among colonized African peoples, belief in "unclean spirits" thus had a self-preserving effect, enabling the people to continue in their traditional way of life, weakened as it was. It also mitigated the tendency, deeply rooted in covenantal thinking, to interpret their suffering as due to their own sins, violations of God's commandments. Focusing on invasive spirits as the cause of their malaise also enabled them to believe that God, though absent or inactive in the present situation, would reassert control in the future. Attributing their malaise to demons, however, was also a mystification of Roman imperial domination, diverting the people's attention from the concrete exercise of powers that violated and controlled their lives and drained away their life energies. This mystification was an important factor in maintaining Roman imperial domination.

Although most of the references to spirit possession and exorcism in the Gospel sources for Jesus' mission are general, three episodes in particular provide a vivid portrayal of the power struggle that was involved as well as how spirit possession and exorcism were understood in terms of (popular) Israelite culture. Two key exorcisms in Mark and the parallel Beelzebul discourses in Mark and Q make unavoidably clear that Jesus' exorcisms were understood not simply as a battle of divine spiritual power versus demonic spiritual power. His exorcisms also involved a demystification of demons that revealed the concrete imperial powers operative in the people's distress. They thus include a political dimension. In the exorcisms Jesus expels the possessing powers of Roman imperial rule and heals its effects. The "acts of power" he performs empower the people in a restoration of their lives under the direct rule (kingdom) of God.[30]

The first exorcism in Mark's narrative (1:21-28) is set in a Sabbath gathering of the synagogue in Capernaum. This was a meeting of the local village assembly for prayer and discussion of community affairs, not a gathering of a cult specifically for exorcism, as in the Sudan. Similar to what takes place in the *zar* cult, however, it is the presence of the exorcist that induces the demon to exhibit the effects of its possession of its host. Forced to manifest its presence, the unclean spirit knows exactly what is happening: "Have you come to destroy us? I know exactly who you are, the Holy One of God" (1:24). The demon thus declares that Jesus is God's agent, whose exorcism as part of a broader program of bringing the "kingdom of God" is bringing defeat for all the demonic forces (note the plural pronoun, "us"). In contrast to typical exorcism stories in other Hellenistic literature, however, the rest of this episode shows no interest in the thaumaturgical techniques of the hero. Jesus merely utters the sharp brief command, "Be silent, and come out of him" (1:25). Thereafter the narrative emphasizes the violence of the struggle engaged: "Convulsing him and crying with a loud voice, the unclean spirit came out of him" (1:26).

The key term in this episode, *epitiman* in Greek, is not used in Hellenistic stories and is distinctive here (9:25; Jesus' exorcisms usually feature "cast out," *ekballein*, Mark 1:34, 39; 3:15, 22; 6:13; 9:18). "Rebuke," the NRSV translation in 1:25, is far too weak and misses the ominous significance of the term *ga'ar* in Hebrew, usually translated as *epitiman*. In many psalms, for example, *ga'ar/epitiman* (synonymously) parallels bold terms such as "destroy, vanquish, trample" in appeals to God as warrior coming in judgment against foreign rulers who conquer Israel (for example, Pss 9:6; 68:31; 106:9). Clearly these psalms are appealing to God to "conquer" or "subject," not to "rebuke," such conquerors. In one late prophetic passage (Zech 3:2) the term is even used with reference to Satan: "May Yahweh subject (*ga'ar/epitiman*) you, O Satan!"

Most significant, moving more fully into the struggle at the spiritual level, is the usage in the Qumran community. The term *ga'ar* is the verb used for Abraham's or God's subjection of evil spirits in the *Genesis Apocryphon* (1QapGen). It is a key term in the struggle between God and Belial (the officer of darkness), as in the *War Scroll* (1QM 14:9-11): "You have driven (*ga'ar*) his [Belial's] spirits [of destruction] far from [us]. You have preserved the soul of Your redeemed [when the men] of his dominion [acted wickedly]." Thus, in Jesus' first public action at the beginning of Mark's Gospel, Jesus has begun to defeat the demonic forces that have been possessing the people, forces that were associated with foreign conquerors in the key verb of the episode. As "the holy one of God," moreover, he is acting in the power of God, which is how he, unlike the scribal representatives of the high priests appointed by the Romans, "teaches" as one possessing "power" (*exousia* means more than "authority").

In both of the two Gospel sources usually deemed the earliest, Mark's Gospel and the Q speeches, Jesus is accused of "casting out demons by Beelzebul the ruler of the demons" (Mark 3:22-27; Luke/Q 22:14-20). Mark's casting of the accusers as "the scribes who came down from Jerusalem" has a certain historical verisimilitude, corresponding to the polarization between the rulers and the ruled attested by the principal sources for

Roman Palestine. The scribes were the representatives of the Jerusalem priestly aristocracy, the client rulers appointed by the Roman governors.

The name *Beelzebul,* used by the scribes, is of Semitic derivation, meaning something like "Baal the Prince." *Ba'al* ("Lord [Storm]"), king of the powers that constituted the cosmic-civilizational order in ancient Canaanite city-states, vilified by the Israelite prophets, had long since been demonized by spokespersons of the Jerusalem temple-state. Like establishment intellectuals in other societies, the Jerusalem scribes looked down upon country people, particularly the Galileans ("Galilee of the Gentiles"; Isa 9:1-2; Matt 4:15), as half pagan. Like the scribes and priests at Qumran, they believed not only in spiritual powers but also in their own version of the diametrical opposition between divine and demonic forces. In their view, the remarkable powers on which Jesus was drawing were not derived from and certainly not approved by the Temple authorities in Jerusalem. They therefore, virtually by definition, derived from the demonic opposition forces headed by Beelzebul. The scribes' accusation parallels how Christian theologians and church authorities, both Protestant and Catholic, defined peasant midwives and healers as witches in collusion with Satan in the witch hunts of the sixteenth and seventeenth centuries. Since Jesus' unusual powers did not derive from and were not approved by the religious and political authorities, they had to be from Beelzebul.

Jesus and his audience also assume that life circumstances involve a struggle between opposing spiritual forces, between God and demonic spirits headed by Satan. They assume, further, that this is a struggle for dominion over people's lives, a spiritual-political war. In formulating his logical argument against the accusation (Mark 3:23-26; cf. Luke/Q 11:17-18), Jesus draws on what were standard (and synonymous) political metaphors in Israelite tradition: "kingdom" and "house." The kingdom of God was central to Israelite tradition, as discussed already. As in the *War Rule* from Qumran, so for Jesus, the kingdom of God was locked in sustained struggle with the rule/kingdom of Satan/Belial/the officer/ruler of darkness. The close synonym "house" was a standing metaphor for a ruling family or dynasty. Jesus argues that it would be absurd to think that Satan, locked in a sustained struggle against God for control of history, would "cast out Satan," thus defeating himself. Having refuted the accusation of the scribes, he states what is really happening in another metaphor or parable (Mark 3:27; cf. Luke/Q 11:21-22). One cannot plunder a strong man's goods without first tying him up. In the exorcisms, Jesus is obviously "plundering the strong man's goods/vessels," that is, Satan's demons. So Satan must have been bound first—by God or by Jesus, who by implication is stronger than Satan.

The point to which Jesus' argument drives is that in Jesus' exorcisms Satan and his demons are being overpowered, defeated. The power they have exercised in people's lives is being taken away. God is winning the struggle. The discourse in Q pushes the argument a significant step further, stating explicitly that the exorcisms are manifestations of the active rule (kingdom) of God. The more concrete (hence probably the earlier) wording in Luke 11:20, "If by the finger of God I cast out demons (which is the case), then the kingdom of God has come upon you," presents the exorcisms as a new exodus, as episodes in the general renewal of Israel under way in Jesus' mission.

The most dramatic and violent exorcism in Mark's Gospel (5:1-20) brings the political dimension of Jesus' power struggle against the "unclean spirits" vividly to the fore. Again, it is the presence of Jesus as exorcist that evokes the mania in the demoniac. No sooner does Jesus step out of the boat in which he has crossed the sea than he is confronted by a man driven utterly berserk by the demon. His violence directed against the community and himself has escalated completely out of control. "He lived among the tombs, and no one could restrain him any more, even with a chain; for he had often been restrained with shackles and chains, but the chains he wrenched apart, and the shackles he broke in pieces; and no one had the strength to subdue him. Night and day among the tombs and on the mountains he was always howling and bruising himself with stones" (5:3-5).

Immediately after wrenching the demon out of the man, itself a violent struggle as well, Jesus is able to elicit its identity. "My name is 'Legion,' for we are many" (5:9). The local onlookers, whose grandparents and parents had witnessed or been killed in the repeated Roman military conquests, understood full well what a Roman legion was. And indeed, the Roman soldiers were many, thousands of heavily armed warriors with orders to destroy and slaughter. Like the possessing spirits in Africa whose names were Lord Cromer or the spirits who insisted on their hosts dressing up like the British army, the force that had been driving the possessed man to such violence against himself and his community was that of the conquering Roman army. As in colonial Africa, this symbolic name of the demon means (to us) that the Roman army was the cause of the distress among the subjected people, including the possession of this man and his violent destructive behavior. Not only is the demon's name symbolic, but the possessed man is representative of the whole society that had been invaded by imperial violence destructive of their persons and communities.

The episode is not yet complete, however. The hearers of the story in Galilean villages and beyond, who are still suffering the effects of Roman conquest and continuing Roman violence, are treated to the image of the Roman "Legion" begging Jesus "not to send them out of the country" they had taken possession of. Clearly, Jesus, as "Son of the Most High God," is the authority figure who holds dominant power in this situation, as in both the first exorcism in Mark and the Beelzebul discourse. More ominously politically, and more empowering for the listeners, Jesus "dismissed" Legion to enter the great "herd/troop" of swine on the hillside, which then impulsively "charged" down the steep bank "into the sea" and "were drowned in the sea." In order to appreciate the fuller political significance of this exorcism, we must understand the special terms used and the connotations of some of them in Israelite culture as they are juxtaposed with the ostensible concrete circumstances. Military imagery continues, confirming that "Legion" refers to a conquering Roman army. The Greek term behind "herd" was often used for a troop of military recruits. "Dismissed" is a command that the commanding officer gives to the troops. "Charged" indicates troops rushing headlong into battle. Here, however, they charged into the sea to their own destruction. "Sea," hardly an appropriate term for the large inland lake of Galilee, has to refer to the Mediterranean Sea across which the Roman legion had come to conquer the people. "Into the sea" and "drowned in the sea," finally, evoked memories of the exodus, when Pharaoh's armies were cast "into the sea" and "drowned in the sea" (Exod 15:1-10).

In the final step of this episode, when the people of the countryside see the man who had been possessed by "Legion" restored to his right mind, they are afraid. And when the swineherds report to them what happened to the herd of swine as well, they beg Jesus to leave the area. Why are they afraid and not rather overjoyed? That they have heard what happened to the "battalion" of swine as well as the demoniac suggests that their fear arose from the revelation of the concrete cause of their distress, which had been veiled by the spirit possession. The demoniac had been the representative figure in their village(s) who had "acted out" the effects of invasive Roman violence on their community(ies). Their chaining him and restraining his violence out among the tombs had been a way of establishing a *modus vivendi* with the Roman imperial power that had invaded and disrupted their lives. Jesus' exorcism had eliminated their means of adjusting and left them facing the concrete cause of their distress.

In the exorcism of "Legion," as in the first exorcism in Mark, Jesus exercises authority/power over the demonic forces that have possessed the people and establishes the rule of God. This episode finally makes explicit what has been implicit in the earlier exorcisms: the concrete political power that corresponds to demon possession. The destructive demonic forces are pointedly identified as the effects of Roman imperial rule. In language that evokes memories of God's original deliverance of Israel from Pharaoh's troops, moreover, the Roman troops are self-destructing as a result of Jesus' exorcism. The identification of the "real" historical power that had been disrupting their common life, however, while liberating (for some) was also threatening (for others).

Many modern Westerners have focused on whether there was anything real behind the stories of Jesus' exorcisms. Exorcism, like the demon possession it purported to "cure," did not conform to reality as defined by the canons of scientific reason. Demon possession was an irrational phenomenon that occurred only among less civilized peoples. Exorcism was a kind of magic or miracle that, by definition, was not susceptible of rational understanding. Ironically, this was the stance taken toward Jesus' exorcisms by interpreters who lived in the Western colonial powers whose invasions of those uncivilized peoples were evoking spirit possession and the need for exorcism. We can now see that the life circumstances of ancient Judean scribes and Galilean Israelite peasants were similar to those of modern African peoples invaded by colonial powers. Roman imperial power had devastated the villages of the Judeans and expropriated the produce of their labor, with debilitating effects on their life energies.

Jesus and the people with whom he interacted took demon possession for granted, and exorcism of "unclean spirits" became one of the principal activities in his mission. The question for Jesus' followers was what was happening in Jesus' exorcisms. The Markan exorcism episodes and the Beelzebul discourse examined above depict demon possession and Jesus' exorcisms as caught up in a sustained struggle between superhuman spiritual forces, divine spirits versus demonic spirits, God versus Satan. Jesus' exorcisms were "acts of power" that brought that struggle to a climax. Jesus, as God's agent in the struggle, in commanding the spirits to "come out" of their hosts was defeating or overcoming the forces that had taken possession of people's lives. Insofar as the people were caught in a struggle between two forces competing for control of their lives, Jesus' exorcisms were manifestations of the demise of the demonic force. The overpowering of the demons, moreover, meant that "the strong man" had been bound, the rule of Satan had fallen. Since it was thus clear that Jesus was casting out demons by the "finger"/spirit/power of God, then the kingdom of God had come upon the people. Finally, pressing the political implications of Jesus' exorcisms in more explicit terms, the identity of the demon across the sea was revealed as "Roman troops," and under the authority of Jesus they proceeded to self-destruct. Jesus' exorcism of the spiritual forces also signaled and manifested the demise of Roman power over the people.

Chapter 6

The Collective Power of Covenant Community

Renewal of the covenant between God and Israel made at Mount Sinai was the very center of Jesus' teaching, according to the Synoptic Gospels. In Matthew, Jesus' first, programmatic speech is a renewal of the covenant, delivered by the new Moses on a mountain (chapters 5–7). Much of the Matthean "Sermon on the Mount," moreover, is paralleled in Jesus' first, programmatic speech in the Gospel of Luke (6:20-49). The two speeches have the same overall structure. It appears that both Matthew and Luke used an already structured speech of covenant renewal, the first and longest in the sequence of Jesus' speeches in Q. Parallel in various ways is the most sustained block of teaching in Mark (10:1-45), a sequence of dialogues two of which explicitly cite the covenantal principles usually known as the Ten Commandments.

The Gospels include additional teaching or dialogues on covenantal issues. In Mark (7:1-13), Jesus insists that the basic commandments of God take priority over the Pharisees' "traditions of the elders," specifically that "honoring your father and mother" requires using a family's resources locally rather than pledging them in "devotion" to the Temple. One of the four petitions in the Lord's Prayer (Luke 11:2-4//Matt 6:9-13) focuses on the cancellation of debts, an economic principle that reinforced covenantal principles. As if ceremonially confirming the renewal of covenant as the core of his teaching, at the celebration of Passover commemorating the exodus Jesus makes his Last Supper a covenantal meal, presenting the cup explicitly as "my blood of the covenant" (Mark 14:22-25; cf. Exod 24:3-8).

Rarely, however, will one find a discussion of Jesus' renewal of the Mosaic covenant in books on the historical Jesus. One reason for this is the Protestant theology in which New Testament studies developed. According to what was previously a standard scheme of Christian origins, "Judaism" was dominated by "the law," which was rooted in the (original or "old") covenant, freedom from which was brought by "the gospel" of Jesus and Paul. Despite the way Matthew framed the "antitheses" in the Sermon on the Mount ("you have heard it was said of old . . . , but I say to you . . .") as the fulfillment of the Law and the Prophets (Matt 5:17-19, 20-48), scholars took them as a break with the Jewish covenantal law. Keying on Paul's wording of the Lord's Supper rather than Mark's, Christian interpreters have traditionally understood Jesus as establishing a *new* covenant (or testament), not a renewal of the Mosaic covenant.[1]

If, however, we abandon this older Protestant theological scheme and focus on whole speeches of Jesus, perhaps we can discern that Jesus thought and taught in broader cultural patterns operative in Israelite tradition. We can discern how Jesus creatively adapted the Mosaic covenant that continued at the center of that tradition in Galilean and Judean society.

ECONOMIC PRESSURES AND THE DISINTEGRATION OF VILLAGE COMMUNITIES

We are attempting to understand Jesus' teaching in the historical context in which he worked. Ancient Galilean society, like other traditional agrarian societies, consisted of many village communities and their component transgenerational families, the fundamental social-economic forms in which people's lives were embedded.

For peasant families, which constituted the basic units of production and reproduction, life was a continuing struggle to sustain themselves from harvest to harvest, ideally on their own family land, traditionally understood as an inalienable gift from God.

Studies of various agrarian societies in different times and areas of the world have shown that, while individual families attempted to feed themselves, the component households of the villages practiced a certain degree of mutual cooperation and reciprocity. Rather than seeking to maximize their own individual livelihood, the families that comprised a village community, concerned that component households remain economically viable, had various ways of supplying aid to needy families.[2]

In Israelite tradition, the Mosaic covenant provided the guiding principles of such a "moral economy" of village communities. The basic principles of the covenant informed various mechanisms of mutual cooperation and support by which the component families might remain viable (as discussed in chapter 2). God's commandments prohibiting murder, coveting, stealing, and adultery protected people's social and economic rights to life, land, livelihood, and family integrity. Israelite families depended on the power of their labor on the land to produce food energy to sustain themselves from one year to the next. The covenant commandments prohibited the relatively more powerful families from taking advantage of periodic weakness of other families, for example, coveting and stealing their produce by charging interest on loans. Covenantal mechanisms of mutual aid, such as generous lending at no interest and periodic cancellation of debts, effected the sharing of produce as needed within village communities (Exod 22:25-27; Lev 25:35-37; Deut 15:1-2, 7-8, 12-15). In addition, ideally the exclusive loyalty to God as the king of the society and the prevention of an ambitious family from gaining power over the others would keep an oppressive kingship from emerging internally.

There is considerable evidence that the covenantal principles and supporting mechanisms of economic adjustment were not simply abstract ideals but were actually practiced in the society in which Jesus worked, at least by many villagers. A considerable number of peasant producers must still have observed the sabbatical rest of the land, judging from Josephus's accounts of how it figured in famines and in payment of the Roman tribute (Exod 23:10-11; *Ant.* 3.12.3 §§280–81; 12.9.5 §378; 13.8.1 §235; 14.10.6 §§202, 206; 14.16.2, §475; 15.1.2 §7). Similarly, observance of the cancellation of debts in the seventh year must have been standard and expected among the people. Otherwise there would have been no need for the leading scholar-teacher Hillel to devise the *prosbul* as a device supposedly to ease credit by allowing creditors to avoid the sabbatical canceling of debts by placing the documents of debts in the hands of a court (*m. Sheb.* 10:3-7; cf. Deut 15:1-6).[3] Especially telling for assessing the covenantal themes and patterns in Mark, Q, and subsequent Gospels are the foundational texts of the Qumran community discovered among the Dead Sea Scrolls. The *Community Rule* and the *Damascus Rule* in particular illustrate how this scribal-priestly movement used the Mosaic covenant as the basis for establishing a community independent of the high priestly rulers in Jerusalem and as the guiding principles for its communal life of mutual sharing.

Peasants in all societies face perpetual difficulties of survival, including insufficient land and the vagaries of weather. But particular actions and arrangements by the Romans ratcheted up the pressures on the Galilean villagers in the decades leading up to Jesus' mission. In their conquests and reconquests the Romans and their client king Herod had destroyed some villages and killed or enslaved some of the people. Given the limitations of our sources, it is difficult to calculate the rate of taxation on villagers' produce. More important in appreciating the pressure on peasant producers were the multiple demands for revenues by multiple layers of rulers. The Roman tribute was imposed on top of the tithes and offerings owed to the priesthood and Temple. The taxes demanded by Herod, the Romans' client king, further exacerbated the economic burdens. Moreover, the efficiency of tax collection would have increased when Herod Antipas established his rule directly in Galilee, from new cities that overlooked most of the villages of lower Galilee.

The very structure of Roman imperial rule thus became a major factor in the disintegration of families and village communities. As more of the produce of the villagers was taken in Roman tribute, royal taxes, and/or tithes and offerings, families had less food (energy) to support themselves. Neighbors' resources were quickly exhausted in loans among villagers, forcing hungry villagers to borrow from those who had access to resources, which in Galilee probably were the Herodian officers. As outsiders to the village communities, these officers had no scruples about charging interest at high rates. Repayment of loans at high interest rates further compounded the demands on the producers. The result was spiraling debts and perpetual hunger for many families. Many sought to supplement their income as day laborers, and some were threatened with the loss of their ancestral land and their membership in the village community. Studies of comparable agrarian societies suggest that it is when villagers are threatened with spiraling debts and the loss of their ancestral land that popular movements or, more rarely, popular revolts emerge.

This is exactly the picture presented in key speeches of Jesus. Ironically, the most sophisticated critical analysis of the sayings of Jesus abstracts

them from these speeches and looks for meaning in the sayings themselves, isolated from particular contexts. In many cases, however, the very
content of the sayings indicates the context to which they were addressed
as components of those speeches.[4] That context is villages in which families are in trouble and the community is disintegrating. In the Lord's
Prayer not only are families hungry, but they are in debt to one another
(Luke 11:2-4//Matt 6:9-13). In one speech, Jesus addresses people's persistent anxiety about having food, clothing, and shelter (Luke/Q 12:22-
31). Many of the longer parables use as familiar illustrations people who
are heavily in debt or have become day laborers or, having lost control
of their land, sharecroppers (for example, Mark 12:1-8; Luke 16:1-8).
The covenant renewal speech that we will examine more closely below
has one reference after another to people who are poor and hungry and
to begging, loans, debts, attempts to collect payments on loans, and the
resultant quarreling, insults, and accusations among neighbors within the
village community (Luke/Q 6:20-22, 27-28, 29, 30, 34, 35, 37-38).

Contrary to recent individualistic constructions of Jesus as having
called his disciples to leave family and village to pursue an itinerant individual lifestyle, the Gospel sources portray Jesus as having sent his disciples into villages to work at the renewal of family and community. In
Mark, Jesus repeatedly visits villages or "towns" and "places" in Galilee
and surrounding areas. Almost in passing, as if it would be obvious, Mark
has Jesus teaching and healing in the village *assemblies,* as noted in chapter 4. Jesus evidently focused his mission in village communities.

The most telling indications of this focus are the parallel but independent "mission discourses" in Mark (6:6-13) and Q (Luke/Q 10:2-16).[5]
The existence of these parallel speeches with the same basic structure
suggests that the sending of Jesus' envoys was a standard practice in early
Jesus movements, originating in Jesus' own mission in Galilee. In both
versions of the commissioning, the workers are sent out in pairs to villages, where they are to stay in a household in the community and accept
subsistence support. It is more clearly stated in the Q mission discourse
than in Mark that the envoys are sent to work in the village communities
(Luke/Q 10:8-11) as well as in their constituent households (Luke/Q
10:5, 7). There is no suggestion that the envoys are to focus on individuals, to "convert" them, in the popular misconception of what early Christian "missionaries" were doing. The individualistic touch in Luke 10:6 is

distinctive to Luke. It is not in the Gospel of Matthew (therefore also not in their mutual Q source) and or in Mark. The envoy's declaration of peace is explicitly on the household (Luke 10:5//Matt 10:13). Given the small houses and crowded conditions in villages, as evidenced from archaeological excavations, even when the envoys were working with families, they could not help but interact with others in the village communities.

Charged to expand Jesus' own mission of exorcism, healing, and preaching the kingdom, these workers were apparently also, in effect, carrying out what might be called "community organizing." Judging from the mission speech in Q, whole villages might turn out to be receptive or hostile. If receptive, a village community apparently became associated with the wider movement. If hostile, curses might be called down upon it for its rejection of the opportunity offered: "Woe to you, Chorazin! Woe to you, Bethsaida!"[6] Jesus' mission of the renewal of Israel was focused not on individuals but on people involved in families and village communities. These fundamental social forms were beginning to disintegrate. This is what Jesus addressed in his renewal of the Mosaic covenant.

JESUS' COVENANT RENEWAL SPEECH IN Q

The basic structure of the Mosaic covenant, as observed in chapter 2, consisted of three major components: (1) a statement of God's deliverance; (2) principles of exclusive loyalty to God and of social-economic relations; and (3) sanctions as motivation for observance.[7] In the covenant made on Sinai (Exodus 20), the covenant renewal ceremony (Joshua 24), and the elaborated covenant in Deuteronomy, the content of these components, respectively, was God's deliverance in the exodus, the Ten Commandments and/or covenantal laws and teachings, and blessings and curses for keeping or not keeping the commandments.

Quite apart from the teaching of Jesus, we know from the *Community Rule* (1QS) and the *Damascus Rule* (CD) from Qumran that the Mosaic covenant was still operative in Roman Palestine. Both Rules not only contain many covenant motifs but also display the same three structural components. But there are two changes in the components that are significant for comparison with Jesus' covenant renewal speech. The declaration of deliverance in the *Community Rule* (1QS 3:15—4:26) concludes with God's final termination of injustice in the near future. In the opening instructions for a covenant renewal ceremony (1QS cols. 1–2), moreover, the blessings and curses that traditionally functioned as sanctions motivating obedience are transformed into part of the declaration of deliverance (or its opposite) in the present and near future rather than in past history.[8] The *Community Rule* and the *Damascus Rule* are not simply pieces of literature; they are (written copies of) directions for (orally performed) ceremonies, including rules and regulations, for the formation and governance of an operating community of priests and scribes independent of the high priestly rulers. The two Rules show that the traditional Mosaic covenant was not only still operative in the society but could be creatively adapted. Scribes and priests, however, had no monopoly on the Mosaic covenant.

While Matthew's Sermon on the Mount and Luke's Sermon on the Plain display the same overall structure, the latter is thought to be closer to the earlier speech that they both adapted. A quick scan of Jesus' speech in Luke/Q 6:20-49 reveals that it contains numerous covenant motifs and is structured by the basic covenantal components.

1. It is not difficult to recognize that the blessings and woes at the beginning constitute the declaration of deliverance, only now in the present-future rather than in the past (6:20-22, 23-26; cf. Matt 5:3-12 + 13-16). This is strikingly similar to the way in which the blessings and curses were transformed in the *Community Rule* at Qumran.

2. The sets of sayings beginning with "love your enemies" (Luke/Q 6:27-36) and "do not judge" (6:37-42) include many allusions to or similarities to covenantal teachings in the "covenant code" (Exodus 21–23) or in Deuteronomy or in sections of Leviticus (esp. Leviticus 19; 25). These admonitions, in the form of "focal instances," are the renewed covenantal principles of social-economic relations (Luke/Q 6:27-36, 37-42; cf. Matt 5:17-48).

3. Finally, in the place of the blessings and curses as the traditional sanction for motivation, Jesus' speech has a double parable of houses built on rock and sand, introduced by "the one who hears and acts" versus "the one who hears and does not act" (Luke/Q 6:46-49; cf. Matt 7:24-27). This double parable in the last step of the speech is clearly now the motivating sanction on keeping the covenantal teachings.

In this covenant renewal speech, Jesus directly addresses the disintegration of village communities under the pressures of Roman imperial rule. Precisely because Galileans, like other Israelites, were deeply rooted in the Mosaic covenant as the guide of their personal and social-economic life, they were evidently blaming themselves for their malaise. The blessings and curses were supposed to function as sanctions to motivate the people to keep the basic commandments, but they easily slipped over into an explanation of people's fortune or misfortune. If people were suffering poverty, hunger, and disease, it must be because they had sinned and broken the covenantal laws; they were therefore receiving the curses. The episode of Jesus' healing of the paralytic (Mark 2:1-12) indicates that this was a common understanding of illness and distress among the people: the man brought to Jesus was paralyzed because either he or his parents had sinned. Jesus' response deals not just with the paralysis but with the people's assumption about its cause. In declaring that the paralyzed man's sins are forgiven, he addresses the debilitating collective self-blame, releasing healing powers that enable the man to "take up his bed and walk."

Similarly in the Q covenant renewal speech, Jesus first addresses the people's broken spirit, their assumption that their poverty and distress are the result of their sinning, of having broken the covenant. In the renewal of the covenant, he transforms the blessings and curses into a new declaration of deliverance that addresses precisely the way the people have become dysfunctional. In addressing the people's self-blame and despair, Jesus pronounces God's blessing for the poor and hungry. Correspondingly, he pronounces woes on the wealthy, whose power and privilege derive from their expropriation of the goods of the peasantry, leaving them poor and hungry.

Having declared God's new deliverance-in-process, Jesus presents covenantal demands specifically aimed at overcoming the internal economic and social conflicts that are further undermining village communities (Luke/Q 6:27-42). He focuses first on economic relations and then on related social relations in the village. "Love your enemies" and the associated sayings that Matthew uses in the six antitheses of the Sermon on the Mount (Matt 5:43-48) have traditionally been taken as commands of nonretaliation against hostile enemies, especially the Roman soldiers. These sayings have formed the basis of Christian pacifism. From the context indicated in the content of the sayings (in Luke/Q 6:27-36, 37-38), however, it is clear that Jesus is addressing economic and social conflicts in local village life—not relations with Roman soldiers, who would not have been present in Galilean villages as occupying troops during the rule of Herod Antipas. Lender families, themselves under pressure of the heavy tax burdens, would soon have been seeking repayment of the loans, but the debtor families would have been unable to pay, leading to local conflicts. Jesus addresses these conflicts with the command to "love your enemies" and then applies the principle in some typical cases of borrowing and lending that focus the covenant renewal on concrete local conflicts.

In direct response to such economic conflicts, Jesus briefly addresses debtors in the community (Luke/Q 6:29). "If someone sues you for your cloak, let him take your shirt as well." The implication, of course, is that the debtor would be standing stark naked, embarrassing the creditor in front of the whole village (Jesus had a sense of humor!). The reference is to the age-old covenant command: "You shall not deal with others as a creditor. If you take your neighbor's cloak in pawn, you shall restore it before the sun goes down, since it is your neighbor's only covering at night" (Exod 22:25-27; Deut 24:10-13).

In these economic teachings, Jesus addresses mainly people in their actual or perpetual role of aiding needy neighbors, insisting that they continue their sharing and generosity (Luke/Q 6:30-36). "To the one who asks from you, give, and from the one who borrows, do not ask back. . . . But love your enemies, and do good and lend." This is a broad exhortation of local economic cooperation and sharing reminiscent of numerous traditional covenantal teachings (for example, Deut 15:7-11). In the command to "be merciful as your Father is merciful," Jesus calls community members to pattern their generosity on God's generosity. This command also resonates with age-old covenantal tradition, particularly with the similar principle enunciated in Lev 19:2. The principles implicit in these focal cases and the accompanying general exhortation also bear a remarkable resemblance to the third petition in the Lord's Prayer: "Cancel our debts, as we herewith cancel the debts of our debtors."

Jesus' admonitions and rhetorical questions, beginning with "love your enemies" (Luke/Q 6:27-36), stand directly in the Mosaic covenantal tradition, build on it, and renew it. The focal instances of lending and borrowing here would have recalled the whole range of such traditional covenantal teachings to the minds of the listeners. To counter the local conflict over borrowing and lending, Jesus thus calls villagers to renew the time-honored values and principles of mutual sharing and cooperation central to covenantal teaching.

Jesus next addresses the social conflicts closely related to the economic difficulties (Luke/Q 6:37-42). "Do not judge and you will not be judged." These admonitions are also derived from the tradition of Mosaic covenantal teaching, as can be seen through the window provided by Lev 19:17-18. The ensuing "parable" and rhetorical questions strongly admonish the people to cease blaming and accusing one another and return to the basic covenantal values of cooperation and mutual support in the community.

The concluding step of Jesus' covenant renewal speech (Luke/Q 6:43-49) provides the motivating sanction. The double parable of houses built on rock and sand (6:46-49) replaces the blessings and curses that had become problematic in that they induced people to blame themselves. The preceding admonitions (6:43-45), again rooted in covenantal tradition, probe the motivational bases of covenantal behavior. They are reminiscent of the prophecy in Jer 31:27-34 of the new covenant written on the heart rather than on stone tablets.[9]

In sum, in his covenant renewal speech, Jesus (as a prophet like Moses) addresses economic and social conflicts between families hard-pressed by the pressures of Roman imperial rule. These conflicts were disintegrating the fabric of reciprocal economic support that had traditionally held village communities together. After declaring the blessings of the imminent kingdom of God that give the people new hope, Jesus restates the fundamental covenantal principles of mutual sharing and cooperation in terms that would have resonated deeply with the people.

The covenant renewal speech, however, was more than teaching. It was a reenactment of the covenant, in "performative speech," which enacts what it states. After pronouncing blessings on the people, Jesus in the role of a prophet like Moses called them to a recommitment to God and to one another in a community of solidarity and mutual support. This restored the communal power of the local community. It was thus also a strategy of resistance to the rulers. By restoring their mutual cooperation and solidarity, villagers could resist the further disintegration of their communities. This mutual support from within the community could enable particularly vulnerable families not to succumb to the outside forces that would turn them into sharecroppers or force them off their ancestral land and from their position in the village community. Jesus' renewal of covenant thus empowered both individual families and the village communities.

JESUS' COVENANT RENEWAL IN MARK

The pace of the story in Mark slows down as Jesus delivers a series of dialogues (10:2-45) focused on the community life of the movement forming in response to his mission.[10] Interpreters have long recognized that Jesus' teaching in these dialogues is concerned with issues similar to those of other social-political movements such as the Qumran community— as in the *Community Rule*, which was clearly a document of covenant renewal.[11] In the first and third dialogues, Jesus refers to or pointedly cites many of the covenantal commandments. In the course of each dialogue, moreover, he articulates general statements of law on issues of central importance to community life (10:10-11, 14, 29-30, 43-44).[12] In the dialogues of Mark 10:2-45, Jesus addresses in succession the issues of marriage, social status of membership in the community, economic relations, and political leadership. In the context of the overall Gospel narrative, this sequence of dialogues thus constitutes a renewed covenantal charter for the communities of the movement that Jesus catalyzed.[13] We should not imagine, of course, that these dialogues represent particular historical interactions of Jesus with followers. The dialogues have been shaped in the ongoing life of communities of a Jesus movement to represent the gist of his covenantal renewal.

In Jesus' covenantal teaching in Mark, as in the original Mosaic covenant, economic relations command the most attention. A sequence of three brief, closely related dialogues that are often separated into three paragraphs in English Bibles (Mark 10:17-22, 23-27, 28-31) develops Jesus' insistence on egalitarian covenantal economics.

Jesus' response to the man who asks how he can inherit eternal life signals the economic focus of the covenantal commandments in unmistakable terms. The man's question indicates that he is wealthy. This is not the kind of question that would have come from a struggling peasant wondering where the next meal would come from. Jesus immediately recites the six commandments that pertain to local social-economic interaction.[14] But he pointedly substitutes "you shall not defraud" for "you shall not covet," inviting the listeners to recognize how the man became wealthy. In an agrarian society, coveting someone else's goods might well lead the coveter to defraud a vulnerable person desperate for wage labor or for a loan to feed his children (cf. Deut 24:14-15). The man's protest that he has piously kept the commandments is exposed as a "fraud" when he cannot respond to Jesus' command to sell his goods and give to the poor. He not only has great possessions but is deeply attached to them. In Israelite covenantal society, the way someone became wealthy was by defrauding the vulnerable, by charging interest on loans (forbidden in covenant law) and eventually gaining control of others' possessions (fields, households).

This episode thus presents a negative example of a man who has gained wealth by defrauding others, by breaking the covenant commandments. This negative example of what not to do—exploiting others to augment one's own wealth—induces the hearers to recommit themselves to the traditional covenantal values of local cooperation and mutual aid. That the negative example is an outsider who had been exploiting the vulnerable villagers to expand his own wealth serves to reinforce the solidarity of the villagers over against the power holders who "defraud" them, against their God-given covenantal rights (in contrast to Jesus' subtlety in Mark, the parallel episode in Luke introduces the man explicitly as a "ruler" in 18:18).

In the next step of the dialogue sequence (10:23-27), Jesus reflects on the negative example of the man who has become wealthy by defrauding others, addressing the disciples who simply don't "get it" (10:23; see 9:33-37) as foils for the important declaration he is about to deliver (10:23-27). Having declared the principle of how extremely difficult it will be for the rich to enter the kingdom of God (10:23), Jesus broadens the application. The stringency of covenantal demands for egalitarian economics applies to everyone (10:24). He then moves back to the rich (10:25). In making a telling analogy, he cannot resist indulging in a bit of typical peasant humor, about the camel going through the eye of the needle. Peasant hostility against wealthy rulers and exploiters is not even veiled in this episode, as often in biblical materials that derive from popular tradition. The point of this step in the dialogues is that criteria for "entering the kingdom" are the simple and straightforward covenantal economic principles.[15]

Jesus' statement in reply to Peter's self-interested query in the concluding dialogue of the sequence must be heard with the ears of Galilean villagers:

> Truly I tell you, there is no one who has left house or brothers or sisters or mother or father or children or fields, for my sake and the gospel's, who will not receive a hundredfold now in this age (houses, brothers and sisters, mothers and children, and fields) with persecutions—and in the age to come eternal life. (Mark 10:29-30)

In contrast to the reading of generations of Christians with their eyes fixed on heaven, Jesus' reassurance to Peter, the disciples, and the whole movement here is astoundingly "this-worldly." The final phrase, "and in the age to come eternal life," is a "throwaway line," an "oh, by the way..." that refers back to the unreal question of the rich man with which the discussion of economics opened. Only people who have become rich by defrauding the poor are interested in "eternal life."

Jesus concludes the sequence of dialogues on covenantal economic relations with the emphasis that the restoration, after all the struggles of the movement, is to occur "now in this age." Nor will the hostile rulers who wield power over them have disappeared. The restoration of family and village life when people will have regained the power to make a good living will happen "with persecutions." Jesus is talking, with wondrous exaggeration but in remarkably concrete terms ("and fields"), about the renewal of village community life under the direct rule of God, which is happening in this age in the face of (in spite of) persecutions, before it comes with power (Mark 9:1). Jesus' final declaration ("There is no one who . . . will not receive," 10:29-30) in this extended dialogue completes the instruction in covenant economics with a clear allusion to the covenantal blessings. In terms of structural components in Jesus' covenant dialogues in Mark, the rewards promised here constitute the motivating sanction, but with sobering realism about the continuing political situation. Observation of egalitarian economic principles, where no one seeks to become wealthy by taking advantage of others' vulnerability, will result in abundance for all in the community, despite continuing imperial domination (cf. Luke/Q 12:22-31).

Corresponding to the egalitarian economic relations in renewed covenantal community (Mark 10:16-31), Jesus declares in the next dialogue
that political power relations within the renewed society are to be egalitarian (10:32-45). Still "without a clue" even after Jesus' third announcement that the Jerusalem rulers will condemn him and the Romans execute
him, James and John request that Jesus appoint them to the highest positions of power at his right and left hands when he comes into his glory.
They are imagining Jesus as receiving the imperial power (presumably
from God), as if that is what Jesus' program of the kingdom of God is all
about. He reminds them that he is headed to a martyr's death by crucifixion—where those "on his right and on his left" will turn out to be fellow
"brigands," similarly executed by the Romans for insurrection against the
imperial order—enunciating his final principle, on political relations in
the renewed covenantal community. He draws a pointed contrast with
the "great ones" of the nations, the high and exalted emperors who use
their power in tyrannical domination. Jesus' program is the opposite
of imperial rule. Not only are there no rulers, no power holders, in the
renewed covenantal society, but its leaders serve others, empowering the
community.

While different in form, Jesus' covenant dialogues in Mark and his covenant renewal speech in Q are closely parallel in their basic concern for
cooperative social-economic relations in community life. They constitute
strong indications that Jesus was engaged in a mission of revitalizing and
reempowering communities in their fundamental social-economic relations, which also enabled them to maintain a certain amount of power
over their own lives as cohesive covenantal communities.

"YOU CANNOT SERVE GOD AND MAMMON"

Jesus' renewal of the Mosaic covenant, while focused on village communities, was a bold move to regenerate local power to withstand the disin-
tegrative effects of imperial power on village communities. The renewal
aimed primarily to revitalize mutual support and solidarity among component families of the villages. Covenant renewal, however, was the central component in the overall program of renewal of Israel over against
the rulers of the people. Explicit in both Jesus' covenant renewal speech

in Q and his covenant renewal dialogues in Mark are condemnations of the wealthy, who further enhance their riches and power by expropriating the people's produce.

In Mark, the principle that "it is easier for a camel to pass through the eye of a needle than for a rich person to enter the kingdom of God" (Mark 10:25) is a prophetic indictment of the wealthy. The immediate context suggests that this is because they have been defrauding the people in violation of the covenantal prohibitions against coveting and stealing. The covenant renewal speech in Q, at least in Luke's version, similarly pronounces condemnation of the wealthy ("Woe to the rich . . . ," Luke/Q 6:23-26). Woes together with blessings would have been part of the symmetry of the speech's covenantal structure, matching the double parable at the end, with a house on the sand corresponding to curses and the house on the rock corresponding to the blessings. The woes, moreover, were not just a rhetorical device. Again in the woes, Jesus' performative speech effects what it states (the condemnation of the wealthy)—at least to an audience of the poor.

Other teachings of Jesus also condemn the rich for accumulating wealth by expropriating the people's labor and produce. Some of these appear in Jesus traditions known only from Luke. And because of Luke's accommodation of Jesus' teaching for urban situations well beyond Galilee, it is sometimes difficult to determine their earlier versions and applications.

The parable of the manipulative steward presents a "slice of life" in an agrarian society similar to the negative example of the rich man in Mark. As with most parables, the assumptions of the telling and appropriate hearing of the parable are either implicit or tacit. Unacquainted with ancient agrarian life, modern interpreters have projected their own inappropriate assumptions onto the parable.[16] Further, the line between the parable itself (is it Luke 16:1-7 or 16:1-8a or 16:1-8b?) and the attached sayings that apply it (16:7, 8a, 8b, 9; 16:10-11, 12, 13a, 13b, 13c, 13d) is very unclear. Modern interpreters have usually assumed that "the lord" is an absentee landlord of large estates and that his "debtors" are tenants (such as sharecroppers). Nothing in the parable itself, however, suggests this.

Taking the parable on its own terms, we may be able to discern how it would have been heard by Galileans on the basis of a more precise understanding of political-economic relationships and Israelite culture in ancient Palestine. The parable focuses on a steward acting as the agent of a wealthy man in making loans to peasants. To hide the interest being charged, which was prohibited by covenant law, the "bills" of what the debtors owed the lord were written to include the interest in the payment due. The going rate was evidently 100 percent on oil (with 100 jars of oil due on 50 borrowed) and 25 percent on grain (100 measures of grain due on 80 borrowed). The large sums involved illustrated the huge gulf between the extremely wealthy and the increasingly impoverished peasants whom they were exploiting with loans at high rates of interest. (In the Galilean context, the master could have been one of Antipas's [Herodian] officers.) When the steward was about to be fired, he knew very well that as a lifelong "white-collar" accountant he could not possibly make it as a manual worker and he could not bear the humiliation of begging. So to ingratiate himself with the debtors, he had them change the amount they owed on their bills to exactly the amount they borrowed, eliminating the hidden and prohibited interest.

In the context of Jesus' mission, the conviction that the kingdom of God was at hand meant also that judgment was at hand, according to covenantal criteria. The parable of the manipulative steward would thus have immediately evoked among the hearers an anticipated judgment of both the lord and his steward for their exploitation of desperate peasants in violation of covenantal law. If Luke 16:8a ("the lord commended the steward") was part of the parable ("the lord" being the rich man, not "the Lord," that is, God), then the rich man, suddenly recognizing that he needed at least to appear to be observing covenantal law, commended his steward. The steward, by manipulating the debtors' bills, had done what the rich man in Mark 10 could not do, that is, give back the wealth he was about to gain by defrauding the debtors to feed the poor (the debtors). Whether Luke 16:8b ("for the children of this age") was an early commentary or not, the saying in Luke 16:13d, or perhaps the two parallel lines in 16:13a and 13d, would be the most obvious principle to be derived from the parable: "No servant can serve two masters. You cannot serve God and mammon (wealth)."

The story of the rich man and Lazarus (Luke 16:19-31) is yet another condemnation of the rich for accumulating huge, ostentatious amounts of wealth while turning a deaf ear to "Moses and the prophets" (16:29, 31). Some modern interpreters have argued that the story does not condemn wealth but rather how wealth blinds the rich to concern for the poor. Such an interpretation simply misses the covenantal content of "Moses and the prophets," as was indicated in the covenantal dialogues in Mark (10:17-22) and in the covenantal speech (Luke/Q 6:23-26, 27-36). Indeed the story of the rich man and Lazarus could be read as an illustration of the blessings and woes in Luke/Q 6:20-26 and the principles articulated in Mark 10:23, 25.

The rich man, who "was dressed in purple and fine linen" (imported luxury items, purple being typically worn mainly by kings) "and feasted sumptuously every day," obviously lived in extreme wealth. In the context of early-first-century Galilee, this was clearly an allusion to Herod Antipas and his "conspicuous consumption" in his lavishly decorated palace in the newly built resort city named after the emperor Tiberius overlooking the Sea of Galilee. Twice elsewhere, Gospel traditions caustically caricature Antipas's ostentatious display of wealth. In one of the Q speeches parallel in Matthew and Luke (Luke/Q 7:25-26), Jesus sarcastically contrasts Antipas as "dressed in soft robes, . . . in fine clothing and living in a royal palace," with John the Baptist as the prophet who had condemned him, as everyone in Galilee would have known. Mark incorporates a popular story that caricatures the elaborate self-staged birthday banquet at which the drunken Herod Antipas, drooling over his stepdaughter's dancing, is manipulated by his new—and unlawful—wife into beheading John (Mark 6:17-29).

In the starkest of contrasts, the story in Luke juxtaposes the rich man and Lazarus, an utterly destitute beggar, covered with sores licked by the dogs, lying at the rich man's gate, hoping to eat whatever crumbs fall from his table. The hearers would have recognized Lazarus as one of the many victims of those mysterious forces that drove villagers into a spiral of indebtedness until they lost control of their land and became so malnourished that they were unable to survive as day laborers. That he lies at the rich man's "gate," the term for a (royal) court, suggests that he is also trying to appeal for justice at the court of the ruler (Antipas) and is being systematically ignored. This experience was well known in Israelite tradition. Through the prophet Amos, YHWH had condemned the king or royal officers who not only "trampled on the poor and took from them levies of grain" in order to "build their mansions of hewn stone," but then "afflicted the righteous, and pushed aside the needy in the gate (court)" (Amos 5:11-12).

That Lazarus is taken to be with Abraham, the original ancestor of Israel, while the rich man descends into Hades (Sheol, not the hell of later Christian culture) turns the tables on standard assumptions and expectations in contemporary culture. Part of the legitimating ideology of the Judean elite, including Herod, who built tombs of the ancestors such as Abraham, and the high priestly aristocracy, was the genealogy by which they claimed descent from the great ancestors such as Abraham, Aaron, or David. This story thus exhibits a close parallel to the prophecy of John the Baptist, which warns (evidently) the Judean elite not to presume that having Abraham as their ancestor is a guarantee of their power and privilege in the face of the impending judgment (Luke/Q 3:8—for "God is able from these stones to raise up children to Abraham"). Even closer is the parallel in Jesus' prophecy of the imminent banquet of the kingdom of God, with Israelites gathered together with "Abraham, Isaac, and Jacob and all the prophets," but those who presume on their ancestry "thrown out" into "wailing and gnashing of teeth" (Luke/Q 13:28-29).

Far from being repentant in his fiery torment, the rich man still presumes upon his privileged status, expects God to grant his request (for relief), and sees Lazarus as belonging to the servant class that caters to the wishes of the wealthy ("dip his finger in the water and cool my tongue"). When told of the chasm that separates him in the agony of punishment from Lazarus in Abraham's solace, he thinks only in terms of his ruling-class family, with Lazarus again in the servant role, warning them about the torment of Hades. But, Abraham answers, they already had "Moses and the prophets," who made abundantly clear the principles of justice in political-economic relations and the criteria by which judgment would be rendered—but they did not listen to them. Those hearing the story, who had heeded "Moses and the prophets," however, knew very well that the only way that people could become wealthy was by exploitation of the people over whom they had gained power.

KEEPING PEOPLE'S PRODUCE FOR
THE WELFARE OF THE PEOPLE

In covenant renewal, the flip side of condemnation of the ruler's expropriation of the produce of the people was the retention of that produce for the support of families and communities. This is implicit in the insistence on mutual support and sharing in Jesus' covenant speech. It is explicit in Jesus' economic dialogue in Mark 10. In two other "covenantal" episodes, Jesus articulates this same insistence on retention of the produce of people's labor for support of the people themselves (as mentioned in chapter 4). In both cases, Jesus' insistence is in direct opposition to the draining of local resources upward in support of the Temple and into the control of the priestly aristocracy, Rome's client rulers in Judea.

In the last episode of Jesus' confrontation with the rulers of Israel in Jerusalem, he first responds to a question from a scribe, then refutes the scribes, and finally accuses them of preying on the poorest of the people (Mark 12:28-34, 35-37, 38-40). The first step in the confrontation is often read as a rather chummy reconciliation between Jesus and at least this one scribe. The second and third steps give the lie to such a reading. The scribe's question is no less a test than the Sadducees' question in the preceding episode: Which commandment is the first/greatest of all? Jesus begins his response satisfactorily enough with the answer that the scribe himself would surely have given. He recites the Shema, the basic Israelite confession of faith in the one God and the fundamental commandment of exclusive love of the one God "with all your heart, . . . soul, . . . mind, and . . . strength" (known in our biblical text from Deut 6:4-5).

Jesus, however, immediately expands his response. He adds a "second" commandment: "You shall love your neighbor as yourself," and then binds them closely together so that they are inseparable as well as incomparable. By adding the second, he is emphasizing it. And his addition of the second command to the official confession of faith makes a bold innovation, judging by comparison with contemporary Judean scribal texts, in which one finds no such close connection between "love God" and "love your neighbor." Both of these commands were contained in Judean texts (that later became biblical), but in different books (Deut 6:4-5; Lev 19:18). In the popular Israelite tradition in which Jesus and his followers were rooted, "love your neighbor" referred to responding to their economic needs, which were also their covenantal rights. This same meaning had been taken up into the official Jerusalem tradition as well. In Lev 19:9-18, "love your enemy" stands as the summary of a whole series of Mosaic covenantal injunctions: to leave crops in the field for the poor to glean at harvest time, not to steal or deal falsely, not to oppress the neighbor, and not to do injustice. It is not by accident that so many parallels to Jesus' covenant teachings are found in this passage. The scribe is forced to agree that Jesus has spoken truly, and he is forced to admit Jesus' point: that love of neighbor is "more important than all whole burnt offerings and sacrifices"—quite an admission by a scribe who was himself economically dependent on Temple offerings. And Jesus acknowledges his admission.

But that does not stop Jesus from proceeding to accusation. He begins by mocking the scribes' pretentious posturing in their self-important positions of authority. But he then indicts them for violating the commandment to "love your enemy": they "devour widows' households/livings." In the next episode, he illustrates the point with the example of a widow who, encouraged by the scribes, donated the last copper coin that remained of her "living" or "household." That is, in the terms of Lev 19:9-18, he accuses them of violating "love your enemy" by stealing and dealing falsely, oppressing the poor, and generally doing injustice. The scribes and the ruling Temple apparatus in which they serve stand in violation of covenant principles for siphoning off to the Temple the people's resources that they need, and that God intended, for their own support.

This is precisely what Jesus declares also in a confrontation with the Pharisees and some scribes in Mark 7:1-13. This episode in Mark is perhaps the prime example of Christian misunderstanding of Jesus as attacking "Jewish law." Such an interpretation can now be seen as a serious oversimplification. In fact, this confrontation is instead the prime illustration of how Jesus appealed to the basic covenantal commandments of God against rulers' devices to expropriate the people's resources to support the ruling institutions.

The framing of the story pointedly designates the Pharisees and scribes as representatives of the high priestly aristocracy who "had come from Jerusalem" to accuse Jesus and his disciples. As a foil for Jesus' response, they accuse his disciples of what Galilean peasants would have considered a ridiculous offense, an excuse to harass the movement: of eating with "common, that is, unwashed hands." That is, they were not observing the purity code of the Pharisees and supposedly of all those Judeans who lived around the Temple. The charge is ridiculous, of course, since according to scriptural purity regulations and later rabbinic rulings, purity codes were of concern mainly to priests who served in the Temple. Except perhaps for Pharisees, who may have aspired to maintain purity regulations, ordinary

Judeans and other Israelites were not expected to maintain purity on a regular basis (but presumably only when they went to the Temple for one of the pilgrimage festivals such as Passover).

The charge against Jesus and his disciples is a rhetorical device to illustrate how ridiculous it is that the Pharisees and scribes charge Jesus and his disciples with not observing the Pharisees' "traditions of the elders," of which the hand-washing requirement was a trivial illustration. As the similar phrase in one of Josephus's discussions of the Pharisees indicates (*Ant.* 13.10.6 §§296–97; cf. 13.16.2 §408), "traditions of the elders" was a reference to the legal rulings that the Pharisees had promulgated over a period of several generations, regulations not written in the laws of Moses. Presumably these "traditions" continued to be authorized by the high priests in Jerusalem as part of official temple-state law, as their (Hasmonean) predecessors had done a hundred years earlier. This is the real target of Jesus' counterattack in this confrontation with the Pharisees and scribes down from Jerusalem. He levels the very serious charge that in holding to their "traditions of the elders," which are merely human precepts, they are abandoning the commandment of God (7:6-8). Then he immediately changes the subject from washing hands before eating to having anything to eat at all.

In order to understand Jesus' charge that the representatives of Jerusalem rule are rejecting, even voiding, the commandment of God, we need a sense of what *korban* meant in first-century Galilee. For the debate to make any sense, *korban* must have been yet another one of the Pharisees' "traditions of the elders." The Markan narrator inserts only the briefest explanation, a term used evidently in an oath formula meaning "dedicated," that is, as "an offering to God" (7:11). In a discussion of various obligations to God, the priests, and the Temple, such as firstfruits and tithes, Josephus mentions people who had been "dedicated" to God or the Temple (debt-slaves?), who then had to pay the priests (thirty to fifty shekels) to be relieved of their obligatory service (*Ant.* 4.4.4 §73; cf. Lev 27:1-8; *Ag. Ap.* 1.22 §167). This suggests that the practice of dedicating people or an animal or other resources to the service of God, that is, to the Temple and the priests, was current at the time of Jesus. An account by the early Christian theologian Origen (third century) illustrates the binding economic implications of "dedicating" something to God/the Temple (even if the details of the report are not trustworthy). His Jewish informant said that in revenge against debtors who could not repay loans, creditors would declare that what was owed was *korban*—thus forgoing repayment themselves but leaving the debtors still obligated to pay their debts.[17]

As a specific example of how the Pharisees and scribes "reject the commandment of God in order to keep [their] tradition," Jesus focuses on what may have been the most sensitive issue for a struggling family: "Honor your father and your mother." To sharpen the charge he also cites the Covenant Code: "Whoever speaks evil of father or mother must surely die" (Exod 21:17). How so? How could their advocacy of *korban* entail that they are guilty of a capital crime? Jesus understands the commandments of God to protect economic rights. The Pharisees and scribes had evidently been urging Galileans to "dedicate" some of their land or probably its produce to God, payment going to the Temple. But that drained away produce needed for support of the multigenerational family. That left people unable to support their aging parents, the most sacred and fundamental duty in any society: "Whatever support you might have had from me is *korban*."

To appreciate the sharpness and urgency of Jesus' charge, it may help to remember that during his lifetime Galilee was under the rule of Herod Antipas, and therefore presumably not under that of the Jerusalem high priesthood. The Temple authorities, however, who had presumably drawn tithes and offerings from Galilee for the previous century during which Jerusalem had ruled Galilee, may have backed off in their efforts at collection, lest it interfere with Antipas's extraction of taxes from the populace. Yet the Temple apparently attempted to keep some revenue flowing from the area, further exacerbating the economic pressure on the people. This would appear to be what Jesus is attacking. In the device of *korban* and in "many things like this," the Pharisees and scribes, as representatives of the Jerusalem Temple, were pressing people to send the produce of their labor to support the Temple and the priesthood. But this was siphoning off resources needed to feed hungry and indebted families, violating the very principles that God had delivered on Sinai for the conduct of family and community life.

Throughout Jesus' covenant renewal speeches and other covenantal teachings, the principal concern is for the welfare of families and village communities. Addressing hungry villagers whose communities were dis-integrating into quarreling over their mutual indebtedness, he declared renewal of the Mosaic covenant. In response to God's new deliverance, bringing the kingdom of God to the poor, villagers recommitted them-selves to mutual cooperation and support. Village communities could regenerate the power of cooperation, mutual assistance, and solidar-ity that would enable them to resist the outside forces that were drain-ing away their resources and leading to their disintegration. The people renewed their commitment to principles and mechanisms of a "moral economy" in which they did not take advantage of others' vulnerability. Renewal of cooperative covenantal community was also a kind of "dec-laration of independence." This included condemnation of the wealthy wielders of power who expropriated the produce of their labor and resis-tance to the devices by which the powerful siphoned off the produce the people needed for the support of family and community life. Jesus' cov-enant renewal aimed to retain and regenerate the people's own power in their local community and to stem the flow of local resources upward to enhance the power of the rulers.

Chapter 7

Speaking Truth to Power

Matthew, Mark, and Luke portray Jesus as dramatically challenging "the powers that be" in Jerusalem. He marches triumphantly into the city with a crowd of Passover pilgrims shouting Hosannas. He forcibly blocks business in the Temple, pronouncing God's condemnation of the ruling aristocracy. He states in barely veiled terms that it was not lawful to render tribute to Caesar, which was tantamount to inciting insurrection. The Gospel of John portrays Jesus as repeatedly confronting the Judean rulers in Jerusalem. All of the canonical Gospels, along with the *Gospel of Peter,* have Jesus crucified as an insurgent leader by the Roman governor. And they all present Jesus' confrontation with the rulers in Jerusalem as the provocation that leads to his crucifixion.

Christian interpretation effectively depoliticized the Gospel accounts. Or perhaps it would be more accurate to say that Christian interpretation shifted the politics in accommodation to political power, exonerating the Romans and blaming "the Jews," in a long process that began in the Gospels. Modern Christian interpretation reduced the Temple to a religious institution and reduced Jesus to a religious reformer carrying out a "cleansing" of the Temple. "Rendering to Caesar" became the proof-text for paying taxes to the state while still giving one's spiritual loyalty to God, who presumably had no jurisdiction in political-economic matters, as in the modern separation of church and state. Jesus' prophetic parable that condemned the high priests tragically became an announcement that God was about to scuttle the violent tenants who killed his son, that is, "the Jews," and give his vineyard to others, that is, the "Christians."

Critical modern scholarship has, perhaps unwittingly, had the effect of perpetuating the depoliticization. Scholars concluded, for example, that insofar as the Gospel narratives are expressions of faith in Christ, they cannot be used as reliable sources for the historical Jesus. But that led to inattention to the very narratives that portray Jesus as engaged in political(-economic-religious) conflict. There has been little investigation into the ways in which the Gospel narratives might display historical verisimilitude, for example, with regard to the structure of power relations that framed Jesus' conflict with the rulers. Some of the most critical examinations of Jesus' individual sayings, moreover, categorized many judgmental sayings as statements of apocalyptic eschatology, having little to do with politics and power relations.

We are left with a Jesus who was politically innocuous, however pithy his sayings. Yet no one would have remembered the teachings had Jesus not mounted a public confrontation of the rulers in Jerusalem and, as a result, been crucified by the Romans as an insurgent leader. Can a critical analysis of the Gospels' portrayal of Jesus' confrontation with those who wielded power in Jerusalem, in the context of what is known of power-relations in Roman Judea from other sources, help explain what led to his crucifixion?

THE DYNAMICS OF POWER RELATIONS IN PALESTINE

On this complex issue more than any other, it will help to broaden our approach to consider factors previously unrecognized and to engage in some critical, multifactor historical reasoning. Among those factors are the structure and dynamics of political-economic power relations in Roman Galilee and Judea, the regional differences, and the emotional as well as ideological results of prolonged relations of domination and subjugation. Not seeing evidence that he was leading an outright revolt against Roman rule, interpreters of Jesus have usually concluded that he must therefore have been politically quiescent. Recent political-anthropological studies of similar agrarian societies, however, have pointed out that such a dichotomy of political possibilities is simplistic. It fails to take into account both the effects of the coercive power wielded by rulers and the forms that popular resistance can take short of outright revolt.

It is important to remember that the Temple, besides being the sanctuary where Judean priests offered sacrifices to God, was also the face and instrument of Roman imperial rule in Judea and, at least until the death of Herod, over Galilee as well. The Romans and their client king Herod kept the high priesthood intact. Herod, moreover, had mounted a massive reconstruction of the Temple as one of the wonders of the Roman imperial world, where the priests conducted sacrifices to Caesar and Rome as well as to God. After Herod died, Roman governors appointed the high priest from one of the four families that Herod had installed in the priestly aristocracy. Thus dependent on the Romans for their positions of power and privilege, the high priestly families consistently collaborated in Roman rule, often against the interests and protests of the people.[1]

While Judeans must have continued to send tithes and offerings to the Temple and priests, there was considerable popular opposition and occasional protest and revolt against the priestly aristocracy and their Roman overlords, as noted in chapter 3. Popular hostility escalated steadily during the first century until it erupted in widespread revolt in 66 C.E. Even scribal groups sharply criticized or opposed the high priests. The circle of scribes that produced the texts collected in the book known as *1 Enoch* had evidently rejected the whole institution of the Second Temple as illegitimate, with "polluted bread on its table," and imagined the future renewal of Israel as not having a temple (*1 Enoch* 89:73; 90:29).[2] A large band of scribes and priests had withdrawn from Jerusalem into the wilderness at Qumran in protest and continued in their alternative community, which they regarded as the true temple through the end the Second-Temple period. As discussed in chapter 3, the radical Pharisees and other scribes of the Fourth Philosophy organized resistance to the Roman tribute in 6 C.E. And at mid-century some of those same discontented scribal teachers formed a terrorist group, the Sicarii, who targeted high priestly collaborators with Roman rule for assassination during festivals. In short, it is difficult to identify any scribal group other than (the majority of) the Pharisees who did not reject or sharply criticize the high priests in late Second-Temple times.

While sharing Judeans' opposition to the high priestly aristocracy as clients of Roman rule, Galileans had their own historical reasons for opposition. The Jerusalem high priesthood based in the Temple had brought

Galilee under its control only about a hundred years before Jesus' birth. Coming under Jerusalem rule for the first time in six centuries may well have increased the Galileans' sense of belonging to the Israelite people, along with the Samaritans and Judeans to the south. To continue living on their land, however, Galileans were required "to live according to the laws of the Judeans" (Josephus, *Ant.* 13.11.3 §§318–19).[3] That presumably meant to pay tithes and offerings to the priests and the Temple, as Judeans were expected to do. Moreover, peasants almost always have a certain degree of resentment about their rulers, who demand a portion of the produce they need to support their families and communities.

During the lifetime of Jesus, however, Galilee was no longer under the jurisdiction of the high priesthood and the Temple. The Romans installed Herod Antipas in control of Galilee. Galilean villagers had reason to resent his rule as well. His construction of two new hilltop cities overlooking the villages of Galilee in the first twenty years of his rule would have placed increased burdens on the Galileans while increasing the efficiency of tax collection. If Jesus had wanted to confront the ruler in Galilee, therefore, he could have marched into Tiberias or Sepphoris. And if he had been apprehended and executed in Galilee, he would presumably have been beheaded, like John the Baptist, not crucified.

Jesus, however, was crucified. To have been crucified, however, he must have gone up to Jerusalem, where the Roman governor had jurisdiction. Moreover, he must have done something seriously threatening to the Roman imperial order that led the Roman governor to crucify him.

Studies of movements in similar circumstances in other societies find that a leader's public articulation of the people's indignation is often what energizes the coalescence and expansion of a movement. It is thus suggestive that the speeches included in the early chapters of Acts, the series of speeches in Q, and the Gospels (as whole stories) represent Jesus' confrontation with the rulers and his crucifixion as the decisive events for his mission and his movement. It may well be that Jesus' confrontation in Jerusalem was the beginning of the "breakthrough" that energized Jesus' movement(s) in its rapid expansion from what had started in Galilee.

We should not imagine that events in Jerusalem happened precisely in the way portrayed in Mark or the other Gospels. More important than details of particular episodes is what the episodes and prophecies reveal about the structural conflict between Jesus and the people (villagers), on the one hand, and the high priestly, Herodian, and Roman rulers, on the other, and particularly the dynamics of their confrontation at the time of Passover.

To understand the rich accounts in the Gospels of Jesus' prophecies against the Temple and his confrontation with the Jerusalem rulers, it will help to appreciate the effects of coercive power on ordinary people and the creative alternative forms of political resistance that they can muster. Modern historians' generalizations about how peasants or slaves accepted the dominant order and their own place in it are based on written sources. In ancient societies where literacy was limited to the cultural elite, however, those sources were produced by the literate elite and reflect the interests of the dominant class. Most written sources therefore provide access to the institutions and ideology of those in power but do not necessarily reveal the views, interests, and ideology of the ordinary people.

In order to get more deeply into the dynamics of power relations it is necessary to consider the effects of domination (power) on what the subordinated say and do, on the one hand, and what they may think, on the other. Political scientist James C. Scott's reflections on his own extensive fieldwork among peasants and the extensive comparative material on which he draws go far to illuminate the dynamics of power relations between the dominant and the subordinated.[4] Even if slaves and peasants had intense resentments of their subjection, they dared not express vocal opposition for fear of the coercive power arrayed against them. Speaking out might evoke subtle or more violent reminders of who was in control. Striking out would bring violent retaliation, probably death and the destruction of the family livelihood. When they are "on stage," in public discourse and interaction with their masters or rulers, therefore, subjugated persons wear masks of compliance. What they may really think and desire is another question. Those feelings could be articulated only when they are safely "off stage," back in their houses and villages among other subjugated people whom they trust.

The experience of subjugation, moreover, produces certain ideas and attitudes. To control subject people and induce them to give up some of their produce, the dominant must impose various indignities on their subordinates. These can range from forced gestures of deference to one's superiors or rituals of subordination to words or acts of humiliation and submission. The resulting indignation produces a popular ideology opposed to the official ideology of the dominant. The people's resentment about the indignities they suffer produces an oppositional emotion that can turn into a powerful motivation. Popular Israelite tradition provided a rich ideology opposed to domination by powerful kings and priests in stories of the exodus, covenantal principles of people's economic rights and provisions for relief of debts, and prophetic oracles against injustice. Jesus drew heavily on these, as noted in the previous chapters.

The generation of people power requires a combination of two factors: sequestered space where oppositional ideas and motivation can be cultivated, and leaders to give articulate and disciplined form to the ideas and emotions in interaction with the people. As in similar agrarian societies, villages in Galilee and Judea were semi-self-governing communities rarely visited by representatives of their rulers except for the collection of taxes. That villages provided off-stage locations for teaching traditions such as covenant renewal was thus another key aspect of Jesus' concentration of his mission in these communities. Jesus, assisted by his envoys sent to work in village communities, transformed the long-standing ideology and the people's resentment into excitement about the coming of God's kingdom of justice and the renewal of covenantal community in their villages.

On the basis of comparative studies of subordinated peoples in similar societies, we can discern three forms of political opposition to the dominant—short of outright revolt, which is rare—in which Jesus and his movement engaged. Just how direct and dangerous the resistance was depended on where it was located and who was watching and listening. One form of resistance remained in the sequestered sites. This was the renewal of village communities already discussed in the previous chapter. Strengthening the cooperation and solidarity of village communities enabled the people to resist further encroachment by the various layers of rulers. This form of political resistance was still located in the village communities, far from the urban centers of power.

The other two forms of opposition moved out into direct resistance to their rulers. In a "politics of disguise and anonymity," Jesus spoke or acted out opposition to the authorities in public, where the rulers could hear or see it, but on occasions and in language that avoided personal culpability and vulnerability to retaliation. In the other action, however, Jesus boldly "spoke truth to power" directly and explicitly. Both of these forms of direct political resistance, but especially the bold declaration of popular opposition in the face of the violent repression sure to follow, had the potential to mobilize the oppositional emotion underneath the oppositional ideology (not usually expressed in public) into expansive momentum.

These distinctions may seem overly subtle, but they make a difference in how powerful the forms of resistance might be. What the subjugated Galileans thought of Antipas or the Jerusalem aristocracy was part of their oppositional ideology, and how Jesus articulated opposition to the rulers reinforced other aspects of his teaching. Where and how he articulated opposition to the dominant, however, made considerable difference in its impact on the people as well as on the rulers.

PROPHETIC CONDEMNATION OF DEREGULATED POWER

Gospel sources offer a good deal of evidence that Jesus prophesied against the Temple and/or Jerusalem rulers. We encountered some of this in the covenant renewal and related covenantal teachings examined in the last chapter, in the woes against the wealthy and the sharp criticism of the scribes' role in siphoning away the people's resources to the Temple. Assuming another traditional prophetic role related to that of covenant renewal, Jesus also pronounced God's condemnation of the high priesthood/Temple. The Q speeches include a still well-defined prophetic lament against the Jerusalem ruling house (Luke/Q 13:34-35a). The Markan narrative and several other sources provide multiple indications that Jesus prophesied against the priestly aristocracy and Temple.

While both Mark and John locate the occasion for Jesus' prophecy against the Jerusalem rulers in the Temple complex itself, such prophetic condemnations could have been articulated outside of Jerusalem as well. The prophetic declaration of God's judgment against the Temple, moreover, was not by itself a disruption of the Roman imperial order serious enough to result in crucifixion. What the Gospel references to Jesus' prophecies against the Temple and high priests do indicate, however, is that Jesus and his movement(s) were convinced that they stood under God's condemnation.

Jesus' prophecy against the ruling "house" of Jerusalem in Q/Luke 13:34-35a is almost verbatim in Matthew's and Luke's parallel texts, suggesting that neither changed it from the tradition they used. The oral poetry of the oracle is almost palpable, with a mournful repetitive address, parallel lines with parallel sounds, and the image of God as a protective mother hen.

> O Jerusalem, Jerusalem!
> You kill the prophets
> and stone those sent to you.
> How often would I have gathered your children together
> As a hen gathers her brood under her wings,
> And you refused.
> Behold, your house is forsaken!
> For I tell you:
> You will not see me until you say:
> "Blessed is he who comes in the name of the Lord."
>   (Luke/Q 13:34-35; cf. Matt 23:37-39)

In delivering this oracle, Jesus steps into the role of an Israelite oracular prophet. He adapts the traditional form of a prophetic lament in which the prophet speaks the words of God. Amos 5:2-3 offers a classic example, in which God's lament anticipates the future lamentation of the ruling city when judgment is finally executed:

> Fallen, no more to rise is the maiden Israel;
> Forsaken on her land with no one to raise her up.
> . . . .
> Therefore thus says the LORD, the God of Hosts:
> In all the squares there shall be wailing;
> And in all the streets they shall say "Alas! Alas!"
> They shall call . . . those skilled in lamentation to wailing.
>   (Amos 5:2-3, 16-17)

Similarly in anticipation of God's imminent judgment, Jesus announces that Jerusalem is already desolate (because destroyed) and in mourning.

Jesus' principal charge in this prophecy is that Jerusalem habitually kills the prophets God has sent. This indictment reverberates outward with wider implications. It resonates with a long Israelite tradition. Historically, kings had at least attempted to kill prophets. Ahab and Jezebel attempted to assassinate Elijah (1 Kings 19). King Jehoiakim even sent agents to Egypt to kill the prophet Uriah son of Shemaiah (Jer 26:20-23). And after Jeremiah pronounced God's condemnation of the Temple for systematic violation of covenantal commandments, officials tried to lynch him (Jer 26:7-23). Legends about the prophets that found their way into the later collection called *The Lives of the Prophets* suggest that Jesus' contemporaries may have believed that most of the prophets had been martyred for their message. This tradition would have been in the forefront of people's memories because both the Roman governors and Roman client rulers in Palestine were killing prophets in their own time. Best known at the time of Jesus, of course, was Herod Antipas's beheading of John the Baptist for his insistence on covenantal justice (Josephus, *Ant.* 18.5.2 §§116–19; cf. Mark 6:17-29).[5]

In his representation of God protecting her children as a mother hen gathers her brood under her wing, Jesus taps into a traditional image familiar to his listeners. In the "Song of Moses," a celebration of the exodus deliverance and covenantal formation of Israel, the people sang of God as "like an eagle that stirs up its nest and hovers over its young, spreading its wings" (Deut 32:11). "Children" (or "daughters") was a standard metaphor for the villages subject to a mother city (as in Isa 51:17-18). Jesus' lament depicts God as a mother grieving because, even though she had tried to protect her children, the Jerusalem rulers had exploited them—and therefore were about to be left forsaken and destroyed.

"House" could be taken as a reference to the Temple, which was indeed the ruling institution in Jerusalem. But "house" had long been a term for a monarchy, dynasty, or temple-state with its whole governing apparatus. "House" also resonated with a long prophetic tradition of declarations of judgment against Jerusalem rulers. Indeed, the whole phrase "your house is forsaken," desolate, abandoned, echoed a prophetic tradition, a glimpse of which can be seen in Jer 22:1-9. In that prophetic oracle, Jeremiah declared God's judgment against (destruction of) the ruling "house of the king of Judah," inclusive of "you [the king himself], your servants [government officials], and your people who enter these gates [other Jerusalemites]."

Because the prophecy takes the form of a lament, modern readers may miss the severity of the indictment and condemnation that Jesus announces here. The lament assumes and announces that God has already condemned Jerusalem as the ruling house of Israel. Jerusalem stands condemned and desolate because of its violent and predatory actions against the people in violation of covenant principles: the rulers had killed the prophets, because the prophets had condemned them for oppressing the people.

The last line of the lament (Luke/Q 13:35a), finally, recites a key line of the highly familiar Passover psalm (Psalm 118) giving thanks for previous deliverance and appealing for future salvation: "Hosanna! Deliver us!" God, speaking through Jesus, declares to the Jerusalem rulers that they will not see him until they welcome "the one who comes in the name of the LORD," presumably Jesus himself. But of course they were not about to do that. Since they have refused/forsaken God, they are about to be refused/forsaken by God.

Three different episodes in Mark, some paralleled in other sources, cite or refer to Jesus' prophesying against the Temple. Some of the witnesses at Jesus' trial in Mark say that they heard him say, "I will destroy this temple that is made with hands and in three days I will build another, not made with hands" (Mark 14:58). Passersby at his crucifixion deride him, saying, "Aha! You who would destroy the Temple and build it in three days" (15:29). It is often assumed that Jesus' saying that "not one stone will be left here upon another, all will be thrown down," in Mark 13:1-2, is a prophetic reference to the destruction of the Temple. The simplest reference is in the *Gospel of Thomas* 71: "Jesus said: 'I shall de[stroy this] house, and no one will be able to build it [again],'" which is close to the report in Acts 6:13-14 that Stephen had said "that this Jesus of Nazareth will destroy this place." That Jesus had prophesied destruction (and rebuilding) of the Temple was so deeply embedded in the tradition that the Gospel of John, unable to suppress the prophecy, carefully explained that Jesus was referring to his body rather than suppress the prophecy (cf. John 2:19-21).

Several attempts have been made to explain—or explain away—this prophecy. Some have argued that at Jesus' trial in Mark the paraphrase of his prophecy is presented as false testimony. Mark's narrative ("But even on this point their testimony did not agree" [15:59]) does not really say that. The assumption at the crucifixion scene is that Jesus had indeed spoken about destroying the Temple. Mark's story had earlier presented Jesus as declaring that the stones would all "be thrown down." It is possible that the "falseness" of the testimony pertains (subtly) to its form. The Markan narrative may be portraying the high priests and elders as unacquainted with the form of prophetic pronouncements and uncomprehending of their ominous import, assuming that Jesus meant that he himself would perform the destruction. If, however, he had been uttering prophecy as the mouthpiece of God in the same way that earlier Israelite prophets had done and in the same way as in Luke/Q 13:34, then it was God who was about to destroy the Temple.[6]

The form of the prophecy in two of the Markan episodes and in John is a double saying, about the destruction and the rebuilding of the Temple. One attempt to mitigate the severity of the prophecy of destruction has been to claim that there was a long-standing expectation of a new temple, and that the destruction in Jesus' prophecy was to prepare for the rebuilt temple. This is a misreading of several Second-Temple Judean texts.[7] In some of those adduced, terms such as *Zion* and *the house* are symbols for the restored people, not the rebuilt temple. In others, the Temple is conspicuously missing in images of the fulfillment of history. The several attempts to explain away Jesus' prophecy of the destruction of the Temple have proven to be flawed and unconvincing.

The temple "not made with hands" was taken as a "spiritual" or "heavenly" temple in earlier Christian interpretation. The appearance of "house" in the *Gospel of Thomas* version, however, suggests another possibility for understanding the prophecy in its double-saying form. "House (of God)" was used in Second-Temple Judean texts not only for the Temple and for the ruling house but also for the people, and often for the restored people of Israel. The discovery of the Dead Sea Scrolls has provided evidence of a Judean community contemporary to the Jesus movement that understood itself as the "temple" (1QS 5:5-7; 8:4-10; 9:3-6; 4QFlor 1:1-13). Terms such as *house, temple, body,* and *assembly* could all function as synonyms, usually with reference to a social body (the people; "the house of Israel").

Jesus' prophecy of destroying and rebuilding the temple can thus be understood as playing on the double meaning of the term *temple* or (more likely, as in the *Gospel of Thomas* version) *house*. His prophecy declared that God was destroying the/God's "house/temple made with hands" in Jerusalem but rebuilding the/God's "house/temple not made with hands," the people of Israel. This fits well with the agenda of Jesus' mission, as attested in Q as well as in Mark, of spearheading a renewal of Israel in opposition to its rulers. If the renewed people itself were understood as the rebuilt "temple" or "house" of God, then of course there would be no need for a temple-state, which, as an instrument of imperial control, was widely resented among the people. The Gospel of John's interpretation of the rebuilt temple as Jesus' "body" can also be understood somewhat in this sense. In John, Jesus is resurrected in the mutual indwelling and love of the "body" of his followers.

The prophetic books of Amos, Hosea, Isaiah, Micah, and Jeremiah indicate that the reason the kings and their officers stood under God's condemnation was that they had oppressed the people in violation of the principles of the covenant (for example, Mic 2:1-5; Isa 3:13-15; Jer 7:5-10). Some of the fragmentary oracles collected in these books contain explicit indictments; in others the covenantal basis of the sentence seems implicit. The kings' use of power was supposedly kept in check by the application of principles of the Mosaic covenant to kingship by Samuel (1 Sam 10:25). As the kings consolidated their power, however, they simply rode roughshod over the covenantal regulations meant to protect the rights of the people. When David conspired to have the pregnant Bathsheba's husband killed and Ahab and Jezebel had Naboth "framed" and stoned to death so that they could seize his ancestral land for their palace garden, all that the people and their prophets could do was to formulate stories of royal abuse of power ("the poor man's lamb" [1 Samuel 11–12]; "Naboth's vineyard" [1 Kings 21]). In the subsequent historical circumstances of the people facing the political-economic power of their rulers that was no longer effectively checked by covenant principles and regulations, individual prophets such as Amos and Jeremiah delivered oracles of God's condemnation of the rulers for violating those principles.

Jesus revives this Israelite prophetic tradition. The destruction of Jerusalem and the First Temple were widely interpreted as the execution of God's condemnation of the rulers of Judah. In connection with the establishment of the temple-state in Jerusalem, circles of priests and scribes made collections of covenantal laws and teachings that were incorporated into the books of the Pentateuch, laws likely intended to function as regulations of the Temple governance of Judea. But long before the time of Jesus, the priestly aristocracy was either ignoring or manipulating the scriptural covenantal regulations that might have protected the people's economic rights. As noted above, the priestly aristocracy, expanded in size under Herod and serving as the instrument of Roman rule, became increasingly predatory in its treatment of the people in the first century.

This was the context in which Jesus pronounced God's condemnation. In his indictments of the scribes and Pharisees, he also opposed the Temple economy's drain on local resources. In his prophesying against the Temple as it appears in Mark's Gospel, the covenantal basis of God's judgment on the temple-state can be inferred from the narrative context (see chapter 6). In the prophetic lament over Jerusalem (Luke/Q 13:34-35a), the covenantal basis of the destruction of the ruling house would have been understood immediately by anyone acquainted with the history of relations between the rulers and the prophets. The reason that Jerusalem had been "killing the prophets" was that they had consistently pronounced God's indictment of the kings and their officers for oppressing the people in violation of the covenant principles.

Although it may be impossible to determine just where and to what audience Jesus made pronouncements against the Temple and high priests, Mark, Matthew, and John place them in Jerusalem, directly in the face of the rulers and/or their scribal representatives. Moreover, the very form of the prophetic oracle, explicit in the lament (in the Q sequence of speeches) and implicit in the Markan accounts of Jesus' prophecy against the Temple, suggests a direct confrontation in Jerusalem. Following the examples of earlier prophets such as Amos or Isaiah or Jeremiah, Jesus as the messenger and mouthpiece of God spoke directly to those upon whom the divine judge was about to execute the sentence. If he uttered such prophetic pronouncements in Jerusalem, they were part of the prophetic demonstration and further declarations in which Jesus spoke truth directly in the face of power.

DIRECT CONFRONTATION

The point bears repeating that, to have been crucified, Jesus must have gone up to Jerusalem and posed a significant threat to the Roman imperial order. It is clear from the Synoptic Gospel tradition in general that he was living and working in Galilee, which was under the jurisdiction of Herod Antipas, not the Jerusalem high priests. Had he intended simply to oppose the ruling house that most directly exploited the people economically, he could presumably have gone into either of Antipas's capital cities, Sepphoris or Tiberias. His agenda must have been broader.

A standard way of downplaying the narratives of Jesus' face-off with the rulers in Judea is to argue that he went to Jerusalem merely as a pilgrim for the festival of Passover. Then, when he arrived in the Temple courtyard, he was supposedly so outraged at the corruption he saw that he carried out an impromptu "cleansing" to restore the Temple as "a house of prayer." Not only would such an outburst not have resulted in his crucifixion, but such a reconstruction makes Jesus into an "accidental" messiah, with no role or mission.

In recent years, we have gained a more precise sense of the history of Galilee and its relations with Jerusalem. It is evident that it would have been rare for Galileans, who had only been under Jerusalem rule for a few generations, to embark on the necessary multiple-day journey to the Temple for the pilgrimage festivals. Clearly one of the principal roles of the prophet in Israelite tradition was to prophesy against the rulers of Israel. Jesus must have had some special reason for making the journey to Jerusalem at Passover time. If the purpose of his mission was the renewal of Israel, then the obvious reason for him to have gone to Jerusalem was to carry out the traditional role of a prophet in confronting the rulers and ruling institutions that, according to other sources, had become increasingly oppressive under Roman rule, as discussed above.

We should not imagine that Jesus' face-off with the Jerusalem and Roman rulers happened more or less as portrayed in the Gospels. Nevertheless, the Gospel accounts contain many historically plausible features, including exchanges between Jesus and the "authorities." These mesh well with information from Josephus about the Passover festival in Jerusalem and comparative evidence from protests by crowds in preindustrial capital cities. The combination makes possible a reconstruction of the main contours of Jesus' confrontation with power.

The Passover festival in Jerusalem under the Roman governors was already a situation of confrontation. Passover was the celebration of the prototypical deliverance of Israelites from bondage under foreign rulers in Egypt. Originally a meal celebrated in the constituent families of Israel, its observance had been centralized in Jerusalem, along with other festivals, as a way of integrating the celebration into the political economy focused on the Temple. Under Roman imperial rule, however, Israelite peoples were again under foreign domination. The very high priests who presided at festival sacrifices were appointed by and collaborated closely with the Roman governors. The Passover festival thus brought celebration of liberation from past imperial domination into vivid juxtaposition with the material forces of present imperial domination.

The potential for the celebration to flow into an uprising was not lost on the Jerusalem and Roman authorities. As Josephus mentions, to control the situation the Roman governors brought extra troops into Jerusalem at Passover time and posted them atop the porticoes of the Temple. But it would have been a further provocation to the people to have the physical presence of armed imperial soldiers above their heads as they celebrated their liberation from imperial bondage. Not surprisingly, as Josephus mentions in an incident under the governor Cumanus, the Roman troops could easily become the trigger for trouble (*Ant.* 20.5.3 §§105–12). The situation of Passover celebration thus featured a blatant "in-your-face" intimidation by Roman troops, which would in turn have intensified the people's indignation. The celebration of Passover in Jerusalem chosen by Jesus for his confrontation with the Jerusalem rulers was a politically-religiously *charged* situation in the extreme.

Jesus' "triumphal entry" into Jerusalem appears to be about the closest he came to stepping into the role of a popular messiah (see chapter 3 above). That Jesus was "role-playing," as part of a joyous procession of the crowd of pilgrims to Jerusalem for Passover, suggests that this bit of theater was an act of political confrontation with at least a veneer of anonymity and disguise. By riding into the city on a donkey, Jesus was alluding to a well-known prophecy of the king coming in victory over enemies ("Behold, your king comes to you; triumphant and victorious is he" [Zech 9:9]). Insofar as he was "humble and riding on a donkey," however, he was a popularly anointed king, leader of a people's militia, not an imperial king in a war chariot. The spreading of cloaks and leafy branches on the road was also reminiscent of welcoming a new king, as when Elijah's protégé Elisha had anointed Jehu to head the overthrow of Ahab and Jezebel (1 Kings 19; 2 Kings 9). Had Jesus done this with several dozen followers at any time other than a pilgrimage festival, it would have been taken as a revolutionary action led by yet another in the series of popular messiahs. The Roman garrison would have immediately marched out of the Jerusalem citadel to put down the audacious (and suicidal) uprising. Jesus and his followers, however, evidently staged the demonstration as part of the pilgrimage procession into Jerusalem for celebration of Passover, with the crowds shouting "Save O Save" in the words of the Hallel Passover psalms remembering the exodus deliverance.

What is portrayed in the Gospels as Jesus' "triumphal entry" was evidently a pointed (political-religious) demonstration, only thinly disguised as a part of the Passover celebration.[8] As part of the procession of pilgrims entering Jerusalem to celebrate the deliverance of Israel from bondage in Egypt, Jesus posed as a popular king leading the people in a mock overthrow of their rulers. He was thus engaging in a pointed political action of anonymity and disguise. Threatening as the demonstration would have been to the Jerusalem and Roman rulers, however, Jesus and his entourage were acting under the "cover" of the Passover celebration and were at least somewhat protected by the anonymity of the crowds. In the ensuing confrontation, Jesus continued to thinly disguise his prophetic declarations in parabolic or semiveiled speech, and the high priests hesitated to arrest him in front of the crowds lest they touch off an actual uprising, at least according to Mark's narrative. The latter is obviously not an eyewitness account of the events in Jerusalem. But judging from how kings and dukes in later preindustrial cities allowed popular riots to run their course, lest their intervention provoke more serious uprisings, Mark's portrayal has a certain degree of historical verisimilitude. The disguise was thin at most. Jesus' opposition was transparent, and the protection of the festival crowd was temporary. The authorities quickly recognized that Jesus' bold direct opposition was dangerous and that they had to take action surreptitiously to avoid unleashing wider indignation from the crowd.

If, as seems likely, Jesus did pronounce his prophecies against the Temple and high priests in Jerusalem, he declared God's condemnation directly in the face of the ruling institutions. These prophecies, however, would not necessarily have provoked the Roman governor to crucify him. Jesus of Nazareth was not the only prophet from the countryside who pronounced God's judgment on Jerusalem and the Temple. Among the few cases of popular prophetic figures that our limited elite sources bother to report was another rustic prophet, Jesus son of Hananiah. Just prior to the great revolt of 66–70, according to Josephus's fascinating account, this other Jesus began taking his stand in the Temple courtyard and voicing another prophetic lament that bears some remarkable resemblances to the earlier lament of Jesus of Nazareth.

> A voice from the east,
> A voice from the west,
> A voice from the four winds:
> A voice against Jerusalem and the Temple!
> A voice against bridegrooms and brides!
> A voice against the whole people!
>   (Josephus, *War* 6.5.3 §§300–309)

In fact, says Josephus, he kept up his dirge for seven years, right into the midst of the revolt and the Roman siege of Jerusalem.

The high priests, understanding how such a prophecy against the city and Temple, their own power base, might resonate with the people, agitated the Roman governor to arrest and execute the fellow. The Roman governor, however, sensed in Jesus son of Hananiah no real threat to Roman imperial order in Judea but merely a raving maniac. So he simply ordered him severely beaten and then released—whereupon the prophet resumed his dirge of imminent destruction. This case of Jesus son of Hananiah, at a time of much greater tension and official paranoia than thirty-some years earlier, suggests that even boldly pronouncing God's condemnation of the Temple and the city was not a sufficiently significant threat to the Roman order that Pontius Pilate would have ordered Jesus of Nazareth crucified.

Jesus of Nazareth, however, went beyond pronouncing judgment on the Temple and city in two major respects. He brought along an entourage. More than a lone oracular prophet, he was a leader of a movement in the tradition of Moses and Elijah, as represented in both Q and Mark, and similar to the prophets such as Theudas, whom the Romans quickly dispatched with military force. Besides pronouncing God's judgment, moreover, Jesus mounted a demonstration of God's condemnation directly in the Temple itself.

Mark, followed by Matthew, and the Gospel of John present Jesus' action in the Temple as forcible. "Making a whip of cords, he drove all of them out of the Temple. . . . He also poured out the coins of the money changers and overturned their tables" (John 2:15). "He began to drive out those who were selling and buying in the Temple, and he overturned the tables of the money changers and the seats of those who sold doves; and he would not allow anyone to carry anything through the temple" (Mark 11:15-16). If anything, because of later political pressures, the Gospels would have toned down the severity of Jesus' action (or "explained" it as merely symbolic, as did John). The disruption must therefore have been at least as forcible as the Gospels describe. The activities that Jesus attacked, moreover, were not "corruptions" but the standard economic transactions in Temple, necessary to make the sacrifices possible. Jesus was thus engaged in the ultimate act of blasphemy and profanation of a super-sacred institution of hoary antiquity. It was also the central institution of the political economy of Judea—with some extension of power in Galilee and Diaspora communities—and the power base of the priestly aristocracy. Insofar as the Temple was also an instrument of Roman rule in Judea, Jesus' action was also a blatant challenge to the Roman imperial order. His forcible disruption of the Temple operations was also an irrevocable action from which there was no retreat.

The action in the Temple, however, was far more than a forcible disruption of Temple operations; it was a profanation of the most sacrosanct institution and a challenge to imperial rule. It was a prophetic action symbolizing God's judgment. It was the latest in a long tradition of symbolic actions by Israelite prophets that dramatized God's judgment on rulers, but more extreme in form. Ahijah the Shilonite tore his new garment in twelve pieces and gave Jeroboam ten, to symbolize that ten of the tribes of Israel would revolt from Solomon's rule in Jerusalem (1 Kgs 11:29—12:20). Isaiah went naked and barefoot for three years to symbolize the fate of the Egyptian imperial regime to which the Judean monarchy was looking for its own defense against the Assyrians (Isaiah 20). Jeremiah wore an ox-yoke around his neck to dramatize God's demand that the Judean monarchy submit to Babylonian rule (Jeremiah 27–28). If Jesus was following prophetic tradition, then his act of disruption in the Temple would evidently have symbolized its condemnation by God. Mark's framing of Jesus' action in the Temple with the analogy of Jesus' curse of the fig tree clearly suggests that this was the way it was understood.

This is confirmed by the reference ("but you have made it a brigands' hideaway") to Jeremiah's famous prophecy of the original Temple's destruction (Jer 7:1-15; cf. chapter 26). Jeremiah had charged the officials of the Temple with stealing the people's goods, in violation of the covenantal commandments, and then seeking refuge in the sacredness of their priesthood and the Temple, like brigands who take refuge in a mountain stronghold after robbing their victims. For this systematic violation of the covenant commandments, God was about to destroy the Temple in Jerusalem. With the reference to Jeremiah's prophecy, Jesus charges the priestly aristocracy based in the Temple with the same exploitation of the people while trusting in their sacred institution as protection.

Less shocking because it took the form of a parable instead of a disruption of the Temple, but also a statement of condemnation of the high priestly rulers, was Jesus' parable of the tenants in the vineyard. A version very close to the one in Mark 12:1-8 is included in the *Gospel of Thomas* (65). Insofar as a parable is told as a story-analogy to induce the hearers to draw the inference for themselves or their own situation, this parable was clearly told against the high priestly aristocracy. This is unmistakable once we recognize that the image of the vineyard was deeply rooted in prophetic tradition as a metaphor or symbol for Israel (Ps 80:8-13; Jer 2:21; 12:10; Ezek 15:1-6; 19:10; Hos 10:1). In what was surely the best-known prophecy, Isaiah 5, the prophet, as the mouthpiece of God, had sung a love song about a vineyard that suddenly shifted into a condemnation of those who "added field to field," as they expropriated the lands of their peasant debtors. In the parable of the tenants Jesus adapted this deeply resonant image and sharpened its focus against those charged to care for the vineyard. If the vineyard evoked Israel, then the tenants evoked those placed in charge of Israel at the time of Jesus, that is, the high priests. But far from caring for the vineyard so that it would yield fruit for the master, the tenants took the produce for themselves.

The application was fairly obvious. The master of the vineyard would take action against the violently exploitative and rebellious tenants. Ironically, the high priestly families, who would have identified with the master of the vineyard, could readily have drawn the intended analogy. As shown by archaeological evidence, high priestly families as well as

Herodian families, probably by foreclosing on loans, had built up large estates farmed by tenants who produced crops for their absentee land-lords who were building themselves lavish mansions in Jerusalem.[9] Quite likely, they had themselves been involved in punitive action against recalcitrant tenants. This parable turned the tables on them. They were the tenants against whom God was now about to execute judgment. Again with historical verisimilitude, Mark has the high priests realize that the parable was told against them, and resolve to arrest Jesus.[10]

Jesus also confronted the Jerusalem rulers about Roman rule (Mark 12:13-17). As we shall see, while Jesus cleverly wriggles out of the trap set by his questioners, the indirection of his answer in no way veils the blunt declaration of independence he makes with regard to the tribute to Caesar. This episode in Mark has been habitually misread by projecting the separation of church and state, religious loyalty and civic duty. Again, we would expect the Gospel of Mark to have toned down rather than invented such a revolutionary statement. So the Markan form of this confrontation on which we are dependent is, if anything, less severe than what Jesus may have said.

Roman domination of subject peoples such as Israel focused on the tribute demanded. In the Markan framing of the issue, the Pharisees and the Herodians (the representatives of the high priestly and Hero-dian client rulers of Rome) escalate the confrontation with Jesus to the question of the tribute. Jesus, the prophetic spokesperson for the people against their Jerusalem rulers and ruling institutions has just proclaimed their condemnation by God. The representatives of the rulers now point to the structure of imperial rule, the imperial power that maintains the high priesthood and temple-state in power: "Is it lawful to pay tribute to Caesar or not?" The confrontation between Jesus and Roman rule is thus placed within the broader confrontation between the Israelite people and Roman domination.

This is what made the Pharisees' question a trap that Jesus—further entrapped by being flattered as a sincere teacher of the way of God who shows deference to no one, regardless of power and position—could not possibly escape. The Pharisees knew very well, on the one hand, that the Romans looked upon failure to pay the tribute as tantamount to rebel-lion and that the high priests who headed the temple-state collected the tribute for the Romans, on whom their own position of power and privilege depended. On the other hand, the Pharisees, as the recognized interpreters of the laws of the Judeans, also knew very well that payment of the tribute to Caesar was *not* lawful according to Israelite tradition. As discussed in chapter 3, two decades or so earlier the Fourth Philosophy, one of whose leaders was a Pharisee and whose members agreed with the Pharisees—except for their intense passion for liberty—had organized resistance to the tribute. If the people were loyal to God as their true, exclusive lord and master, they said, it was not possible to render tribute to Caesar. That was simply an application of the first two commandments of the Mosaic covenant. In their attempt at entrapment, the Pharisees evidently assumed that Jesus would answer sincerely and truthfully, that it was not lawful, which would be inciting rebellion against Roman rule, thus making him susceptible to arrest and execution.

Jesus, however, comes up with a clever circumlocution that eludes the trap but states the implications of Israel's exclusive loyalty to God with unmistakable clarity: "Give to Caesar the things that are Caesar's, and to God the things that are God's." Everyone listening, whether the high priests and Pharisees or the crowds, would have understood exactly what he had said: Since, according to Israelite tradition, everything belonged to God as the people's exclusive God and king, and nothing to Caesar, then payment of the tribute was not lawful. Jesus' crafty formulation was, to be sure, not a call to arms. But it was a clear declaration of independence of Roman rule and of life directly under God's rule.

A BREAKTHROUGH BEGINS

Speaking the truth of the people's intense indignation at their prolonged oppression directly to the face of power not only drew down violent repression, the arrest and execution of Jesus. It also was the beginning of the breakthrough to open and active resistance by his followers, leading to the rapid expansion of the movement he had started. We have not appreciated this before because we have not been sensitive to the popular indignation produced by prolonged domination, which makes subjugated people feel increasingly powerless. People endure indignities because the coercive power of their rulers gives them no alternative and in some cases because they have become habituated to the ideology and rituals that enforce their subordination. Our usual historical sources, documents produced by the elite, seldom offer clues as to how eager the subjugated are to express their indignation. Only on rare occasions does a spokesperson become emboldened to step forward in defiance of domination. Depending on the circumstances, such an act of defiance can transform the collective indignation into an excitement and energy that continue the resistance. Such a religious-political breakthrough can then escalate into a significant movement and/or energize a nascent movement into sudden expansion.

The moment when a spokesperson suddenly gives voice to the people's resentment and opposition on the public stage, directly in the face of the dominant, immediately becomes a politically charged occasion.[11] In Jesus' confrontation with the priestly aristocracy and Roman governor in Jerusalem, a number of factors intensified the impact of his "speaking truth to power." First, he chose as the occasion for his politically charged confrontation the already highly religiously-politically charged festival of Passover. Second, he not only spoke out but acted out demonstratively and forcibly his and the people's anger at the way their resources were being drained away to the Temple and the Roman tribute. Third, his forcible demonstration of the people's indignation was a blatant profanation of a long and deeply institutionalized sacred space and of sacred rituals of subordination.

Fourth, Jesus spoke and acted out of a long tradition of previous profanation of the Temple, the high priesthood, and sacred rituals of subordination by Israelite prophets who claimed divine inspiration. This tradition had long since itself gained a sacred authority in the books of the prophets as well as in popular oral tradition. The traditional prophetic forms in which he spoke and acted resonated with the memories of earlier prophetic heroes and the more recent announcement by John the Baptist that one was coming after him who would baptize with fire as well as with Spirit.

Finally, as Scott points out,[12] the energy released by such a confrontation with domination flows from "the sense of personal release, satisfaction, pride, and elation" that indignant subjugated people feel when their spokesperson speaks truth instead of more submissive lies and equivocations. The release may even be double. Identifying with their leader's challenge to the dominant, they too are finally talking back and resisting rather than submitting. But they also experience the release of finally expressing the response they had on many previous occasions choked back to avoid repressive consequences.

The rapid expansion of the Jesus movement began with Jesus speaking truth to power at Passover time in Jerusalem. Of course, when the Roman governor crucified him as an insurgent leader, Jesus also became a martyr to his mission of renewal and resistance.

Chapter 8

The Power of the Crucifixion

Crucifixion was a public display of power, intended to terrorize. In crucifixion, Rome sought to display its absolute power over human life by rendering those who resisted utterly powerless. In response to his bold confrontation of their client rulers in Jerusalem, the Romans crucified Jesus. The crucifixion of Jesus, however, as I shall argue in this chapter, became the catalyst for the rapid spread of the movement he had started and its continuing opposition to the imperial order. The expanding movement was still subject to the overwhelming power of Roman rule in various ways. Paradoxically, however, in the crucifixion of Jesus the display of power that Rome used to render subjects powerless was transformed into the power to form communities of an alternative social order and, when necessary, to maintain solidarity against repressive measures by the local or imperial authorities.

Our exploration will diverge from three standard (and frequently combined) paths often taken in the interpretation of the death of Jesus. One is to try to discern "what really happened," if anything, behind each of the episodes that now appear in the Gospels' "passion narratives" by cutting critically through what are clearly embellishments. Another is to offer the simple explanation that Jesus was crucified because he claimed to be or was acclaimed as "the Messiah." Yet another is to find in the "Easter faith" (alone) the motivating force of the spread of the Jesus movement after the supposed crushing defeat of the crucifixion. This last line of interpretation is deeply rooted in what became orthodox Christian faith in the West. As we shall see, however, it is not well grounded in what are usually deemed the earliest sources.

Historical understanding of Jesus' crucifixion, like that of his mission in Galilee, requires a "wide-angle" focus on his relationship with followers in the historical context, including how it is related both to prior events and to subsequent developments.

A PUBLIC DISPLAY OF POWER

Crucifixion was the most severe form of punishment and execution practiced by the Romans, "the most wretched of deaths" (Josephus *War* 7.6.4 §203). Under the Roman Empire, the victims were beaten before being crucified. Then they were required to carry the cross or the crossbeam to the place of execution, they were stripped naked, and their forearms were nailed or bound to the beam, which was raised up and affixed to the stake, or they were simply nailed to the stake. The body was partly supported by being seated on a peg on the upright, and the feet were bound or nailed to the stake with an iron nail through the heels. Death would come slowly, by asphyxiation, often after several days of excruciating pain. The process could be hastened by breaking the lower legs with a severe blow. Variations depended on the sadistic ingenuity of the executioners. While hung on crosses, the victims might well become carrion for birds and animals of prey. Being "fastened to the accursed tree," said Seneca, meant "wasting away in pain, dying limb by limb, letting out life drop by drop, . . . swelling with ugly weals on shoulders and chest, and drawing the breath of life amid long-drawn-out agony" (*Ep.* 101). Crucifixion was thus a method of slowly torturing the victims to death.[1]

The Persians had used crucifixion as an execution for actions against the imperial regime. The Romans practiced crucifixion much more systematically against people of low status, especially disobedient slaves, and against subject peoples, especially those they viewed as insurgents. It was an utterly degrading, dehumanizing form of execution. For Roman citizens themselves, crucifixion was thus "that most cruel and disgusting penalty" (Cicero, *Verr.* 2.5.165). At points, even Roman citizens were crucified for treason or other serious offenses against the state. Ordinarily, however, more respectable forms of execution or simply ostracism (deportation) was used against Roman citizens, especially patricians. In defending a Roman noble, Cicero argued that the very words "cross" or "executioner" should not even be mentioned with regard to a Roman citizen (*Rab. Perd.* 16).

In Italy and Rome itself the Roman authorities used crucifixion against mutinous troops, criminals, and especially slaves. Roman historians cite several cases of crucifixion to punish slave conspiracies or to deter revolts among the ever larger gangs of slaves on the expanding estates of the Roman patricians (Livy 22.33.2; 33.36.3). After the first slave revolt in Sicily, 450 slaves were crucified; after the revolt led by Spartacus in 71 B.C.E., Crassus ordered more than six thousand slaves crucified along the Appian Way from Capua to Rome. Over a century later, under Nero, the Senate revived the custom of executing all the slaves of a household (which might be hundreds) if a slave killed the master (Tacitus, *Ann.* 13.32.1). The Romans clearly practiced crucifixion as a method of terrorizing slaves and other lower orders into acquiescence. As Quintilian (c. 35–95 C.E.) commented, "Whenever we crucify the guilty, the most crowded roads are chosen, where the most people can see and be moved by this fear. For penalties relate not so much to retribution as to their exemplary effect" (*Decl.* 274).

The Romans also used crucifixion as a way of trying to terrorize subject peoples into submission. Partly because of their passion for independence, Galileans and Judeans became very familiar with crosses along the roadsides and in Jerusalem. In the brutal Roman suppression of the revolts that framed the mission of Jesus, the crosses numbered in the thousands. In 4 B.C.E., after destroying villages and slaughtering their residents, Varus had his soldiers round up the leaders of the insurrection and crucified about two thousand (Josephus, *War* 2.5.2 §75; *Ant.* 17.10.10 §295; cf. *T. Mos.* 6:9). During the Roman siege of Jerusalem toward the end of the great revolt of 66–70 C.E., the Roman general Titus sent out cavalry to capture desperate Jerusalemites who crept outside the walls to look for food. He then had them "scourged and subjected to torture of every description, before being crucified opposite the walls. . . . His main reason [for crucifying many each day] was the hope that the spectacle might perhaps induce the Judeans to surrender, for fear that continued resistance would involve them in a similar fate" (*War* 5.11.1 §§446–51).

In the intervening decades of the first century, Roman governors used crucifixion to punish insurgents and to deter further resistance. Just before mid-century the governor Tiberius Alexander tried and crucified James and Simon, sons of Judas of Gamala, who had led resistance to the Roman tribute (*Ant.* 20.5.2 §102). Five or six years later, Quadratus, legate of Syria, crucified both the Samaritans and the Judeans taken prisoner by the governor Cumanus in suppression of their internecine battles (*War* 2.12.6 §241; *Ant.* 20.6.2 §129). Later in the 50s, the governor Felix captured and sent to Rome the brigand chief Eleazar, who had for a time led a local insurgency, and crucified many other "brigands" (*lēstai,* the Roman term for insurgents and brigands alike; *War* 2.13.2 §253; *Ant.* 20.8.5 §§160–61). In the increasingly volatile atmosphere of the mid-60s, the governor Florus, having provoked abuse from Jerusalemites, held the Jerusalem high priests and other eminent figures responsible for handing over the troublemakers. After sending out his soldiers for a retaliatory massacre in the upper city, he had several Jerusalemites beaten and crucified, including some of those eminent figures (*War* 2.14.6–9 §§293–308). When it came to provincials, Roman governors were prepared to use crucifixion even against their own client rulers who claimed (the equivalent of) equestrian rank. Judging from the repeated agitation against Roman rule and the repeated emergence of popular renewal movements, however, crucifixion and other Roman measures do not appear to have been sufficient to repress resistance among Galileans and Judeans, with their strong cultural tradition of independence under the rule of God.

There can be no question that in first-century Judea and Galilee crucifixion was a *Roman* form of execution used to punish and intimidate insurgency; it was not an instrument of capital punishment in the hands of the Jerusalem high priests. It is true that prior to the Roman takeover, the Hasmonean high priest Alexander Jannaeus (Yannai) "had eight hundred of his [opponents] crucified in [Jerusalem], and their wives and children butchered before their eyes, while he looked on, drinking, with his concubines" (Josephus, *War* 1.4.6 §97; *Ant.* 13.14.2 §380). The *Pesher* (Interpretation) on Nahum (4QpNah) found among the Dead Sea Scrolls confirms that (some of) these were Pharisees, for whom the code name is "seekers of smooth things." Herod the Great clearly executed many of his subjects, although not by crucifixion. When Rome imposed direct rule in Judea a decade after Herod's death, however, they reserved the power of execution for their governors. The Jerusalem high priests were thus no longer allowed to order someone stoned to death, much less crucified. The crucifixion of Jesus, therefore, cannot be attributed to "the Jews."

THE CRUCIFIXION OF JESUS

Although Jesus was crucified by the Roman governor as a threat to the imperial order, we should not imagine that events proceeded in just the way they are portrayed in the Gospels. That the Gospels include embellishments is hardly surprising. The crucifixion of Jesus was a hugely significant traumatic event for the movement(s) focused on Jesus, an event that became increasingly fraught with meaning as the movement(s) expanded. Like any such formative event, it demanded increasingly elaborate interpretation in ever new circumstances. The parts of the Gospels' narratives most important for Christian faith—the passion narratives—are thus, ironically, the most problematic as historical sources. Much of the detail in the passion narratives is embellishment for the edification of faith.[2] It would thus be beside the point to try to establish, by intricate analysis, "what really happened" behind each episode. Yet it may be important to separate some of the major embellishments that lack historical credibility from the basic reality of Jesus' crucifixion—in order then to focus on how the crucifixion of Jesus, resulting from his confrontation in Jerusalem, became the breakthrough event in Jesus' mission and movement(s).

Several major embellishments in the passion narratives are readily discernible. Most important for "setting the historical record straight" are the episodes and aspects that not only were historically diversionary but also later became historically dangerous. Foremost among these is the episode in which Pilate offered to set free either Jesus or Barabbas (Mark 15:6-15) and the related motifs of Pilate's innocence (washing his hands, in Matthew) and the attribution of guilt for Jesus' crucifixion to "the Jews." There is no evidence external to the Gospels that Pilate, or any other Roman governor, customarily released a prisoner at Passover. Nor would any Roman governor likely have released "a rebel who had committed murder during the insurrection" any more than he would have released an agitator who had just disrupted Temple business.

The Pilate portrayed in the Gospel passion narratives, moreover, is utterly out of character from what we know of him from other sources. Josephus supplies accounts of a shrewd hard-bitten governor who on different occasions sent his troops into Jerusalem with their objectionable army standards; who expropriated Temple funds to construct an aqueduct, over strenuous objections from the Judeans; and who resorted to deception for brutal crowd control (Josephus, *War* 2.9.2–4 §§169–77; *Ant.* 18.3.1–2 §§55–62). This Pilate would hardly have "wished to satisfy the crowd" (Mark 15:15). He would hardly have needed to be reminded by the high priests that an insurgent was acting against the interest of the emperor (John 19:12). He would hardly have found such a man innocent (Luke 23:13-22), or have "washed his hands" of the matter (Matt 27:24). It is also difficult to imagine a Roman governor holding a trial open to the mass of Passover pilgrims.

While the high priests could well have attempted to influence a Roman governor, moreover, it is quite incredible that a Passover crowd engaged in the celebration of liberation would have agitated for the crucifixion of a prophet who had just protested against official injustices. In fact, the crowd's crying for the crucifixion of Jesus in the Barabbas episode is utterly out of character for the crowd as Mark has depicted them in the preceding narrative of Jesus' last days in Jerusalem. At the beginning and end of Jesus' confrontation with the high priests, a "whole/large crowd was spellbound by his teaching" or "listening with delight" (Mark 11:18; 12:37), and the high priests and elders were afraid of the crowd (11:32; 12:12). It is thus inconsistent with Mark's portrayal of the crowd in the previous days when, in the Barabbas episode (thought to be quite unhistorical for other reasons), they suddenly shout, "Crucify him!" Matthew even has "the people as a whole" say "His blood be on us and on our children" (Matt 27:25). Both Mark (15:11) and Matthew (27:20), perhaps sensing the inconsistency, attribute the crowd's evidently fickle turn against Jesus to persuasion by the high priests. However, that people who had come into Jerusalem from the countryside would be amenable to such persuasion lacks historical credibility. Some of the ordinary people of Jerusalem, of course, who were economically dependent on Temple business, may have been persuadable by their high priestly patrons. But the Judean historian Josephus, as well as all of the Gospels, represent the people from the countryside as opposed and sometimes even hostile to the high priestly rulers in Jerusalem (e.g., Mark 11:27-33 and par.).[3]

Pilate's declaration of Jesus' innocence (Luke 23:4) and the portrayal of his own innocence of Jesus' death, which effectively place the blame instead on "the Jews," were later inventions of the movements of Jesus' followers. This apology vis-à-vis the Romans probably developed after the widespread Judean and Galilean revolt against Roman rule and the ensuing Roman destruction of Jerusalem and the Temple (66–70 c.e.). These depictions were parts of a larger effort in the Gospel narratives to reduce or eliminate any impression of Roman responsibility for Jesus' death. The apostle Paul, in his letters written about twenty years after the event, has no hesitation about identifying with the "crucified Christ" or asserting that "the rulers of this age" (the Romans) were responsible for Jesus' crucifixion (see especially 1 Cor 2:6-8). After the great Judean revolt, however, those who produced the Gospels—people who by then were sometimes called "Christians"—were eager to dissociate themselves from the rebellious Judeans and Galileans in Palestine and were uneasy about being identified with one who had been crucified as an insurgent against Roman rule. In one of the great horrors of history, these inventions—the Barabbas episode and the other apologetic aspects of the passion narratives—became a principal basis for later Christian doctrine that the Jews were guilty of deicide and for centuries of Christian anti-Judaism, which eventually resulted in Christian acquiescence in the Nazi Holocaust.

The Psalms, which were often understood by Judeans and Galileans in the late Second-Temple period as prophecy, have also exerted a strong influence on the embellishment of the crucifixion in the passion narratives. The latter make numerous allusions to psalmic and other scriptural phrases and images, including many phrases from Psalm 22. That the soldiers cast lots for his garments (Mark 15:24; John 19:23-25; *Gos. Pet.* 4:12; *Barn.* 6:6), for example, was clearly suggested by Ps 22:18 ("for my clothing they cast lots"). The references that those who passed by at the crucifixion shook their heads at him and that the others crucified with him taunted him (Mark 15:29, 32) were influenced by Ps 22:6-8.

Some features of the Gospels' portrayal of Jesus' crucifixion may not be entirely attributable to the perceived "fulfillment of (scriptural) prophecy," however, and may well be rooted in historical memory. This may be true of two features that would have been typical of crucifixions. One is that two "bandits" were crucified at the same time. The Romans used the Greek term *lēstai* not only for those who fled their villages to become brigands but also for agitators and rebels against Roman rule, such as Eleazar ben Dinai, a "bandit" who became the leader of a local insurgency (Josephus, *War* 2.12.4–5 §§235–36; 2.13.2 §253; *Ant.* 20.6.1 §121; 20.8.5 §161).[4] Another episode with some historical credibility is that the crucified Jesus' legs were not broken (*Gos. Pet.* 4:13-14; John 19:31-33). Since it was standard procedure to break the legs of the victim (to hasten the victim's death by suffocation), it may have been memorable that Jesus' legs were *not* broken, for whatever reason (see the distinctive christological twist added in John 19:31-37).

While we have no way of knowing what may have gone on at a possible trial before a high priestly council or at a possible hearing before Pilate, it seems likely that there was some sort of collaboration by the Jerusalem high priests in the arrest and handing over of Jesus. One of the credible sentences in Josephus's account of Jesus and his movement suggests as much: "Pilate, upon hearing him accused by men of the highest standing among us, condemned him to be crucified" (*Ant.* 18.3.3 §63). Such collaboration, moreover, would have been typical between the high priest Caiaphas and Pilate. A high priest usually remained in office only a few years before a new governor replaced him. Once Pilate became governor, however, Caiaphas lasted another ten years, through the entire tenure of Pilate, who otherwise often offended Judean sensibilities (see above, and Philo, *Legat.* 302).

Judging from two later trials of figures that the high priests considered dangerous, it seems likely that there was some sort of hearing at least before the Roman governor once the agitator had been arrested and handed over. According to Josephus, just before Albinus was appointed governor (62–64 C.E.) the high priest Ananus II took the opportunity of the temporary absence of a governor to "convene the judges of the council and brought before them a man named James, the brother of Jesus who was called the Christ, and certain others. He accused them of having transgressed the law and delivered them up to be stoned" (*Ant.* 20.9.1 §200). When Albinus arrived to take up his duties, however, he quickly deposed Ananus. Somewhat later, the rustic prophet Jesus son of Hananiah was arrested, chastised, and beaten by the new high priests, and then handed over to the governor Albinus. The latter interrogated him but concluded that he was merely a maniac and released him (*War* 6.5.3 §§302–5). While we cannot determine, on the basis of these other cases, whether Jesus would have had a trial before a council convened by the high priest, it seems likely that he would have been interrogated by Pilate. It also seems likely that he would have been beaten, perhaps even twice. It does appear clear from these later cases that even if a high priest had authority to convene a council, he certainly did not have authority to issue and carry out the death penalty. Imposing the death penalty was a power reserved for the Roman governors. Moreover, that Jesus was crucified, not stoned, is yet another clear indication that he was executed by the Romans and not "the Jews."

WHY JESUS WAS CRUCIFIED

One of the most prominent interpretations of Jesus' death is that he was crucified because he claimed to be, or was acclaimed by his followers as, "the Messiah" ("the Anointed One," *Christos* in Greek). This view is deeply rooted in the previously standard traditional Christian belief that Jesus fulfilled the long-standing expectation of "the Messiah" in "Judaism," but was rejected (and killed) by "the Jews." Indeed, that Jesus was "the Messiah/Christ" was an early claim of some of the leaders and texts that shaped what developed into orthodox Christianity. In his letters, composed only twenty years after the crucifixion, the apostle Paul refers to Jesus as "Jesus Christ the Lord," almost as if "Christ" is part of his name, with "Lord" as his principal title. Those who believe that Jesus was crucified because he claimed to be (or was acclaimed as) "the Messiah" find proof-texts in the Gospels. Matthew, Luke, and John all portray Jesus as an/the anointed one as well as a prophet (like Moses), and as belonging to the lineage of David, the prototypical "anointed" king of Judah and Israel. The Roman inscription on the cross, "Jesus of Nazareth, King of the Judeans," has also been a factor in the assumption that Jesus was crucified as "the Messiah."

Critical examination of "early Christian" texts over the last century or so challenged the previously standard view that Jesus' first followers generally understood him as "the Messiah," however. The texts produced by various movements or communities that later developed into Christianity articulated different understandings of Jesus. Paul, for example, knew of early creedal statements focused on the "crucifixion and resurrection" or "humiliation and exaltation" of "(Jesus) Christ the Lord" (1 Cor 15:3-5; Phil 2:5-11). But the Q speeches behind the speech material in Matthew and Luke understood Jesus primarily as a prophet, while the *Gospel of Thomas* viewed him as a teacher-revealer.

To get at the historical Jesus, however, scholars attempted to cut critically through the various representations in the texts to the figure behind them. For over a century, many critical scholars have come to one or another of two almost opposite conclusions, that Jesus must have been an apocalyptic visionary or that he was a wisdom teacher. It is hard to imagine, however, that either a visionary or an itinerant teacher would have been sufficiently threatening to the Roman imperial order that he would have been crucified. Not surprisingly, therefore, to explain why Jesus was crucified, some still argue that Jesus must have claimed to be or must have been acclaimed by followers as "the Messiah" (presumably at the "triumphal entry" into Jerusalem).[5]

Historical research and critical examination of the sources in the last forty or fifty years suggest that this last position is highly unlikely, however, for two principal reasons: (a) there is little textual evidence for a standard Judean expectation of "the Messiah," which means that the question must be reformulated; and (b) the earliest sources for Jesus' death do not present him as (claiming to be or acclaimed as) an anointed one or king during his mission or in its climax in Jerusalem.

Little more than a generation ago, it was commonly assumed among critical biblical scholars that there was a standard "Jewish expectation" of "the Messiah." In the standard Christian view, Jesus supposedly fulfilled that expectation, adapting it in a more spiritual direction, and was accepted as "the Messiah" by his followers, mostly Gentiles, while being rejected by "the Jews." During the last forty years, however, we have come to a much more precise sense of Judean and Galilean culture at the time of Jesus. Very few Judean texts in late Second-Temple times make any reference to an anointed one. Even in the Judean texts closest to the time of Jesus, most of which were produced by circles of dissident scribes unhappy about imperial rule, only a few passages used the term *messiah*. In one of those, *Psalms of Solomon* 17, the anointed king, the son of David, is portrayed with scribal features. The various references to (plural) anointed figures in some of the Dead Sea Scrolls are to symbolic royal and/or priestly leaders of the restored Israel in the future, whereas the leaders of the Qumran community are represented as prophets and teachers of torah. There thus appears to have been no standard expectation of "the Messiah" in first-century Judea and Galilee.[6]

While there are few texts to attest expectations of anointed figures produced by the literate elite, however, the Judean historian Josephus offers (hostile) accounts of several popular figures who were acclaimed as "kings" by their followers, both a generation before and a generation after Jesus of Nazareth, as discussed in chapter 3. In Galilee and Judea, when the people formed movements to assert their independence of Roman and Jerusalem rulers, they acclaimed one or another of their leaders as king, evidently following the pattern in Israelite popular tradition of their ancestors who "anointed" the young David as their king to lead them against the Philistines (1 Sam 2:1-4; 5:1-4). To suppress these popular "messianic" movements, which effectively controlled their own lives and territory for months or even years, the Romans sent large military forces to slaughter and enslave the insurgents and their leaders. Somewhat parallel, but different in form according to Josephus's accounts, were the popular prophetic movements that emerged in Judea in mid-first century c.e., in which villagers followed a Moses- or Joshua-like leader in hopes of experiencing a new deliverance patterned after the exodus and/or entry into the land. Again, the Roman governors sent out their military forces to suppress the movements and kill the prophets who led them. Judging from the multiple movements of each kind, the informal unwritten "scripts" of both of these kinds of movements were clearly operative in popular Israelite tradition at the time of Jesus, and both were clearly threats to the imperial order, which led the Romans to use military force against them.[7]

This more precise sense of what was happening in Judean and Galilean society at the time leads to a reformulation of the question: Was Jesus crucified because he was acting and/or acclaimed by the people as a king leading a popular insurrection? We can take a fresh, critical look at the earliest sources (Q, Mark, and the traditions evident in the earliest chapters of Acts)—now quite apart from the anachronistic concept of "the Messiah."

The Q speeches. The series of speeches paralleled in Matthew and Luke (Q) is straightforward and unambiguous. These speeches give not a hint that Jesus was understood or crucified as a popular king, much less as acclaimed (or "anointed") by his followers. Rather, the Q speeches depict Jesus as the latest and most important in a long line of Israelite prophets, and at points the speeches present him as killed by the rulers as many of the prophets had been (Luke/Q 7:18-35; 11:47-51; 13:34).

Mark's Gospel. The Gospel of Mark, at first reading, presents what may appear to be a somewhat confusing picture: that while Jesus acted and spoke consistently throughout the Gospel as a prophet like Moses and Elijah, at a crucial point he posed as a king and was crucified by Pilate as "king of the Judeans." After closer examination of Mark, however, it is clear, first, that while some disciples may have pictured Jesus in the role of a popular king, Jesus pointedly rejected such a role; and, second, that Jesus' arrest and execution are the rulers' responses not to his or his followers claims of messiahship, but to his actions and pronouncements as a prophet.

It is not surprising that one of the earliest critical readings of the Gospel of Mark as a whole, toward the end of the nineteenth century, found its theme to be "the messianic secret." It was simply assumed that Jesus was "the Messiah" and that the earliest Gospel would, of course, have presented him as "the Messiah." But it is difficult to find Jesus represented as "the Messiah" and impossible to find episodes in which he claims to be or is acclaimed as an anointed king who is therefore arrested and killed for this reason. The ostensible title, "The beginning of the Gospel of Jesus Christ, the Son of God" (1:1), was probably a later scribal addition to the Gospel. Mark's account may not, in its earliest use, even have carried the title "Gospel"—as suggested by the many variations at the beginning of early manuscripts of Mark and the evidence that Matthew may not have found the term *Gospel* in the text of Mark that he used.[8]

The only episode in Mark's Gospel in which Jesus even momentarily *appears* to step into the role of a popular king is the entry into Jerusalem, where he rides on the donkey, in an allusion to the prophecy of Zechariah about the humble king "coming to you" (Mark 11:1-10; cf. Zech 9:9). The Hosanna of the crowd entering the city with him comes from the Hallel psalms, which were traditionally sung by Passover pilgrims (Ps 118:26). The pilgrims shout, as they well might at the festival of liberation from foreign rule, of "the coming kingdom of our ancestor David." But if this is supposed to be an acclamation of *Jesus* as king, it is indirect at best and "disguised." In Mark's narrative, this seeming "messianic demonstration" is not what leads the rulers to move against Jesus.

Earlier in the story, Jesus has decisively *rejected* acclamation as "the messiah." Indeed, the only time that the term *messiah* (*christos,* in Greek) is mentioned, in Peter's confession, Jesus sharply rebukes Peter, clearly rejecting the role of a popular king leading an insurrection for independence (8:31-33). Further, without mentioning the term, in the episode where James and John ask for positions of power in Jesus' kingdom, Jesus sharply rejects the whole idea of a kingship of power holders (10:32-45). Far from representing Jesus as crucified because he claimed to be a/the messiah (a king), Mark's Gospel depicts Jesus decisively rejecting such a role and program.

Mark indicates explicitly and repeatedly, however, that what provokes the high priestly rulers to arrest Jesus and hand him over to Pilate for crucifixion are his bold public actions and pronouncements as a prophet. Already early in the story, as Jesus carries out exorcisms and healings and commissions representative leaders in his prophetic program of the renewal of Israel, the Pharisees and Herodians conspire on how to destroy him (3:6). Once he enters Jerusalem and the Temple, the very center of high priestly control, the official plotting to kill him escalates in response to his repeated prophetic condemnations of Temple, high priesthood, and the Roman tribute. In reaction to his demonstrative condemnation of the Temple and again in reaction to his prophetic parable that condemned the high priestly aristocracy, the high priests and scribes are looking for a way to kill him but are restrained by their anxiety about the adverse reaction of the crowd (11:18; 12:12). The Pharisees and Herodians try entrapment, which Jesus wriggles out of (12:13-17). Finally, following the sustained confrontation, the high priests and scribes lay a plot to arrest Jesus by stealth and kill him (14:1-2). This portrayal of the reason why the Judean client rulers and their representatives want to have Jesus killed fits squarely into the main plot of the overall narrative presented in Mark: as *a prophet like Moses and Elijah,* Jesus is carrying out a renewal of Israel in opposition to the Roman and Jerusalem rulers of the people, who take action when his opposition becomes public and provocative in the capital.

So what is to be made of the episodes of the trials before the high priests and Pilate and the crucifixion scene in the passion narrative? As noted above, these are the least historically reliable parts of the Gospel narrative, suspect in their attribution of motives and in their accounts of what was said. There is no way we could know what transpired in a trial before the high priestly council, if there was such a hearing. Yet, whatever their historical credibility, these episodes in Mark do not suggest that Jesus claimed to be a messiah or king, even though they may suggest that Pilate condemned Jesus to death on the charge of leading an insurrection as "the king of the Judeans."

In Mark 14:61-65, the high priest asked Jesus, "Are you the messiah, the son of the Blessed One?" Jesus answered, "I am, and. . . ." In previous generations, the "I am" has been taken by itself as a proof-text that Jesus claimed to be "the Messiah." In addition to the problematic language in both the question and the answer as they appear in the authorized (modern) text,[9] however, the "I am" must be understood as superseded by the rest of Jesus' answer in the flow of the narrative. He immediately added, "and you will see the human one ['son of man'] seated at the right hand of Power, and 'coming with the clouds of heaven.'" It was in response to those words that "the high priest tore his clothes and said, 'You have heard his blasphemy!'" and the council condemned him as deserving death. The offense for which he is condemned to death is evidently his having blurted out the prophetic vision of "the human one seated at the right hand of Power," which might have implied the imminent destruction of the Temple (by God, not Jesus) but was certainly *not* a claim to be a king (messiah). "The human one seated at the right hand of Power," to which he called their urgent attention, was a reference to a vision that we know from the book of Daniel (7:1-14). In Daniel itself, "the one like a human" enthroned beside God was interpreted as a symbol for the imminent restoration of "[the people] of the holy ones of the Most High" to sovereignty, as the beastly empires were condemned to destruction by God (7:15-27). At the time of Jesus, the image was also probably a symbol of the divine court of judgment. Invoking either the restoration of the people of God to sovereignty or the divine court of judgment as imminent would have been threatening to the high priests, who were dependent on and collaborating in Roman imperial rule. Of course, either or both fit well with the overall agenda of Jesus' mission, according to the Gospel of Mark.

In the next episode in Mark, when the council handed Jesus over to Pilate, the high priests "accused him of many things," yet no particular charges such as claiming to be "king" or "messiah" or committing "blasphemy" are mentioned. But Pilate immediately asked him, "Are you the king of the Judeans?" And Jesus answered, "You say so." The formulation of the question is clearly by an outsider, the Roman governor, who viewed the people in Israelite Palestine generally as "Judeans." Herod had been appointed by the Romans as "king of the Judeans," and Pilate may well have known of those upstart petty "kings" who had led revolts thirty-some years earlier. That Pilate posted "king of the Judeans" on Jesus' cross suggests that it was the official charge for which he was crucified, whatever he had done. Other features of Mark's narrative, however, suggest that, however official the charge may have been, it was (also) done in mockery. Mark presents the Roman soldiers' treatment of Jesus explicitly as mockery (dressing and crowning him as a king and bowing down in homage [15:16-20]) and then presents the high priests and scribes as mocking Jesus hanging on the cross as "the anointed king of Israel" (the insiders' term [15:31-32]). This strongly suggests that Pilate's charge, "the king of the Judeans," is also a contemptuous mocking.

So the earliest Gospel story does not present Jesus as having been crucified because he claimed to be or was acclaimed as the Messiah or a popular king. The Markan narrative of the confrontation (Mark 11–12; 14:1-2) states rather that the high priests and scribes sought to arrest Jesus because of his public condemnation of the Temple and ruling aristocracy, that is, as a prophet, which is consistent with his role throughout the Gospel story as a prophet.

Early views carried in the speeches in Acts. The speeches supposedly delivered by Peter in the first chapters of the book of Acts, while overwritten by Luke, carry early tradition that Jesus was not understood as "(the) anointed (one)" (*messiah*) when he was crucified, but only after his vindication or exaltation by God.[10] One speech does not even give him the title of "Messiah" (Acts 5:30-31). In another, Jesus is called "the messiah appointed," but evidently this appointment happened only *after* he was killed and raised up (Acts 3:11-21). Yet another speech represents God as making Jesus "both Lord and Messiah" only after he was raised up and exalted at the right hand of God (Acts 2:32-36). This speech presents Jesus' actions that led up to his being handed over for crucifixion as "deeds of power, wonders, and signs," that is, as aspects of a renewal of Israel carried out by a prophet like Moses.

Our earliest sources for Jesus (other than Paul), the series of speeches in Q, Mark's Gospel, and "Peter's" speeches in Acts, thus offer no support for the view that Jesus was crucified because he or his followers claimed he was a messiah or king. In fact, the speeches in the early chapters of Acts indicate that at least some in the early Jesus movement(s) came to the conclusion that Jesus had been appointed "Lord" and "Messiah" only after he was killed and raised. They understood the sequence of events not as crucifixion-as-messiah and then resurrection, but as crucifixion followed by resurrection and only *then* divine appointment of the exalted Jesus as *Messiah*. All three of the early sources, however, represent Jesus as having been killed for his prophetic actions, that is, squarely in the context of his broader mission of renewal of Israel in opposition to the rulers of Israel. The Gospel of Mark, the only extended narrative, presents the arrest and crucifixion as the response of the high priests and the Roman governor to Jesus' public pronouncements against the Temple, the high priests, and the tribute to Rome.

RESURRECTION

In what may be the most prominent theological construction of Christian origins, the crucifixion of Jesus is linked in an inseparable sequence with his "resurrection." In this view, Jesus' crucifixion was a debilitating defeat for his disciples. But the resurrection appearances supposedly evoked faith that sparked the formation of a community and the missionary enterprise of preaching the gospel of Christ and expanding the movement. This scheme, which attributed the motive of the formation and expansion of the movement to the resurrection faith, effectively reduces or even eliminates the historical (social-political) significance of Jesus' crucifixion as a force in the dynamics of his movement. This standard scheme of "Christian origins," however, is highly problematic as a historical construction, in three (closely related) fundamental ways.

First, it is difficult to discern any basis in the sources for the view that the crucifixion was a debilitating defeat for the disciples. Only by having been taken utterly out of literary context as proof-texts could a handful of references have lent the impression that a significant stage of the disciples' discouragement preceded the resurrection, which then inspired a dynamic group formation. Mark's narrative has Jesus, after the Last Supper, predict that the disciples will all become deserters after he is arrested, which indeed they do (14:27, 50). Their desertion, however, is a response to his arrest, not to his crucifixion, and the motif is influenced by, if not based on, the quotation of the prophecy in Zech 13:7. In addition, the desertion of the disciples, along with their failure to watch with Jesus in Gethsemane and Peter's denial, is the climax of the Markan subplot of the disciples' inability to understand and follow Jesus, which develops steadily through the narrative following their initial commissioning, and thus cannot be taken simply as a memory of the disciples' desertion before the crucifixion.

Matthew more or less follows Mark's narrative and provides no independent representation on this question.

In the "Emmaus road" episode in Luke (24:13-35), two followers of Jesus express disappointment that Jesus, "a prophet mighty in deed and word," who they hoped "was the one to redeem Israel," was handed over to be crucified (24:19-21). This narrative, however, follows the empty tomb episode, in which the two men "in dazzling robes" announce that Jesus is risen. And the two followers' account to the "stranger" continues directly from Jesus' death and the disappointment of their hope to the women receiving the angels' reassurance that Jesus was indeed alive. The Emmaus road episode then flows seamlessly into the scene of the eleven, with their companions, recounting the Lord's appearance to Simon. The temporary disappointment, then, is a passing motif in a story within a story within the larger Gospel narrative. There is no indication that their disappointment is a significant stage in the overall story.

In John, one of the episodes in which the risen Jesus appears begins with the disciples meeting in a house with "the doors locked for fear of the Judeans" (20:19-23). But this meeting behind locked doors cannot indicate that disciples are in a defeated mood, for the meeting follows after the scene of the empty tomb, in which "the other disciple . . . saw and believed," and Mary Magdalene encountered the risen Jesus and then told the disciples. That the doors were locked for fear of the Judeans is only to be expected in an overall Gospel story in which the Judean high priests have been hostile to Jesus and his movement throughout. The Gospel sources simply do not offer any hints or memories of the disciples being devastated after the crucifixion.

Second, there is no clear and consistent representation of what happened to Jesus after the crucifixion in New Testament texts. Portrayals range from an empty tomb to the simple assertion that he "rose" or "was raised" to accounts of what are clearly visions, "appearances" of an earthly or a heavenly Jesus, particularly to the disciples or the women closely familiar with him. "The resurrection" of Jesus as a singular event is a modern synthetic concept, often used without any clear referent in New Testament texts, which themselves vary considerably. The concept of or belief in "resurrection" in "Judaism," in which the followers of Jesus were supposedly rooted, is also a modern synthetic construct from textual references that are equally varied.[11] The concept of resurrection that is standard in biblical studies often lumps together three evidently separate but often interrelated Judean concepts of future fulfillment and their respective proof-texts. Key in this connection is the appearance of all three concepts in Dan 12:1-3, the classic proof-text for the idea of "resurrection" prior to Paul's letters and the Gospels. The three interrelated Judean hopes, however, appear separately both in Judean texts prior to the mission of Jesus and in the portrayals of Jesus in the Gospels and "Peter's" speeches in Acts.

a. "The dead" coming to life in Isa 26:19 and "the dead bones" again becoming living people in Ezekiel 37 are images of *the restoration of the people* of Judah/Israel, and not strictly of the resurrection of dead bodies. In the historical visions usually classified as "apocalyptic" texts, such as the Animal Vision in *1 Enoch* 85–90 and Daniel 7, and in *Psalms of Solomon* 17, the restoration of the people is the final resolution, expressed in different images, of the crisis of imperial domination. For example, "one like a son of man" seated beside the Ancient of Days in the vision in Daniel 7 is interpreted as "[the people of] the holy ones of the Most High" being given sovereignty when the beastly empires are punished at the divine judgment. A brief speech about the renewal of Israel may have been the final component in Q (Luke 22:28-30; Matt 19:28 has the term "restoration of all [people]"). All of these texts express a hope of the renewal/restoration of the people without being associated with a special resuscitation of the dead.

b. Images of the *vindication of those who are killed by the authorities* because of their firm commitment to the traditional way of life or the movement are often confused with the idea of resurrection. However, the statement in Dan 12:3 that "those who are wise will shine . . . like the stars" and similar expectations in *1 Enoch* 102:4-6 are anticipations of vindication at the divine judgment. Speeches of Jesus warning his followers about the commitment necessary when facing repressive action also have images of vindication in the heavenly court (Mark 8:34-35; Luke/Q 12:2-9). With the exception of Dan 12:3, these images of vindication are separate from any expression of the resurrection of the dead.

c. More difficult to find in Judean texts are images of the (collective) *resurrection of the dead*, proper. The story of the seven martyred brothers and their mother in 2 Maccabees 7 appears to attest a resurrection of bodies ("to die at the hands of mortals and to cherish the hope God gives of being raised again by him" [7:14; cf. 7:9, 11]). In addition, Dan 12:2 has the image of "those who sleep in the dust of the earth" awakening, some to life and some to shame, in between the restoration of the people and the vindication of the wise. Matthew has such a resurrection, of "the saints who had fallen asleep" coming "out of their tombs" at a great earthquake, as the effects of a "theophany" (an ominous, terrifying appearance of God) that occurs as Jesus breathes his last (Matt 27:50-54; 28:2). Paul offers both a visionary reassurance and a discursive elaboration of the general resurrection (1 Thess 4:15-18; 1 Corinthians 15). All of these texts, few as they are, refer to a general resurrection; Paul thinks of Christ's resurrection as included in the general resurrection, only as its "firstfruits."

Thus, although we find in various texts the different expectations of the collective restoration of the people, the vindication of people who were killed for their commitment to God or the covenant, and a general resurrection of the dead, these distinctive expectations appear together only rarely. It would be difficult to argue that there was a common, widespread, unified concept of or belief in "resurrection" among the Judeans and Galileans that might have been shared by Jesus and his followers.

Further, as noted above, the Gospels and Paul present different representations of what happened with Jesus after his death. These range from reports of his tomb being empty to simple assertions that he "rose" or "was raised," either solo or as the first in a general resurrection, to accounts of visions of appearances of Jesus on earth (for example, in a community) or in/from heaven. Only some of these correspond to one of the three different expectations attested in Judean texts. There is thus no basis in the sources for imagining that there was some single, unitary, commonly experienced event, "the resurrection."

Third, it is almost impossible to find in the sources any support for the view that it was some sort of "resurrection" that motivated the (formation and) rapid expansion of the Jesus movement(s). In all of the Gospels, *the renewal of Israel is already under way*—indeed is the principal agenda of Jesus' mission. There is little or no indication that some sort of resurrection was decisive in inspiring formation or expansion.

The very existence of the Q speeches attests a movement or community that continued to recite them. But these speeches seem to have no knowledge of any sort of resurrection of Jesus.

Mark has three brief "predictions" of Jesus being killed and raised (8:31; 9:31; 10:32-34). But after Jesus' extensive confrontation with the rulers in Jerusalem and the elaborate portrayal of his arrest, trials, mocking, and crucifixion, Mark includes only a short episode at the empty tomb, in which the young man briefly states that Jesus "has been raised" and is going ahead of his disciples to Galilee, presumably where they would continue the movement of renewal that he and they had already started (Mark 16:1-8).

Matthew has little more. To the empty tomb scene he adds a brief mention that "Jesus met them," that is, the disciples (28:9), and ends the Gospel with the short commission to "go make disciples of all peoples." But the renewal of Israel was already well under way *before* Jesus' death, and the continuing renewal of Israel is the principal concern of Matthew.

To the empty tomb story, Luke adds visionary appearances of Jesus (24:13-35). But Jesus' role in these scenes is only revelatory and instructional for a movement of the renewal of Israel that is already under way and that, at the opening of the book of Acts, will now expand. After Jesus ascends into heaven, the movement receives further inspiration, but from the outpouring of the Holy Spirit, not from "the resurrection."

John is the only Gospel with extensive and clearly bodily resurrection appearances. In the scene in which Jesus meets the disciples behind locked doors, he breathes on them so that they receive the Holy Spirit (20:19-23). But again, the community is (already) formed and well under way, having been specially empowered by the "farewell discourses" (John 13–17).

Nor do the short speeches in the book of Acts suggest that it was the resurrection faith that drove the rapid expansion of the Jesus movement(s).

According to the speech in Acts 2:22-36, God raised Jesus up as a vindication (2:23-24), but this is simply to set up God's appointment of Jesus as "both Lord and Messiah" (2:36), which is the decisive event in world history. In the speech in Acts 5:29-32, God's raising of Jesus is a vindication for his having obeyed God rather than human authority, and it leads to God's exaltation of Jesus into the heavenly office of "Leader and Savior." Again, Jesus' raising is an ancillary step toward the principal event, his installation into heavenly office, after which the renewal of Israel begun by Jesus continues and expands.

All of these sources attest a *continuation* of the movement begun by Jesus following his crucifixion and vindication/raising/appearance(s). But none of them suggests that "the resurrection" was the decisive motivating experience or event that led to the *formation* or *expansion* of the movement.

BREAKTHROUGH

Another look at our earliest Gospel sources suggests that *the crucifixion* was the decisive event in the historical breakthrough begun in Jesus' confrontation with the rulers in Jerusalem that gave impetus for the expansion of the Jesus movement(s). The effect of the crucifixion of Jesus on the movement he started was to transform the power that was intended to intimidate and dominate into the power that inspired commitment and solidarity in forming an alternative social order.

In the chapters above, we have been attempting to discern how the various aspects and steps of Jesus' mission were related to the historical context and to one another. A tentative picture has begun to take shape: Roman conquest followed by harsh Herodian rule and multiple demands for tribute, taxes, and tithes had induced a deep-running indignation among Jesus' Galilean and Judean contemporaries. That indignation resonated with the Israelite tradition of opposition to foreign imperial rule and of stories of deliverance. Jesus not only adapted and sharpened an oppositional discourse of a renewed covenantal society of justice rooted in that Israelite tradition. He also tapped the yearning and drive to realize that renewal. Simultaneously he mediated life-restoring and energizing power in healings and exorcisms. The new hope, the promise of blessing, and the sense that a more equitable and just social order was possible would only have intensified the people's indignation at their oppression in violation of God's covenantal will. Jesus' mission and movement of renewal of Israel were thus able to gain considerable momentum in the villages of Galilee and beyond—to generate considerable social-political power—without publicly challenging or being checked by Antipas or other rulers.

Finally, however, Jesus brought his prophetic opposition face to face with the high priestly representatives of Roman imperial power in the Temple. He staged his confrontation with imperial power, moreover, at the festival in which the people celebrated their historical deliverance from foreign domination directly under the oversight of the Roman military posted on the porticoes of the Temple. Jesus' forcible demonstration of God's condemnation of the Temple and other prophetic pronouncements of divine judgment against the rulers began a "breakthrough" expression of the deep popular indignation about oppression that had long been bottled up by coercive power. As noted in the last chapter, Jesus' confrontation with the rulers, as the beginning of the breakthrough, brought a release of energy that had previously been used for self-restraint, energy that could now be channeled into expansion of the movement of renewal and resistance.

Jesus' bold prophetic confrontation, however, led quickly to his crucifixion. In some early sources, the crucified Jesus is represented as having been raised or otherwise vindicated. But with or without such vindication, Jesus' crucifixion in Jerusalem became the key event in the breakthrough. It further intensified the transformation of collective indignation into a force that drove the expansion of the movement. The prophetic leader of the renewal of the people had boldly endured the torturous execution intended to intimidate and suppress resistance. The effect of his crucifixion, however, was to release all the more energy, which the threat of crucifixion had previously helped contain, into the expansion of the renewal movement. Insofar as Jesus' followers identified with their crucified leader, thus weakening the power of the threat of crucifixion to intimidate them, the crucifixion of Jesus inspired further resistance and steadfast commitment in repressive circumstances.

That the killing of Jesus became the breakthrough event is evident at several points both in the Q speeches in Matthew and Luke and in the Gospel of Mark. It is seen especially in the way the followers of Jesus identified with his opposition to the rulers that led to his death, and themselves imitated that opposition, even if it led to their own crucifixion. This relationship between Jesus and his followers is a prime example of why it is essential that we stop imposing the assumptions of modern Western individualism in a quest for precisely which sayings Jesus the individual figure may have uttered, and move instead to a more historical *relational and contextual* approach. Only because Jesus *communicated* with people did he become a historically significant figure. Only because his teaching on particular issues *continued to resonate* with his followers did those shorter or longer speeches continue to be recited in community settings—so that they were eventually included in the Gospel story of Mark, the sequence of speeches called Q, and the more complex Gospels of Matthew and Luke. What the Gospel sources offer us are not individual sayings that *might* go back to Jesus, but Jesus-in-relation-with communities or movements of followers. What the Gospel sources offer is how Jesus is remembered as addressing key issues of importance to the people who responded to his speeches. It is of particular importance when both of the earliest Gospel sources, Mark and Q, independently represent Jesus as addressing the same issue that his followers were struggling with.

The series of speeches in Q indicate awareness that Jesus was put to death on the cross (Luke/Q 14:27), even though they do not dwell on the form of his execution. The relationship between follower and paradigmatic prophet is stated in stark terms: "Whoever does not take up his/her cross and follow after me cannot be my disciple" (14:27). Beyond that blunt statement, the Q speeches are remarkable for the way in which the death of Jesus, as the climactic result of his opposition to the rulers, is embedded in the identity of his movement.

When Jesus speaks of the long line of prophets that God (or Wisdom) had sent to Jerusalem (Luke/Q 13:34; 11:49-51), it seems clear that he is speaking as the latest in that line. This is implicit, at least, in the speeches insofar as (we may presume that) they were being repeatedly performed in communities of Jesus' followers who knew that he had been executed and why. That Jesus was prophesying against the Jerusalem ruling house is explicit in the prophetic lament directed against Jerusalem (13:34). The Jerusalem ruling house is implicated as well in the series of woes against the scribes and Pharisees that concludes with God's declaration that the blood of all the prophets (including that of Jesus) will be required of "this type/kind/ilk [*genea*]," that is, those representatives of Jerusalem's interests.

The "Q people," who heard and recited these speeches, also understood themselves, then, as collectively continuing the prophetic line in their identification with Jesus. This stands out prominently at the outset in the foundational covenant renewal speech with which the series of Q speeches begins. "Blessed are you when they (exclude and) reproach you and speak evil of you on account of me/'the human one.' . . . For so their fathers did to the prophets" (6:22-23). In their own prophetic role, the followers of Jesus, who continued proclaiming the kingdom of God and pressing the renewal of Israel, were prepared to undergo arrest, trial, and possible death. One speech in the series focuses specifically on this contingency (12:2-9). In this speech, their founding prophet "Jesus" admonishes his followers to be bold in their proclamation, not worrying about possible execution, but trusting in God's providential care. The motivating sanction on their bold persistence in proclamation indicates that their movement was now out in the open. They, like Jesus, were being hauled before courts, where they had to declare their loyalty in public and be prepared to suffer the consequences.

The Gospel of Mark also attests how the crucifixion of Jesus, as the imperial response to his public confrontation in Jerusalem, was the key event in the breakthrough that energized the movement. While Mark includes the episode of the empty tomb, in which the young man's announcement sends the disciples back to Galilee to continue the movement, the climax of the overall story comes earlier in the arrest and crucifixion of Jesus in response to his confrontation of the rulers. This emphasis on the crucifixion is reinforced by Mark's inclusion of the divine vindication of Jesus in the rending of the curtain of the Temple just at the moment of Jesus' death on the cross, followed by the centurion's recognition that Jesus was truly "a son of God."[12]

The most important indication in Mark that Jesus' crucifixion became the empowering event for the dynamic expansion of the movement he had begun is surely his word over the cup at the Passover meal with the disciples. His declaration, "My blood of the covenant, which is poured out for many," reenacts the making of the covenant on Sinai, evoking memory of the basins of blood that symbolically bound God and the people, who promised to observe the principles of social-economic justice (Exod

24:3-8). In Mark, Jesus' crucifixion is the event that seals the renewal of the Mosaic covenant, remembered in the binding and empowering ceremony of the Lord's Supper in anticipation of full realization of the direct rule of God. Instead of decisively weakening the movement, the Roman crucifixion of Jesus for his pronouncement of God's judgment on the rulers became the central, symbolic event that empowered its solidarity and further expansion.

How this happened can be seen in Mark, as in the Q speeches, in the ways the followers not only continued his program of renewal of the people but also identified with his opposition to the rulers despite the risk of repressive action. The two Marys who witness the empty tomb are instructed to tell his disciples "that he is going ahead of you to Galilee," where they will see him, just as he had told them (16:7; 14:28). The open ending of Mark's narrative suggests that the "Markan" (branch of the) movement had returned to "Galilee," where Jesus "met them" as they continued the renewal of the people. As in the Q speeches, moreover, so in Mark's Gospel, Jesus' movement continued his program of renewal in intentional opposition to the imperial order. The leadership of the movement, for example, is to be a self-conscious alternative to hierarchical relations of power. The paradigm for this alternative form of leadership is Jesus' sharp rejection of James's and John's request for positions of political power. "The cup he drinks" and "the baptism with which he is baptized" are symbols of commitment to the common good even to the point of being crucified (10:35-45).

Once we recognize that Mark's Gospel consists not of mere reminiscences but of the active remembering of a community that is still resonating with and living out Jesus' teachings, we can see that Mark also portrays Jesus' followers as expanding the renewal of the people in open opposition to the rulers. At the end of the dialogue focused on egalitarian covenantal economic relations (10:17-31), Jesus reassures the disciples of the restoration of the families and lands that they have left temporarily while pursuing the mission. The restoration is not "apocalyptic" or "eschatological," as interpreters often claim. While represented with considerable hyperbole ("a hundredfold"), it is to come "now in this age." And far from being a panacea of peaceful rest, the restoration of household and fields is to involve continuing struggle, "with persecutions." Jesus' confrontation and crucifixion had dramatically brought the movement to the attention of the rulers, so that it now had to contend with active opposition from the rulers. This means that Jesus' followers continue their movement in opposition to the imperial order in imitation of Jesus, in full awareness that they too may face crucifixion. Mark's Gospel places the key admonition by Jesus immediately after his first announcement of the crucifixion and his rebuke of Peter's misunderstanding about "messiahship" (8:34—9:1). Jesus' followers must expect that they may be required to "take up their [own] cross," boldly facing their own condemnation—but in the confidence that they will be vindicated in the divine judgment and that the direct rule of God will soon be "coming with power."

Conclusion

Jesus and the Struggle with the Powers

We in the modern West have been limiting our understanding of the historical Jesus by continuing to read the Gospel sources according to our own habits of thought and definition of reality. Having categorized Jesus as a religious figure, we have difficulty appreciating his conflict with the Jerusalem and Roman rulers, which was inseparably political-religious. Assuming modern Western individualism, we have conceived of Jesus as an autonomous individual relatively unconstrained by social-political relations. We thus do not even investigate how Jesus *communicated* and *interacted* with his followers and his opponents in a historical situation of crisis—so that he became a historically significant figure. As indicated even in the most recent standard translations of the Gospels, we assume that Jesus was "curing" "diseases," imposing Western biomedical definitions. In recent decades, however, there is increasing recognition that illnesses are responses to a complex matrix of social, political, and economic influences on communities as well as on individual persons, and that illness and healing are defined by the cultures in which they occur.

In the exploration of Jesus in the chapters above, we have adopted an alternative strategy: attempting to appreciate the way the Gospels and other sources portrayed ancient Galileans, Judeans, and other peoples in their own life circumstances. Judging from a wide range of sources, from myths to monuments, it seems that ancient societies and civilizations involved a dynamic interaction of multiple powers that affected peoples' lives and livelihood, and people's interaction with those powers. The vast majority of these forces or spirits had only local or other limited functions. Most important were the major powers that, in their dynamic interaction, determined the life circumstances of whole civilizations, such as Storm-Kingship in ancient Mesopotamia, Lord Storm (*Ba'al*) in the Canaanite city-states, and Caesar, the Lord and Savior, in the Roman Empire.

These powers were often what made civilized life possible. They included the forces of fertility and productivity and those of political-economic stability and organization. Because they were culturally shaped by those who wielded power in the name of the powers, however, they could become economically demanding and politically threatening. The great powers wielded what we would call political and economic power, through their representatives' enforcement of order and expropriation of produce and labor. Closely related and often inseparable, however, were the religious manifestations of the powers in the massive monuments and elaborate ceremonies managed by their representatives.

There was yet another important cultural manifestation of the powers, often unrecognized, in the struggle of subjected peoples in response to the invasion of their lives by outside powers. In military conquests and demands for taxes, the invasive powers were political and economic to be sure. Closely corresponding to the political-economic impact, however, was subject peoples' experience that their culture had been invaded by alien spirits. In comparative cases from East Africa, corresponding to the British military invasion led by Lord Cromer, a number of people were possessed by a spirit named "Lord Cromer." And corresponding to the aggressive Christian mission, numerous people were possessed by the spirit named *Kijesu*. For many people, the alternative to submission to the outside powers—and perhaps an expression of it—was possession by outside spirits.

In all of these aspects, moreover, we can discern that power was relational. The power of Storm-Kingship in Mesopotamia or of Caesar in the Roman Empire was developed, consolidated, and expanded by extracting the produce and labor of subject peoples. The extracted produce and labor were transformed into power over the people that was used to support coercive military forces. This power also took a combination of institutionalized and symbolic forms in impressive monumental structures that constituted and ensured the continuing or increasing centralization of power. Because power is relational in this way, however, it is always possible that some of the subject people could withhold (some of) their support from the system—that is, the powers and institutionalized power—or even withdraw altogether, perhaps weakening the powers and threatening the "power structure."

The people of Israel, according to their cultural tradition, present a distinctive history in the midst of the field of powers that determined the civilizations of the ancient Near East. The early narratives of the Hebrew Bible depict them being led by a force that came from outside these civilizations to escape from hard bondage under the pharaoh in Egypt. They established an alternative social-economic order of mutual aid and cooperation under the direct rule of YHWH, the power who had liberated them and who prohibited them serving the great centralized powers of civilization and commanded principles that protected the people's livelihood.

Israelites' centralization of military power, undertaken in an attempt to maintain their independence, led to the centralization of power generally in monarchy. Israel and then Judah could not avoid being conquered and subjected to one great empire after another. In Judean texts composed as part of the effort to maintain the traditional way of life, we can see how scribal circles struggled with the impact of the outside cultural forces, of spirits and heavenly agents that corresponded to the imperial political-economic powers that dominated their lives. In popular movements of resistance in early Roman times, we can see the Judean and Galilean people's mobilization of their own collective power, their refusal to yield up resources to the power holders and at least the temporary reassertion of their independence.

Appreciating the way ancient sources portray their life circumstances in this way sets up new possibilities for understanding the mission and impact of Jesus in ways less limited by the modern Western dichotomy between politics and religion and the abstraction of the autonomous individual from social forms and relationships.

In his mission among the people, Jesus was not working in a social and cultural vacuum. People of Israelite heritage had long cultivated their tradition in their own semi-independent and self-governing village communities. By telling and retelling stories of the exodus and of prophets such as Elijah and by teaching covenantal principles, they reinforced both the memory and the ideals of an independent life of dignity. Cultivation of Israelite tradition in the sequestered sites of the village communities kept alive a sense of indignation about their circumstances and longings for deliverance and justice. In proclaiming the kingdom of God at hand Jesus declared that those longings were now being fulfilled. Speaking with authority in the traditional role of a prophet, Jesus declared the imminent blessings of the kingdom for the poor in performative speech. The imminent blessings of the kingdom, moreover, offered empowerment in the concrete sense of enough to eat (daily bread) and relief from debilitating debts. The kingdom of God was happening, becoming a social-economic reality in the people's response, such as their mutual cancellation of debts even as they prayed for the kingdom. The power of rekindled hope for restoration and renewal gained social extension as rumor of fulfillment spread from village to village.

The most striking manifestation of the coming of the kingdom of God was Jesus' exorcism of "unclean spirits." In their possession of particular people, the spirits were wreaking violence on whole communities, just as the invading Roman troops had wrought destruction of whole villages. As indicated in the story of the spirit identified as "Legion," the alien possessing force was a reflection of the Roman military. The exorcism of particular spirits brought relief for the people generally as well as for possessed individuals. Jesus' acts of power, however, were understood as more than exorcisms. In these acts, Jesus was defeating the demons. Indeed, the Beelzebul discourse represents the exorcisms as evidence that God, through Jesus, had defeated Satan, the "prince of demons," and it portrays the battle between the spirits as a political struggle between ruling "houses" or "kingdoms." In response to Jesus' exorcisms, moreover, the Galileans were acclaiming Jesus as acting with authority (power), in contrast to the supposedly authoritative scribal representatives of the Jerusalem high priests. That is, in his "acts of power" mediating divine power to subjected people, Jesus was generating power among the people. This was not lost on the representatives of the Jerusalem temple-state, who accused Jesus of working in the power of the prince of demons.

In addition to possession by alien spirits, the effects of Roman rule, with its multiple demands for tribute to Caesar, taxes to the Herodian kings, and tithes and offerings to the Temple, were to diminish the resources available to the people to sustain their own lives. The economic pressures not only weakened individuals with malnutrition but also weakened the wider social fabric. Families and village communities began to disintegrate, as impoverished people could no longer aid their hungry neighbors and began quarreling over debts. Again drawing on Israelite tradition, Jesus declared a renewal of the Mosaic covenant. Proclaiming blessings to the poor, for whom God was offering the kingdom, he renewed the covenantal demands for mutual aid and cooperation among members of village communities. As in his prophetic statements, the covenantal speech in Q was not just teaching, as it is often described today. Addressing the people in performative speech, Jesus in effect *enacted* covenant renewal in the listening community. Confident that God was again delivering them from distress, they could now respond with recommitment to the covenant principles according to which the people took responsibility for each other's welfare and maintained mutual support in the village community.

The renewal of covenantal community, however, also meant that the people were regenerating the power of local solidarity. That enabled them as families and village communities to resist the further encroachments of tax collectors and creditors that would bring them deeper into debt or even force them off their land and out of their villages. Jesus reinforced the renewal of covenant community locally by condemning, on covenantal principles, both creditors' expansion of their own wealth by exploiting the poor and the measures taken by the representatives of the rulers to extract even more resources from families and villages to support the Temple.

Having catalyzed the empowerment of the people in the villages of Galilee, Jesus finally challenged the rulers publicly in Jerusalem, which was both the capital of Israel and the face of Roman power in Judea. The challenge was hardly innocent or innocuous. It was not a revolt, much less an armed insurrection. But Jesus' prophetic pronouncements and demonstration of God's judgment against the Temple and high priests generated a countervailing power threatening to the high priests' control of the people and the Roman imperial order in Judea. Like the Israelite prophets in whose role and tradition he was acting, Jesus was speaking not only for God, but for the people as well, and the two were closely related. In his pronouncement of God's condemnation of the Temple and the high priesthood, he was giving voice to the collective resentment of the people who were forced to suffer various indignities in the expropriation of their goods.

This public demonstration, moreover, was staged during the Passover festival, the celebration of the people's historic deliverance from foreign domination during which collective popular indignation at their subjugation by the Romans at times erupted in protest. The Passover celebration initially provided a protective anonymity and disguise for the "show of force" by Jesus and his followers. Like Jeremiah and other prophets before him, however, Jesus spoke and acted out God's condemnation of the Temple directly in the face of the rulers and ruling institutions. His "speaking truth to power" was not simply the annoyance of an individual outcry. Rather, in giving voice to the popular indignation, he generated power among the people in opposition to the rulers. His prophetic speech and action transformed the previously festering energy of indignation, along with the energy previously used for self-restraint, into collective power channeled into the expanding movement of renewal and resistance.

Contrary to the previous view that Jesus' death meant defeat for the disciples, the Roman crucifixion of Jesus only served to intensify the collective energy of his followers generated by his confrontation of the rulers in Jerusalem. It became the key event in the movement's breakthrough from its beginning in more "hidden" renewal and resistance to its public opposition to and by the rulers. According to the Gospel sources, the crucifixion was not a defeat for the disciples, to which the resurrection was the answer that inspired them for the first time to form a movement. As represented in the sources, the crucifixion, the Roman ruler's response to Jesus' pronouncement of God's judgment, led directly to the expansion the movement. The prophetic leader of the renewal had boldly endured the torturous execution intended to intimidate resistance. The effect was to release all the more energy, which the threat of crucifixion had previously helped contain, into the rapid extension of the movement of renewal. Insofar as Jesus' followers identified with their crucified leader, thus lessening the power of the threat of crucifixion to intimidate them, the crucifixion of Jesus inspired further resistance and steadfast commitment in the extension of the renewal of the people.

The mission of Jesus generated a collective power among the people rooted in the conviction that God was again acting for their deliverance, fulfilling their longings for a life of dignity. The movements that formed in response to Jesus' mission were thus empowered to revitalize their covenantal communities as an alternative society under the direct rule of God. They were further emboldened by Jesus' public confrontation of the rulers and martyrdom at the hands of the Romans. The cooperative power generated among the people enabled them to expand the movements in resistance to, and despite periodic repression by, the powers that still determined the conditions of their lives.

Notes

INTRODUCTION: "YOU SHALL NOT BOW DOWN AND SERVE THEM"

1. An early, important, and very accessible presentation is Werner H. Kelber, *Mark's Story of Jesus* (Philadelphia: Fortress Press, 1979).

2. See, for example, the elementary analysis in Jack Dean Kingsbury, *Conflict in Mark: Jesus, Authorities, Disciples* (Minneapolis: Fortress Press, 1989).

3. On Mark, see the fuller discussion in Richard A. Horsley, *Hearing the Whole Story: The Politics of Plot in Mark's Gospel* (Louisville: Westminster John Knox, 2001), ch. 5.

4. For discussion, see ibid., ch. 6.

5. The most sophisticated development of standard critical analysis of Jesus' sayings is John Dominic Crossan, *The Historical Jesus: The Life of a Mediterranean Jewish Peasant* (San Francisco: HarperCollins, 1991).

6. See the critical discussion of the understanding of religion in the modern West by Talal Asad, *Genealogies of Religion: Discipline and Reasons of Power in Christianity and Islam* (Baltimore: Johns Hopkins University Press, 1993), ch. 1, especially pp. 45–46.

7. See Crossan, *Historical Jesus*, 282–93.

8. See the sharply critical discussion in Elisabeth Schüssler Fiorenza, *Jesus and the Politics of Interpretation* (New York: Continuum, 2000).

9. This is my principal concern in *Hearing the Whole Story*.

10. For fuller analysis and discussion, see Richard A. Horsley, *Galilee: History, Politics, People* (Valley Forge, Pa.: Trinity Press International, 1995), ch. 4.

11. For a brief summary of the political-economic structure of Roman Palestine, see Richard A. Horsley, *Sociology and the Jesus Movement* (New York: Crossroad, 1989).

12. For a preliminary attempt to deal with how people are so embedded in

fundamental social forms of family and village community, which is usually ignored in the interpretation of Jesus, see Horsley, *Galilee*, chs. 8–10.

13. For a preliminary statement of a relational and contextual approach to the historical Jesus, see Richard A. Horsley, *Jesus and Empire: The Kingdom of God and the New World Disorder* (Minneapolis: Fortress Press, 2003), ch. 3. For fuller discussion of the roles or "scripts" operative in Galilean and Judean society around the time of Jesus, see Horsley, *Hearing the Whole Story*, ch. 10.

14. This will be more complicated than a simple reversal of the old "criterion of dissimilarity" from "Jewish" teaching previously applied in establishing the "authentic" sayings of Jesus. Cultural tradition/social memory almost certainly operates in patterns broader than can be detected in sayings taken in isolation. An influential discussion of the criterion of dissimilarity from a generation ago was Norman Perrin, *Rediscovering the Teaching of Jesus* (New York: Harper & Row, 1967), 39–45.

15. See now William V. Harris, *Ancient Literacy* (Cambridge, Mass.: Harvard University Press, 1987); and Catherine Hezser, *Jewish Literacy in Roman Palestine,* Texte und Studien zum antiken Judentum 81 (Tübingen: Mohr Siebeck, 2001).

16. For an attempt to begin such exploration, see Richard A. Horsley, *Jesus in Context: Power, People, and Performance* (Minneapolis: Fortress Press, 2008), chs. 5–7.

17. For a discussion of "hard power" and "soft power," see Joseph Nye, *Soft Power: The Means to Success in World Politics* (New York: Public Affairs, 2004).

1. THE POWERS OF EMPIRE

1. Some of the classic studies on which the following depends are A. Leo Oppenheim, *Ancient Mesopotamia: Portrait of a Dead Civilization,* rev. ed. by Erica Reiner (Chicago: University of Chicago Press, 1976); and H. W. F. Saggs, *The Greatness That Was Babylon: A Sketch of the Ancient Civilization of the Tigris-Euphrates Valley* (New York: Praeger, 1962). Surveys of more recent studies can be found in A. Kirk Grayson, "Mesopotamia, History of," *Anchor Bible Dictionary,* ed. David Noel Freedman, 6 vols. (New York: Doubleday, 1992), 4:732–77; and Norman Yoffee, "Political Economy in Early Mesopotamian States," *Annual Review of Anthropology* 24 (1995): 281–311.

2. For a fuller exposition of the imperial tributary system of ancient Mesopotamian/Babylonian civilization, in comparison with advanced consumer capitalism, see Richard Horsley, "Christmas: The Religion of Consumer Capitalism," in

Christmas Unwrapped: Consumerism, Christ, and Culture, ed. Richard Horsley and James Tracy (Harrisburg, Pa.: Trinity Press International, 2001), 165–87.

3. Roman historians, including that most infamous of warlords Julius Caesar, describe many similar scenes of Roman "shock and awe." See, for example, Julius Caesar, *Bell. Gall.* 4.19; Cassius Dio 68.6.1–2; Pliny, *Ep.* 2.7.2.

4. Susan P. Mattern, *Rome and the Enemy: Imperial Strategy in the Principate* (Berkeley: University of California Press, 1999), 117–22; quotation from 119.

5. See the compact and incisive account of the American ideology in Anders Stephanson, *Manifest Destiny: American Expansion and the Empire of Right* (New York: Hill & Wang, 1995,) especially the statements in ch. 3 by mainline American religious leaders, senators, and presidents that are strikingly parallel to statements by distinguished Romans such as Cicero.

6. Eisenhower, who had been the commander of the Allied forces in the Second World War, prophetically warned that the "defense" industry had grown so powerful that it could not only steer U.S. foreign policy, but also channel resources needed for other purposes into its own self-aggrandizement, thus further expanding its power.

7. The following discussion is dependent on the elaborate analysis, with extensive documentation, by Keith Hopkins, *Conquerors and Slaves,* Sociological Studies in Roman History 1 (Cambridge: Cambridge University Press, 1978), ch. 1.

8. Ibid., 7.

9. Ibid., 67.

10. Ibid., 9.

11. The classic study is Paul Veyne, *Bread and Circuses: Historical Sociology and Political Pluralism* (London: Penguin, 1990). The following is indebted also to Peter Garnsey and Richard Saller, *The Roman Empire: Economy, Society and Culture* (Berkeley: University of California Press, 1987), esp. 83–85, 95–96; and Peter Garnsey, *Famine and Food Supply in the Graeco-Roman World: Responses to Risk and Crisis* (Cambridge/New York: Cambridge University Press, 1988), esp. 231.

12. The following depends heavily on Veyne, *Bread and Circuses.*

13. The contemporary American equivalent of these games would be something like a combination of Easter or Passover services and Fourth of July fireworks displays with NASCAR races, the Superbowl, and the Academy Awards, organized and presided over by prominent figures who combine the functions of archbishop, the NFL commissioner, Superbowl sponsors, and big-city mayors.

14. Veyne, *Bread and Circuses,* 210, 212.

15. For treatments of patronage, patron-client relations, and patron-protégé relations, see especially Richard Saller, *Personal Patronage under the Early*

Empire (Cambridge: Cambridge University Press, 1982); and Garnsey and Saller, *Roman Empire*, 148–59.

16. On the expansion of patronage networks into the empire, see especially John Rich, "Patronage and Interstate Relations in the Roman Republic," in *Patronage in Ancient Society,* ed. Andrew Wallace-Hadrill, Leicester-Nottingham Studies in Ancient Society 1 (London: Routledge, 1989), 125–38; David Braund, "Function and Dysfunction: Personal Patronage in Roman Imperialism," in Wallace-Hadrill, *Patronage in Ancient Society,* 139–49; and the summary discussion in Richard A. Horsley, "Introduction, Part II: Patronage, Priesthoods, and Power," in *Paul and Empire: Religion and Power in Roman Imperial Society,* ed. Richard A. Horsley (Harrisburg, Pa.: Trinity Press International, 1997), 88–95.

17. The emperor Augustus is reported to have cracked, similarly, that he "would rather be Herod's pig [*hus*] than his son [*huios*]"—prefiguring President Franklin Delano Roosevelt's comment about Anastasio Somoza, the U.S.–supported dictator in Nicaragua, "He may be a son-of-a-bitch, but he's *our* son-of-a-bitch."

18. The following is based on the groundbreaking analysis of the emperor cult in S. R. F. Price, *Rituals and Power: The Roman Imperial Cult in Asia Minor* (Cambridge: Cambridge University Press, 1984); and Paul Zanker, *The Power of Images in the Age of Augustus,* Jerome Lectures, 16th Series (Ann Arbor: University of Michigan Press, 1988). Excerpts and further discussion as it bears on nascent Christianity can be found in Horsley, ed., *Paul and Empire* (op. cit. n. 16); part 1, pp. 10–86.

19. *Corpus inscriptionum graecarum,* ed. August Boeckh et al., 4 vols. (Berlin: Ex Officina Academica, 1828–77), 3957b, translation in Hopkins, *Conquerors and Slaves,* 207.

20. On this point, see Richard Gordon, "The Veil of Power: Emperors, Sacrificers, and Benefactors," in *Pagan Priests: Religion and Power in the Ancient World,* ed. Mary Beard and John North (London: Duckworth, 1990; reprinted in Horsley, *Paul and Empire,* ch. 7), as well as Price, *Rituals and Power* (excerpted in *Paul and Empire,* ch. 3).

2. ISRAEL'S COVENANT
AND PROPHETIC PROTEST

1. The following account is heavily indebted to Norman K. Gottwald, *The Tribes of Yahweh: A Sociology of the Religion of Liberated Israel, 1250–1050 B.C.E.* (Maryknoll, N.Y.: Orbis Books, 1979), and subsequent scholarly debate about the history of early Israel.

2. See Renita J. Weems, "Reading *Her Way* through the Struggle: African American Women and the Bible," in *Stony the Road We Trod: African American Biblical Interpretation,* ed. Cain Hope Felder (Minneapolis: Fortress Press, 1991), 57–77; reprinted in *The Bible and Liberation: Political and Social Hermeneutics,* ed. Norman K. Gottwald and Richard A. Horsley, Bible and Liberation Series (Maryknoll, N.Y.: Orbis Books, 1993), 31–50.

3. Careful analysis and discussion of the key passages may be found in Gottwald, *Tribes of Yahweh;* idem, "Social Class and Ideology in Isaiah 40–55: An Eagletonian Reading," reprinted in *The Bible and Liberation,* 329–42.

4. For a fuller discussion, see Richard A. Horsley, *Covenant Economics: A Biblical Vision of Justice for All* (Louisville: Westminster John Knox, 2009), ch. 2; which in turn depends on earlier analysis and discussion by George E. Mendenhall, *Law and Covenant in Israel and in the Ancient Near East* (Pittsburgh: Presbyterian Board of Colportage of Western Pennsylvania, 1955); and "Covenant," *Interpreter's Dictionary of the Bible,* ed. G. A. Buttrick, 4 vols. (Nashville: Abingdon, 1962), 1.714–23 .

5. On the eighth-century prophets, see especially the essays of Marvin L. Chaney, "Bitter Bounty: The Dynamics of Political Economy Critiqued by the Eighth-Century Prophets," in Gottwald and Horsley, *Bible and Liberation,* 250–63; and idem, "Whose Sour Grapes? The Addressees of Isaiah 5:1-7 in the Light of Political Economy," *Semeia* 87 (1999): 105–22. On Amos, see Robert M. Coote, *Amos among the Prophets: Composition and Theology* (Philadelphia: Fortress Press, 1981).

6. For a reassessment of the history of Judea in the Persian period from archaeological evidence, see Charles E. Carter, *The Emergence of Yehud in the Persian Period: A Social and Demographic Study,* Journal for the Study of the Old Testament Supplement Series 294 (Sheffield: Sheffield Academic Press, 1999).

7. On the Persian period, see the discussion, on the basis of recent research, in Richard A. Horsley, *Scribes, Visionaries, and the Politics of Second-Temple Judea* (Louisville: Westminster John Knox, 2007), ch. 1.

8. See further Norman K. Gottwald, "Social Class and Ideology in Isaiah 40-55," *Semeia* 59 (1992): 43–57.

3. HEAVENLY POWERS AND PEOPLE POWER

1. For fuller discussion, see Richard A. Horsley, *Scribes, Visionaries, and the Politics of Second-Temple Judea* (Louisville: Westminster John Knox, 2007), chs. 8–9; and idem, *Revolt of the Scribes: Resistance and Apocalyptic Origins* (Minneapolis: Fortress Press, 2009), chs. 3–5.

2. See especially Samuel P. Huntington, *The Clash of Civilizations and the Remaking of World Order* (New York: Simon & Schuster, 1996); and Bernard Lewis, *The Crisis of Islam: Holy War and Unholy Terror* (New York: Modern Library, 2003).

3. The pathbreaking critique of Orientalism is Edward W. Said, *Orientalism* (New York: Pantheon, 1978). Some of the intellectuals who helped shape Orientalism were leading philologists of Semitic ("Oriental") languages, such as Ernest Renan, who also wrote the widely read *The Life of Jesus* (orig., 1863; ET London: Mathieson, 1864), which strongly influenced popular understanding of Jesus in Western Europe and North America well into the twentieth century.

4. See Samuel K. Eddy, *The King Is Dead: Studies in the Near Eastern Resistance to Hellenism, 334–31 BC* (Lincoln: University of Nebraska Press, 1961); and Horsley, *Scribes, Visionaries*; and *Revolt of the Scribes*.

5. On the following, see the fuller discussion, with references to sources and recent research, in Horsley, *Scribes, Visionaries,* chs. 3–5.

6. On the following, see the fuller discussion, with references to sources and previous scholarship, in Horsley, *Scribes, Visionaries*, ch. 2.

7. For further investigation and discussion, see Horsley, *Scribes, Visionaries*, 157–61, 179–85.

8. It has become standard in biblical studies to classify texts such as Daniel and *1 Enoch* as "apocalyptic" and to interpret their images and motifs as features of "apocalypticism." The latter, however, is a modern scholarly concept constructed from a synthesis of text fragments taken from a wide range of Judean and other texts from antiquity. "Apocalyticism" is said to be oriented toward "otherworldly" realities in anticipation of a "cosmic catastrophe," in despair over history, which is hopelessly under the force of evil. A fresh reading of complete texts such as Daniel 7; 10–12, or the Book of the Watchers (*1 Enoch* 1–36), however, shows that their principal concern is to explain the historical situation in which they are involved and to discern how they can take action consistent with their traditional Judean faith. Since the standard construct of "apocalypticism" often blocks discernment of how such texts respond to their historical context, I urge readers not to allow it to determine their reading of these texts in historical context. See the fuller discussion in Horsley, *Revolt of the Scribes*.

9. For further discussion, see Richard A. Horsley, *Jesus and the Spiral of Violence: Popular Jewish Resistance in Roman Palestine* (San Francisco: Harper & Row, 1987; repr., Minneapolis: Fortress Press, 1993), 143–44.

10. For further recent discussion of these three protests by scribal retainers see Horsley, *Revolt of the Scribes,* ch. 10.

11. Josephus's other account makes the grounds of their action even more explicit in traditional terms: "We believe it is less important to observe your decrees than the laws that Moses wrote as God instructed him" (*Ant.* 17.6.3 §159). My translations.

12. Modern scholarly treatment of the Fourth Philosophy was misled by Josephus's tirade about madness that led to the widespread revolt against Rome in 66–70; see, for example, Martin Hengel, *The Zealots: Investigations into the Jewish Freedom Movement in the Period from Herod until 70 A.D.*, trans. David Smith (Edinburgh: T&T Clark, 1989; German orig., 1961). The result was the modern scholarly construct of "the Zealots," which lumped together a number of different smaller movements, such as the Fourth Philosophy and the Sicarii, into one supposedly widespread and sustained armed insurrection against the Romans. If we read Josephus's accounts and other sources more carefully, it is clear that the coalition of peasant groups called "the Zealots" did not emerge until the middle of the revolt against Rome in 67–68 and that the scribal Fourth Philosophy did not advocate armed insurrection. See further Richard A. Horsley with John S. Hanson, *Bandits, Prophets, and Messiahs: Popular Movements in the Time of Jesus* (1985; repr., Harrisburg, Pa.: Trinity Press International, 1999), ch. 5; and Horsley, "'The Zealots,' Their Origin, Relationships, and Importance in the Jewish Revolt," *Novum Testamentum* 28 (1986): 159–92.

13. See Martin Goodman, "The First Jewish Revolt: Social Conflict and the Problem of Debt," *Journal of Jewish Studies* 33 (1982): 418–26; and Magen Broshi, "The Role of the Temple in the Herodian Economy," *Journal of Jewish Studies* 38 (1987): 31–37.

14. Further analysis of evidence and discussion is in Richard A. Horsley, "High Priests and the Politics of Roman Palestine: A Contextual Analysis of the Evidence in Josephus," *Journal for the Study of Judaism* 17 (1986): 435–63; and more general discussion in Martin Goodman, *The Ruling Class of Judaea: The Origins of the Jewish Revolt Against Rome, A.D. 66–70* (Cambridge: Cambridge University Press, 1987).

15. For a fuller analysis and discussion of the situation in Judea in the mid-first century C.E., see Horsley, *Jesus and the Spiral of Violence*, ch. 2.

16. See especially Eric R. Wolf, *Peasant Wars of the Twentieth Century* (New York: Harper & Row, 1969).

17. See, for example, John H. Kautsky, *The Politics of Aristocratic Empires* (Chapel Hill: University of North Carolina Press, 1982).

18. Analysis of sources and discussion is in Horsley, *Bandits, Prophets, and Messiahs*, chs. 2–4; and idem, *Jesus and the Spiral*, 110–16.

19. On the fundamental social forms of village community and family, see the more extensive discussion in Richard A. Horsley, *Galilee: History, Politics, People* (Valley Forge, Pa.: Trinity Press International, 1995), chs. 8–10.

20. On the following, see the more extensive discussion in Horsley, *Galilee*, 148–56. A most suggestive analysis and presentation of the "little tradition" for biblical studies is James C. Scott, "Profanation and Protest: Agrarian Revolt and the Little Tradition," *Theory and Society* 4 (1977): 1–38, 211–46.

21. The following analysis draws heavily on the theory and comparative knowledge in James C. Scott, *Domination and the Arts of Resistance: Hidden Transcripts* (New Haven: Yale University Press, 1990), as applied to ancient Judean and Galilean society and the Gospels as sources for Jesus in Richard A. Horsley, *Jesus in Context: Power, People, and Performance* (Minneapolis: Fortress Press, 2008), especially chs. 8–9.

22. See the critical discussion and documentation in Richard A. Horsley, "Popular Messianic Movements around the Time of Jesus," *Catholic Biblical Quarterly* 46 (1984): 471–93; idem, "'Like One of the Prophets of Old': Two Types of Popular Prophets at the Time of Jesus," *Catholic Biblical Quarterly* 47 (1985): 435–63; and, in more accessible form, in Horsley with John S. Hanson, *Bandits, Prophets, and Messiahs: Popular Movements in the Time of Jesus.*

23. The implied dating before the Fourth Philosophy in Acts 5:33-39, however, is surely a confusion.

24. Luke's statement in Acts 21:38 that "the Egyptian" had stirred up a revolt and led four thousand men of the Sicarii out into the wilderness can be explained simply as his confusion of two groups active at the same time. Note that they appear in successive accounts in Josephus's narrative. Josephus's accounts of Theudas also indicate that even an unarmed popular movement appeared to the authorities to be a serious threat to the Roman imperial order.

25. See further analysis and discussion in Horsley, "The Zealots."

4. THE POWER OF HOPE

1. For a fuller discussion of the Gospel of Mark, see Richard A. Horsley, *Hearing the Whole Story: The Politics of Plot in Mark's Gospel* (Louisville: Westminster John Knox, 2001); for further analysis of the parallel speeches in the Gospels of Matthew and Luke, see Richard A. Horsley with Jonathan A. Draper, *Whoever Hears You Hears Me: Prophets, Performance, and Tradition in Q* (Harrisburg, Pa.: Trinity Press International, 1999).

2. Indian historians of the modern history of India, in what they call "subaltern studies," have sharply criticized "colonial" as well as Marxist historians for

not recognizing that what they dismiss as politically irrelevant "religious" movements were the forms of popular resistance to colonial rule. See, for example, Ranajit Guha, *Elementary Aspects of Peasant Insurgency in Colonial India* (Delhi: Oxford University Press, 1983).

3. For fuller analysis and discussion of Galilean village communities and their assemblies, see Richard A. Horsley, *Galilee: History, Politics, People* (Valley Forge, Pa.: Trinity Press International, 1995), chs. 8–10.

4. On the following, see James C. Scott, *Domination and the Arts of Resistance: Hidden Transcripts* (New Haven: Yale University Press, 1990); idem, "Profanation and Protest: Agrarian Revolt and the Little Tradition," *Theory and Society* 4 (1977): 1–38, 211–46; and their application to Jesus and the Gospels in Richard A. Horsley, *Jesus in Context: Power, People, and Performance* (Minneapolis: Fortress Press, 2008), chs. 8–9.

5. See further the discussion in Horsley, *Hearing the Whole Story*, 101–9.

6. The following discussion depends on the fuller analysis in Horsley with Draper, *Whoever Hears You Hears Me*, 95–96. Standard scholarship on the Gospels and Jesus has yet to come to grips with recent research that demonstrates that literacy was limited to scribal circles; that scrolls were expensive, unwieldy, and not widely available; and that books later included in the Hebrew Bible did not yet have standardized texts. It seems unlikely that the early followers of Jesus would have been directly acquainted with written copies of scriptural books.

7. The following paragraph depends on the more extensive discussion in Horsley, *Hearing the Whole Story*, 208–12.

8. For more extensive analysis, see Horsley with Draper, *Whoever Hears You Hears Me*, 285–91.

9. Scott, *Arts of Resistance*, 145–46; Georges Lefebvre, *The Great Fear of 1789: Rural Panic in Revolutionary France,* trans. Joan White (New York: Vintage Books, 1973).

10. Scott, *Arts of Resistance*, 147.

11. Guha, *Elementary Aspects of Peasant Insurgency*, 251.

12. Scott, *Arts of Resistance,* 147.

5. JESUS AND THE STRUGGLE FOR POWER

1. In this chapter, I am dependent on the more extensive research, analysis, and discussion in Richard A. Horsley, "Jesus' Healing and Exorcism: Key Aspects of the Renewal of Israel in Response to the Impact of Roman Domination," *Neotestamentica* 44 (2010, forthcoming); and "'My Name Is Legion': Spirit Possession and Exorcism in Roman Palestine," in *Experientia,* vol. 1, *Inquiry into*

Religious Experience in Early Judaism and Early Christianity, ed. Frances Flannery, Colleen Shantz, and Rodney Werline; SBL Symposium Series 40 (Atlanta: Society of Biblical Literature, 2008), 41–57.

2. A prominent example is John Dominic Crossan, *The Historical Jesus: The Life of a Mediterranean Jewish Peasant* (San Francisco: HarperCollins, 1991), 303–32.

3. Morton Smith, *Jesus the Magician* (San Francisco: Harper & Row, 1978); Crossan, *Historical Jesus.*

4. Felicitas D. Goodman, *How about Demons? Possession and Exorcism in the Modern World,* Folklore Today (Bloomington: Indiana University Press, 1988), 15–23.

5. Stevan L. Davies, *Jesus the Healer: Possession, Trance, and the Origins of Christianity* (New York: Continuum, 1995), 86–93; John Dominic Crossan, *Jesus: A Revolutionary Biography* (San Francisco: HarperSanFrancisco, 1994).

6. Goodman, *How About Demons?* 5–6; Crossan, *Jesus,* 87–88; John J. Pilch, "Altered States of Consciousness: A 'Kitbashed' Model," *Biblical Theology Bulletin* 26 (1996): 33–38.

7. Some scholars, such as Davies (*Jesus the Healer*), have simply dismissed the possibility that the demon possession addressed by Jesus could have been related to Roman domination of Palestine.

8. Arthur Kleinman, *Patients and Healers in the Context of Culture: An Exploration of the Borderland between Anthropology, Medicine, and Psychiatry,* Comparative Studies of Health Systems and Medical Care 3 (Berkeley: University of California Press, 1980), 72.

9. Merrill Singer, "Reinventing Medical Anthropology: Toward a Critical Realignment," *Social Science and Medicine* 30 (1990): 181. Cultures are not simply systems of meaning that orient humans to one another and their world. They are also "webs of mystification" that disguise political and economic realities, particularly the power relations that determine sickness and the possibility of healing. See further Roger M. Keesing, "Models, 'Folk' and 'Cultural,'" in *Cultural Models in Language and Thought,* ed. Dorothy Holland and Naomi Quinn (Cambridge/New York: Cambridge University Press, 1987), 369–95.

10. The reflections on power by Frantz Fanon precede the work of Michel Foucault; see Fanon, *The Wretched of the Earth,* trans. Constance Farrington (1963; repr., New York: Grove Press, 1968); James C. Scott, *Domination and the Arts of Resistance: Hidden Transcripts* (New Haven: Yale University Press, 1990).

11. Fritz W. Kramer, *The Red Fez: Art and Spirit Possession in Africa,* trans. Malcolm Green (orig. 1987; New York: Verso, 1993), chs. 1–2, especially 71–72.

12. Ibid., 97, 99.

13. Ibid., 100.

14. Janice Boddy, *Wombs and Alien Spirits: Women, Men, and the Zār Cult in Northern Sudan* (Madison: University of Wisconsin Press, 1989), 269–70.

15. Ibid., 291–94.

16. Ibid., 289–90.

17. Kramer, *Red Fez*, 116–17.

18. See the extensive description and notes from actual exorcism sessions in Boddy, *Wombs and Alien Spirits*.

19. Kramer, *Red Fez*, 125.

20. Ibid.

21. Bengdt G. M. Sundkler, *Bantu Prophets in South Africa,* 2nd ed. (Oxford: Oxford University Press, 1961), 248–49.

22. Kramer, *Red Fez*, 126.

23. Ibid., 134–35.

24. On the following, see Frantz Fanon, "Concerning Violence," in *Wretched of the Earth*, 35–94.

25. In addition to "Concerning Violence," see the case studies in Fanon, *Wretched of the Earth*, 249–310. Paul Hollenbach ("Jesus, Demoniacs, and Public Authorities: A Socio-historical Study," *Journal of the American Academy of Religion* 49 [1981]: 567–88) boldly pioneered the exploration of the social-psychological and ideological pertinence of Fanon's analysis. It remains to explore the political-historical relevance of Fanon. For some first steps, see Richard A. Horsley, *Hearing the Whole Story: The Politics of Plot in Mark's Gospel* (Louisville: Westminster John Knox, 2001), 141–48.

26. Fanon, *Wretched of the Earth*, 56.

27. For more extensive analysis and discussion, see Richard A. Horsley, *Scribes, Visionaries, and the Politics of Second-Temple Judea* (Louisville: Westminster John Knox, 2007), ch. 2.

28. See George W. E. Nickelsburg, *1 Enoch: A Commentary on the Book of 1 Enoch, Chapters 1–36; 81–108*, Hermeneia (Minneapolis: Fortress Press, 2001), 174, 178–81. For precise exegesis of key passages in the Book of the Watchers, see further Nickelsburg's commentary. For more general analysis of the book's explanation of what was happening in Judean history, see Horsley, *Scribes, Visionaries*, ch. 8.

29. See the fuller analysis and discussion of the struggle between the two spirits and how it related to the Romans in Richard A. Horsley, *Revolt of the Scribes: Resistance and Apocalyptic Origins* (Minneapolis: Fortress Press, 2009), ch. 7.

30. For fuller discussion of the following, see Horsley, *Hearing the Whole Story*, 136–48.

6. THE COLLECTIVE POWER OF COVENANT COMMUNITY

1. The scholarly tendency to separate or even contrast Jesus' teaching and the Mosaic covenant stands in striking contrast to the way the Bible was understood in the formative history of the United States. After their "exodus" from under the English monarchy, the English Puritans who came to New England understood their settlements as new covenantal communities. As their guide for social-political affairs they took not only the covenant given to Moses on Sinai, but the Sermon on the Mount, which they understood as Jesus' renewal of the Mosaic covenant. These covenantal texts in the Bible strongly influenced the American colonists' sense of their divinely endowed "inalienable rights," which they articulated in the Declaration of Independence and attempted to protect in the framing of the Constitution. In discerning the similarity and continuity between the major speech of Jesus in the Gospels and Israel's covenant with God on Sinai, those English Puritans may have understood something that has escaped Jesus scholars. Unfortunately they also found in their English translation of the Bible what they claimed as a justification for killing the Native Americans already living on the land. For fuller discussion, see Richard A. Horsley, *Covenant Economics: A Biblical Vision of Justice for All* (Louisville: Westminster John Knox, 2009), ix–xvi.

2. James C. Scott, *The Moral Economy of the Peasant: Rebellion and Subsistence in Southeast Asia* (New Haven: Yale University Press, 1976), is the foundational study, based on Scott's own fieldwork in Southeast Asia and comparative material from many studies of peasant societies by historians and anthropologists.

3. There is a good discussion of the *prosbul* in Martin Goodman, *The Ruling Class of Judaea: The Origins of the Jewish Revolt against Rome, A.D. 66–70* (Cambridge/New York: Cambridge University Press, 1987), 57–58.

4. See Richard A. Horsley, *Jesus and the Spiral of Violence: Popular Jewish Resistance in Roman Palestine* (San Francisco: Harper & Row, 1987), 255–73.

5. For fuller analysis of the mission discourses, see Richard A. Horsley with Jonathan A. Draper, *Whoever Hears You Hears Me: Prophets, Performance, and Tradition* (Harrisburg, Pa.: Trinity Press International, 1999), ch. 10.

6. Building a movement by sending envoys to work in village communities sounds similar to the activities of at least two known organizations, Der

Bundshuh and Der Arme Konrad, which sent delegates to towns up and down the Rhine valley in the decade prior to the Peasant War of 1524–25 in southwest Germany. See Peter Blickle, *The Revolution of 1525: The German Peasants' War from a New Perspective,* trans. Thomas A. Brady Jr. and H. C. Erik Midelfort (Baltimore: Johns Hopkins University Press, 1977).

7. This section depends on the more extensive analysis and discussion in Horsley with Draper, *Whoever Hears You Hears Me,* ch. 9; see now the more accessible discussion in Horsley, *Covenant Economics,* ch. 7.

8. This can be seen in the very structure of the *Community Rule* from Qumran (1QS), as laid out by Klaus Baltzer, *The Covenant Formulary in the Old Testament, Jewish, and Early Christian Writings,* trans. David E. Green (Philadelphia: Fortress Press, 1971). The *Damascus Rule* begins with a lengthy declaration of deliverance emphasizing the group's own (recent) origins (1:1—6:11). A brief section of principles and rulings for communal life is followed by declarations of long life and God's salvation for those who keep the covenant and retribution for those who do not (7:4-6, 8-10 + recension B, 2:28-36; and perhaps the rest of the document), which is the sanction without explicit form of blessings and curses.

9. Jesus' admonitions in Luke/Q 6:43-45 offer yet another similarity to the renewed covenant in the Qumran *Community Rule,* which lists the dispositions that result in certain behavior (see 1QS 4:2-7, 9-12).

10. This section depends on the more extensive analysis and discussion in Richard A. Horsley, *Hearing the Whole Story: The Politics of Plot in Mark's Gospel* (Louisville: Westminster John Knox, 2001), ch. 8.

11. John R. Donahue, *The Theology and Setting of Discipleship in the Gospel of Mark* (Milwaukee: Marquette University Press, 1983), 39; Ernest Best, *Following Jesus: Discipleship in the Gospel of Mark,* Journal for the Study of the New Testament Supplement Series 4 (Sheffield: JSOT Press, 1981), 99.

12. Ernst Käsemann, "Sentences of Holy Law in the New Testament," in idem, *New Testament Questions of Today* (Philadelphia: Fortress Press, 1969), 66–81.

13. For more extensive discussion, see Horsley, *Hearing the Whole Story,* 186–95.

14. Not surprisingly, American and European biblical interpreters who assume the separation of economics and religion tend to miss the centrality of economics in the Mosaic covenant. Not only do "you shall not covet," "you shall not steal," and "you shall not bear false witness" protect peoples' economic resources and rights in the interaction of community members, but "you shall not murder," "you shall not commit adultery," and "honor your father and mother" include economic aspects as well. See discussion in ch. 3 above; and in Horsley, *Covenant Economics,* chs. 2–3.

15. There is a similar discussion of covenantal economics in Mark in Ched Myers, *Binding the Strong Man: A Political Reading of Mark's Story of Jesus* (Maryknoll, N.Y.: Orbis Books, 1988), 271–76.

16. On the parables in historical context, see especially the analysis and interpretation of William R. Herzog, *Parables as Subversive Speech: Jesus as Pedagogue of the Oppressed* (Louisville, KY: Westminster John Knox, 1994).

17. See further Albert I. Baumgarten, "*Korban* and the Pharisaic *Paradosis*," *Journal of the Ancient Near Eastern Society* 16–17 (1984–85): 6–14.

7. SPEAKING TRUTH TO POWER

1. See further Martin Goodman, *The Ruling Class of Judaea: The Origins of the Jewish Revolt against Rome, A.D. 66–70* (Cambridge/New York: Cambridge University Press, 1987); Richard A. Horsley, "High Priests and the Politics of Roman Palestine: A Contextual Analysis of the Evidence in Josephus," *Journal for the Study of Judaism* 17 (1986): 23–55.

2. See Richard A. Horsley, *Revolt of the Scribes: Resistance and Apocalyptic Origins* (Minneapolis: Fortress Press, 2009), ch. 4.

3. For analysis and discussion, see Richard A. Horsley, *Galilee: History, Politics, People* (Valley Forge, Pa.: Trinity Press International, 1995), 42–52.

4. James C. Scott, *Domination and the Arts of Resistance: Hidden Transcripts* (New Haven: Yale University Press, 1990). Several colleagues and I have applied Scott's reflections to Jesus' mission in Richard A. Horsley, ed., *Hidden Transcripts and the Arts of Resistance: Applying the Work of James C. Scott to Jesus and Paul,* Semeia Studies 48 (Atlanta: Society of Biblical Literature, 2004); and *Oral Performance, Popular Tradition, and Hidden Transcript in Q,* Semeia Studies 60 (Atlanta: Society of Biblical Literature, 2006). My own articles in those volumes are reprinted in revised form in Richard A. Horsley, *Jesus in Context: Power, People, and Performance* (Minneapolis: Fortress Press, 2008), chs. 8–10.

5. In other cases, mentioned in chapter 2 above, the Roman governors quickly sent out the military to slaughter such figures as the "Egyptian" prophet who returned to Judea to lead his followers up to the Mount of Olives. And just before the great revolt in 66 the high priests sought to have Jesus son of Hananiah executed, even though the Roman governor Albinus thought he was merely a maniac (Josephus, *Ant.* 20.8.6 §§169–71; *War* 2.13.5 §§261–63; 6.5.3 §§300–309).

6. By no means am I suggesting that we revert to trusting Mark's "passion narrative" as a reliable historical report. Episodes in the passion narrative are surely some of the least historically reliable parts of Mark's narrative. Since the

motif of "false testimony" in the trial episode is often claimed as good evidence that Jesus did not take a stance against the Temple, hence was not opposed to the rulers and politically innocuous, however, we should make every effort to understand Mark's representation here. Far from portraying Jesus as politically innocent and innocuous in the trial episode, Mark ends it with Jesus pointing the high priests and elders to their impending judgment, of which "the son of man coming with the clouds of heaven" was a standing image.

7. For fuller discussion of the following, see Richard A. Horsley, *Jesus and the Spiral of Violence: Popular Jewish Resistance in Roman Palestine* (1987; repr., Minneapolis: Fortress Press, 1993), 286–92.

8. A possible analogy from more recent history would be the demonstrations against the shah of Iran, who had been put in power and supported by the United States. The demonstrations took the form of Shi'ite funeral processions, as explained briefly in Richard A. Horsley, *Religion and Empire: People, Power, and the Life of the Spirit* (Minneapolis: Fortress Press, 2003), 64–66.

9. See further Richard A. Horsley, *Galilee: History, Politics, People* (Valley Forge, Pa.: Trinity Press International, 1995), 132–37, 205–21.

10. Later Christian interpretation latched onto the line that the master would "give the vineyard to others" as a proof-text for Christian supersession of Judaism. It is difficult to judge whether this line belonged to the parable or to developing comment on it. If it was part of the parable, then in the more original context of the parable told to the Jerusalem aristocracy, with a crowd of Judean and Galilean peasants listening in, the implications were more immediate. Many of those peasant pilgrims would have had relatives and neighbors who had been reduced to serving as sharecroppers of their wealthy creditors. The crowd overhearing the parable would have drawn the conclusion that the "others" to whom the vineyard was given were people who had been dispossessed of the land that God had given to their ancestors as a family inheritance, as their inalienable right.

11. Scott, *Domination,* 207.

12. Ibid., 208.

8. THE POWER OF THE CRUCIFIXION

1. For more extensive coverage of crucifixion, see Joseph A. Fitzmyer, S.J., "Crucifixion in Ancient Palestine, Qumran Literature, and the New Testament," *Catholic Biblical Quarterly* 40 (1978): 493–513.

2. For extensive analysis of the passion narratives in the Gospels, see Raymond E. Brown, *The Death of the Messiah: From Gethsemane to the Grave: A*

Commentary on the Passion Narratives in the Four Gospels, 2 vols., Anchor Bible Reference Library (New York: Doubleday, 1987); and the sharply critical reply by John Dominic Crossan, *Who Killed Jesus: Exposing the Roots of Anti-Semitism in the Gospel Story of the Death of Jesus* (San Francisco: HarperSanFrancisco, 1995). A literary-theological analysis of the Gospels' portrayal of the death of Jesus is found in John T. Carroll and Joel B. Green, *The Death of Jesus in Early Christianity* (Peabody, Mass.: Hendickson, 1995).

3. With significant exceptions such as John 8:31 and 11:45, "the Judeans" in John's Gospel, who are hostile to Jesus, are the Jerusalem officials, not the ordinary people; see, for example, John 7.

4. On ancient Judean and Galilean bandits (including Eleazar ben Dinai), who sometimes incited revolt, see Richard A. Horsley with John S. Hanson, *Bandits, Prophets, and Messiahs: Popular Movements in the Time of Jesus* (Minneapolis: Winston, 1985; repr., Harrisville, Pa.: Trinity Press International, 1999), ch. 2.

5. This has been argued again recently by Paula Fredriksen, *Jesus of Nazareth: King of the Jews: A Jewish Life and the Emergence of Christianity* (New York: Knopf, 1999), especially ch. 5.

6. On the lack of evidence for a standard expectation of "the Messiah" and the diverse representation of future leadership, see the survey by Marianus de Jonge, "The Use of the Word 'Anointed' in the Time of Jesus," *Novum Testamentum* 8 (1966): 132–48; and the many particular studies in Jacob Neusner, William Scott Green, and Ernest Frerichs, eds., *Judaisms and Their Messiahs at the Turn of the Christian Era* (Cambridge/New York: Cambridge University Press, 1987); and in James H. Charlesworth, ed., *The Messiah: Developments in Earliest Judaism and Christianity: The First Princeton Symposium on Judaism and Christian Origins* (Minneapolis: Fortress Press, 1992). John J. Collins (*The Scepter and the Star: The Messiahs of the Dead Sea Scrolls and Other Ancient Literature*, Anchor Bible Reference Library [New York: Doubleday, 1995]) attempts a partial rehabilitation of the more synthetic scholarly construction of the concept of the Messiah. On the *Psalms of Solomon* and the Dead Sea Scrolls as products of circles of dissident scribes, see further Richard A. Horsley, *Revolt of the Scribes: Resistance and Apocalyptic Origins* (Minneapolis: Fortress Press, 2009).

7. For analysis and further discussion of popular messianic and prophetic movements, see Richard A. Horsley, "Popular Messianic Movements around the Time of Jesus," *Catholic Biblical Quarterly* 46 (1984): 471–93; and "'Messianic' Figures and Movements in First-Century Palestine," in *The Messiah: Developments in Earliest Judaism and Christianity: The First Princeton Symposium on Judaism and Christian Origins*, ed. James H. Charlesworth (Minneapolis: For-

tress Press, 1992), 276–95; and "'Like One of the Prophets of Old': Two Types of Popular Prophets at the Time of Jesus," *Catholic Biblical Quarterly* 47 (1985): 435–63. For discussion of these popular patterns in Mark, see Richard A. Horsley, *Hearing the Whole Story: The Politics of Plot in Mark's Gospel* (Louisville: Westminster John Knox, 2001), ch. 10.

8. See the critical discussion by Helmut Koester, *Ancient Christian Gospels: Their History and Development* (Philadelphia: Trinity Press International, 1990), 12–14.

9. The language in both the question and the answer in Mark 14:61-62 are unique in the Gospel passion accounts and raise a host of questions. "The messiah, the son of the Blessed One" is liturgical language, which could be "speech in character" appropriately attributed to the high priest. The only other occurrence in the Gospels of "Blessed" with reference to God comes in the psalm blessing/praising God by the priest Zechariah in Luke 1:68. Paul twice pauses briefly in his arguments to reverence God the Creator and deliverer as "Blessed be" (Rom 1:25; 9:5). And "Blessed be the God and Father of our Lord Jesus Christ" has become standard in the opening blessings of "Paul's" letters in "Pauline Christianity" (2 Cor 1:3; 11:31; Eph 1:3; compare 1 Pet 1:3). That neither Matthew nor Luke follows Mark in this sacerdotal language ("son of the Blessed One") in their parallel accounts leads to suspicions about a reworking of language in Mark 14:61-62 under influence of later "Christian" language. Further, both Matthew, more closely following Mark's account, and Luke, in diverting from it, agree against Mark in having Jesus reply "You have said so" to the question of the high priest(s) about being the Messiah. Thus Jesus replies to the high priest(s) as he replies to Pilate's question about being "the king of the Judeans," "you say so."

10. Two generations ago, these speeches of "Peter" in Acts were thought to be early examples of apostolic preaching about Jesus separable from their literary context, as in C. H. Dodd, *The Apostolic Preaching and Its Development* (London: Hodder & Stoughton, 1936), 17–29. More recent literary analysis has led to the recognition that the book of Acts has many similarities to Hellenistic historiography, and that the speeches in particular resemble typical "speech in character" that Greek and Roman historians attributed to their historical subjects. The speeches of "Peter" in Acts may be viewed critically either as compositions of Luke according to what he thought Peter would have preached in the years immediately following the crucifixion about what had happened to Jesus, or a Lukan reworking of earlier (oral) traditions. Either way, because of their distinctive representations of how Jesus had become Messiah and Lord only after his exaltation, which is so different from later, more "orthodox" representations, they represent early tradition.

11. The key study of Judean texts is George W. E. Nickelsburg, *Resurrection, Immortality, and Eternal Life in Intertestamental Judaism and Early Christianity,* Harvard Theological Studies 56 (1972; expanded ed., Cambridge, Mass.: Harvard University Press, 2006).

12. Note: not the "messianic" title "*the* Son of God."

Bibliography

Asad, Talal. *Genealogies of Religion: Discipline and Reasons of Power in Christianity and Islam.* Baltimore: Johns Hopkins University Press, 1993.

Baltzer, Klaus. *The Covenant Formulary in the Old Testament, Jewish, and Early Christian Writings.* Translated by David E. Green. Philadelphia: Fortress Press, 1971.

Baumgarten, Albert I. "*Korban* and the Pharisaic *Paradosis.*" *Journal of the Ancient Near Eastern Society* 16–17 (1984–85): 6–14.

Best, Ernest. *Following Jesus: Discipleship in the Gospel of Mark.* Journal for the Study of the New Testament Supplement Series 4. Sheffield: JSOT Press, 1981.

Blickle, Peter. *The Revolution of 1525: The German Peasants' War from a New Perspective.* Translated by Thomas A. Brady Jr. and H. C. Erik Midelfort. Baltimore: Johns Hopkins University Press, 1977.

Boddy, Janice. *Wombs and Alien Spirits: Women, Men, and the Zār Cult in Northern Sudan.* Madison: University of Wisconsin Press, 1989.

Braund, David. "Function and Dysfunction: Personal Patronage in Roman Imperialism." In *Patronage in Ancient Society,* edited by Andrew Wallace-Hadrill, 139–49. Leicester-Nottingham Studies in Ancient Society 1. London: Routledge, 1989.

Broshi, Magen. "The Role of the Temple in the Herodian Economy." *Journal of Jewish Studies* 38 (1987): 31–37.

Brown, Raymond E. *The Death of the Messiah: From Gethsemane to the Grave: A Commentary on the Passion Narratives in the Four Gospels.* 2 vols. Anchor Bible Reference Library. New York: Doubleday, 1987.

Carroll, John T., and Joel B. Green. *The Death of Jesus in Early Christianity.* Peabody, Mass: Hendickson, 1995.

Carter, Charles E. *The Emergence of Yehud in the Persian Period: A Social and Demographic Study.* Journal for the Study of the Old Testament Supplement Series 294. Sheffield: Sheffield Academic Press, 1999.

Chaney, Marvin L. "Bitter Bounty: The Dynamics of Political Economy Critiqued by the Eighth-Century Prophets." In *The Bible and Liberation: Political and Social Hermeneutics,* edited by Norman K. Gottwald and Richard A. Horsley, 250–63. Bible and Liberation Series. Maryknoll, N.Y.: Orbis Books, 1993.

———. "Whose Sour Grapes? The Addressees of Isaiah 5:1-7 in the Light of Political Economy." *Semeia* 87 (1999): 105–22.

Charlesworth, James H., ed. *The Messiah: Developments in Earliest Judaism and Christianity: The First Princeton Symposium on Judaism and Christian Origins.* Minneapolis: Fortress Press, 1992.

Collins, John J. *The Scepter and the Star: The Messiahs of the Dead Sea Scrolls and Other Ancient Literature.* Anchor Bible Reference Library. New York: Doubleday, 1995.

Coote, Robert M. *Amos among the Prophets: Composition and Theology.* Philadelphia: Fortress Press, 1981.

Corpus inscriptionum graecarum. Edited by August Boeckh et al. 4 vols. Berlin: Ex Officina Academica, 1828–77.

Crossan, John Dominic. *The Historical Jesus: The Life of a Mediterranean Jewish Peasant.* San Francisco: HarperCollins, 1991.

———. *Jesus: A Revolutionary Biography.* San Francisco: HarperSanFrancisco, 1994.

———. *Who Killed Jesus: Exposing the Roots of Anti-Semitism in the Gospel Story of the Death of Jesus.* San Francisco: HarperSanFrancisco, 1995.

Davies, Stevan L. *Jesus the Healer: Possession, Trance, and the Origins of Christianity.* New York: Continuum, 1995.

Dodd, C. H. *The Apostolic Preaching and Its Development.* London: Hodder & Stoughton, 1936.

Donahue, John R. *The Theology and Setting of Discipleship in the Gospel of Mark.* Milwaukee: Marquette University Press, 1983.

Eddy, Samuel K. *The King Is Dead: Studies in the Near Eastern Resistance to Hellenism, 334–31 BC.* Lincoln: University of Nebraska Press, 1961.

Fitzmyer, Joseph A., S.J. "Crucifixion in Ancient Palestine, Qumran Literature, and the New Testament." *Catholic Biblical Quarterly* 40 (1978): 493–513.

Fredriksen, Paula. *Jesus of Nazareth: King of the Jews: A Jewish Life and the Emergence of Christianity.* New York: Knopf, 1999.

Garnsey, Peter. *Famine and Food Supply in the Graeco-Roman World: Responses to Risk and Crisis.* Cambridge/New York: Cambridge University Press, 1988.

Garnsey, Peter, and Richard Saller. *The Roman Empire: Economy, Society and Culture.* Berkeley: University of California Press, 1987.

Goodman, Felicitas D. *How about Demons? Possession and Exorcism in the Modern World*. Folklore Today. Bloomington: Indiana University Press, 1988.

Goodman, Martin. "The First Jewish Revolt: Social Conflict and the Problem of Debt." *Journal of Jewish Studies* 33 (1982): 418–26

———. *The Ruling Class of Judaea: The Origins of the Jewish Revolt against Rome, A.D. 66–70*. Cambridge/New York: Cambridge University Press, 1987.

Gordon, Richard. "The Veil of Power: Emperors, Sacrificers, and Benefactors." In *Pagan Priests: Religion and Power in the Ancient World*, edited by Mary Beard and John North, 199–234. London: Duckworth, 1990.

Gottwald, Norman K. *The Tribes of Yahweh: A Sociology of the Religion of Liberated Israel, 1250–1050 B.C.E.* Maryknoll, N.Y.: Orbis Books, 1979.

Grayson, A. Kirk Grayson. "Mesopotamia, History of." In *Anchor Bible Dictionary*, edited by David Noel Freedman. 6 vols. New York: Doubleday, 1992, 4:732–77.

Guha, Ranajit. *Elementary Aspects of Peasant Insurgency in Colonial India*. Delhi: Oxford University Press, 1983.

Harris, William V. *Ancient Literacy*. Cambridge, Mass.: Harvard University Press, 1987.

Hengel, Martin. *The Zealots: Investigations into the Jewish Freedom Movement in the Period from Herod until 70 A.D.* Translated by David Smith. Edinburgh: T&T Clark, 1989. German orig., 1961.

Hezser, Catherine. *Jewish Literacy in Roman Palestine*. Texte und Studien zum antiken Judentum 81. Tübingen: Mohr Siebeck, 2001.

Hollenbach, Paul. "Jesus, Demoniacs, and Public Authorities: A Socio-historical Study." *Journal of the American Academy of Religion* 49 (1981): 567–88.

Hopkins, Keith. *Conquerors and Slaves*. Sociological Studies in Roman History 1. Cambridge: Cambridge University Press, 1978.

Horsley, Richard A. "Christmas: The Religion of Consumer Capitalism." In *Christmas Unwrapped: Consumerism, Christ, and Culture*, edited by Richard Horsley and James Tracy, 165–87. Harrisburg, Pa.: Trinity Press International, 2001.

———. *Covenant Economics: A Biblical Vision of Justice for All*. Louisville: Westminster John Knox, 2009.

———. *Galilee: History, Politics, People*. Valley Forge, Pa.: Trinity Press International, 1995.

———. *Hearing the Whole Story: The Politics of Plot in Mark's Gospel*. Louisville: Westminster John Knox, 2001.

———, ed. *Hidden Transcripts and the Arts of Resistance: Applying the Work of James C. Scott to Jesus and Paul*. Semeia Studies 48. Atlanta: Society of Biblical Literature, 2004.

234   Bibliography

————. "High Priests and the Politics of Roman Palestine: A Contextual Analysis of the Evidence in Josephus." *Journal for the Study of Judaism* 17 (1986): 23–55.

————. "Introduction, Part II: Patronage, Priesthoods, and Power." In *Paul and Empire: Religion and Power in Roman Imperial Society,* edited by Richard A. Horsley, 88–95. Harrisburg, Pa.: Trinity Press International, 1997.

————. *Jesus and Empire: The Kingdom of God and the New World Disorder.* Minneapolis: Fortress Press, 2003.

————. *Jesus and the Spiral of Violence: Popular Jewish Resistance in Roman Palestine.* San Francisco: Harper & Row, 1987. Reprint, Minneapolis: Fortress Press, 1993.

————. "Jesus' Healing and Exorcism: Key Aspects of the Renewal of Israel in Response to the Impact of Roman Domination." *Neotestamentica* 44 (2010, forthcoming).

————. *Jesus in Context: Power, People, and Performance.* Minneapolis: Fortress Press, 2008.

————. "'Like One of the Prophets of Old': Two Types of Popular Prophets at the Time of Jesus." *Catholic Biblical Quarterly* 47 (1985): 435–63.

————. "'Messianic' Figures and Movements in First-Century Palestine." In *The Messiah: Developments in Earliest Judaism and Christianity: The First Princeton Symposium on Judaism and Christian Origins,* ed. James H. Charlesworth, 276–95. Minneapolis: Fortress Press, 1992.

————. "'My Name Is Legion': Spirit Possession and Exorcism in Roman Palestine." In *Experientia,* vol. 1, *Inquiry into Religious Experience in Early Judaism and Early Christianity,* edited by Frances Flannery, Colleen Shantz, and Rodney Werline, 41–57. SBL Symposium Series 40. Atlanta: Society of Biblical Literature, 2008.

————, ed. *Oral Performance, Popular Tradition, and Hidden Transcript in Q.* Semeia Studies 60. Atlanta: Society of Biblical Literature, 2006.

————. "Popular Messianic Movements around the Time of Jesus." *Catholic Biblical Quarterly* 46 (1984): 471–93.

————. *Religion and Empire: People, Power, and the Life of the Spirit.* Minneapolis: Fortress Press, 2003.

————. *Revolt of the Scribes: Resistance and Apocalyptic Origins.* Minneapolis: Fortress Press, 2009.

————. *Scribes, Visionaries, and the Politics of Second-Temple Judea.* Louisville: Westminster John Knox, 2007.

————. *Sociology and the Jesus Movement.* New York: Crossroad, 1989.

————. "The Zealots: Their Origin, Relationship, and Importance in the Jewish Revolt." *Novum Testamentum* 28 (1986): 159–92.

Horsley, Richard A., with John S. Hanson. *Bandits, Prophets, and Messiahs: Popular Movements in the Time of Jesus.* Minneapolis: Winston, 1985. Reprint, Harrisburg, Pa.: Trinity Press International, 1999.

Horsley, Richard A., with Jonathan A. Draper. *Whoever Hears You Hears Me: Prophets, Performance, and Tradition in Q.* Harrisburg, Pa.: Trinity Press International, 1999.

Huntington, Samuel P. *The Clash of Civilizations and the Remaking of World Order.* New York: Simon & Schuster, 1996.

Jonge, Marianus de. "The Use of the Word 'Anointed' in the Time of Jesus." *Novum Testamentum* 8 (1966): 132–48.

Käsemann, Ernst. "Sentences of Holy Law in the New Testament." In idem, *New Testament Questions of Today,* 66–81. Philadelphia: Fortress Press, 1969.

Kautsky, John H. *The Politics of Aristocratic Empires.* Chapel Hill: University of North Carolina Press, 1982.

Keesing, Roger M. "Models, 'Folk' and 'Cultural.'" In *Cultural Models in Language and Thought,* edited by Dorothy Holland and Naomi Quinn, 369–95. Cambridge/New York: Cambridge University Press, 1987.

Kelber, Werner H. *Mark's Story of Jesus.* Philadelphia: Fortress Press, 1979.

Kingsbury, Jack Dean. *Conflict in Mark: Jesus, Authorities, Disciples.* Minneapolis: Fortress Press, 1989.

Kleinman, Arthur. *Patients and Healers in the Context of Culture: An Exploration of the Borderland between Anthropology, Medicine, and Psychiatry.* Comparative Studies of Health Systems and Medical Care 3. Berkeley: University of California Press, 1980.

Koester, Helmut. *Ancient Christian Gospels: Their History and Development.* Philadelphia: Trinity Press International, 1990.

Kramer, Fritz W. *The Red Fez: Art and Spirit Possession in Africa.* Translated by Malcolm Green. New York: Verso, 1993. German orig., 1987.

Lefebvre, Georges. *The Great Fear of 1789: Rural Panic in Revolutionary France.* Translated by Joan White. New York: Vintage Books, 1973.

Lewis, Bernard. *The Crisis of Islam: Holy War and Unholy Terror.* New York: Modern Library, 2003.

Mattern, Susan P. *Rome and the Enemy: Imperial Strategy in the Principate.* Berkeley: University of California Press, 1999.

Myers, Ched. *Binding the Strong Man: A Political Reading of Mark's Story of Jesus.* Maryknoll, N.Y.: Orbis Books, 1988.

Neusner, Jacob, William Scott Green, and Ernest Frerichs. *Judaisms and Their Messiahs at the Turn of the Christian Era.* Cambridge/New York: Cambridge University Press, 1987.

Nickelsburg, George W. E. *1 Enoch: A Commentary on the Book of 1 Enoch, Chapters 1–36; 81–108.* Hermeneia. Minneapolis: Fortress Press, 2001.

———. *Resurrection, Immortality, and Eternal Life in Intertestamental Judaism and Early Christianity.* Harvard Theological Studies 56. 1972. Expanded ed., Cambridge, Mass.: Harvard University Press, 2006.

Nye, Joseph. *Soft Power: The Means to Success in World Politics.* New York: Public Affairs, 2004.

Oppenheim, A. Leo. *Ancient Mesopotamia: Portrait of a Dead Civilization.* Rev. ed. by Erica Reiner. Chicago: University of Chicago Press, 1976.

Perrin, Norman. *Rediscovering the Teaching of Jesus.* New York: Harper & Row, 1967.

Pilch, John J. "Altered States of Consciousness: A 'Kitbashed' Model." *Biblical Theology Bulletin* 26 (1996): 33–38.

Price, S. R. F. *Rituals and Power: The Roman Imperial Cult in Asia Minor.* Cambridge: Cambridge University Press, 1984.

Renan, Ernest. *The Life of Jesus.* 1863. ET London: Mathieson, 1864.

Rich, John. "Patronage and Interstate Relations in the Roman Republic." In *Patronage in Ancient Society,* edited by Andrew Wallace-Hadrill, 125–38. Leicester-Nottingham Studies in Ancient Society 1. London: Routledge, 1989.

Saggs, H. W. F. *The Greatness That Was Babylon: A Sketch of the Ancient Civilization of the Tigris-Euphrates Valley.* New York: Praeger, 1962.

Said, Edward W. *Orientalism.* New York: Pantheon, 1978.

Saller, Richard. *Personal Patronage under the Early Empire.* Cambridge: Cambridge University Press, 1982.

Schüssler Fiorenza, Elisabeth. *Jesus and the Politics of Interpretation.* New York: Continuum, 2000.

Scott, James C. *Domination and the Arts of Resistance: Hidden Transcripts.* New Haven: Yale University Press, 1990

———. *The Moral Economy of the Peasant: Rebellion and Subsistence in Southeast Asia.* New Haven: Yale University Press, 1976.

———. "Profanation and Protest: Agrarian Revolt and the Little Tradition." *Theory and Society* 4 (1977): 1–38, 211–46.

Singer, Merrill. "Reinventing Medical Anthropology: Toward a Critical Realignment." *Social Science and Medicine* 30:2 (1990): 179–87.

Smith, Morton. *Jesus the Magician.* San Francisco: Harper & Row, 1978.

Stephanson, Anders. *Manifest Destiny: American Expansion and the Empire of Right.* New York: Hill & Wang, 1995.

Sundkler, Bengt G. M. *Bantu Prophets in South Africa.* 2nd ed. Oxford: Oxford University Press, 1961.

Veyne, Paul. *Bread and Circuses: Historical Sociology and Political Pluralism.* London: Penguin, 1990.

Weems, Renita J. "Reading *Her Way* through the Struggle: African American Women and the Bible." In *Stony the Road We Trod: African American Biblical Interpretation,* edited by Cain Hope Felder, 57–77. Minneapolis: Fortress Press, 1991. Reprinted in *The Bible and Liberation: Political and Social Hermeneutics*, edited by Norman K. Gottwald and Richard A. Horsley, 31–50. Bible and Liberation Series. Maryknoll, N.Y.: Orbis Books, 1993.

Wolf, Eric R. *Peasant Wars of the Twentieth Century.* New York: Harper & Row, 1969.

Yoffee, Norman. "Political Economy in Early Mesopotamian States." *Annual Review of Anthropology* 24 (1995): 281–311.

Zanker, Paul. *The Power of Images in the Age of Augustus.* Jerome Lectures, 16th Series. Ann Arbor: University of Michigan Press, 1988.

Index of Ancient Literature

General Index